CONTEXT
and
CONTINUITY

The Korean Adventist Church in North America and Its Future Generations

Won K. Yoon

ANDREWS
UNIVERSITY PRESS

BERRIEN SPRINGS, MICHIGAN

Andrews University Press
Sutherland House
Berrien Springs, MI 49104-1700
Telephone: 269-471-6134
Fax: 269-471-6224
Email: aupo@andrews.edu
Website: http://universitypress.andrews.edu

ISBN 978-1-883925-60-4

Printed in the United States of America

12 11 10 09 08   5 4 3 2 1

Library of Congress Cataloging-in-Publication Data

Yoon, Won K.
  Context and continuity : the Korean Adventist Church in North America and its future generations / Won K. Yoon.
      p. cm.
  Includes bibliographical references (p.   ) and index.
  ISBN 978-1-883925-60-4 (pbk. : alk. paper) 1. Korean American Seventh-day Adventists--Religious life. I. Title.

  BX6153.2.Y66 2008
  286.7'73089957--dc22
                              2008007205

Project Director	Ronald Alan Knott
Project Editor	Deborah L. Everhart
Typesetter	Thomas Toews
Indexer	Ann Parrish
Cover Designer	Doris Bruey, DB Graphic Design Services

Typeset: 11/15 Goudy Old Style

CONTEXT
and
CONTINUITY

Dedicated to
the Korean parents and their children
who have kept their faith and courage
during their struggles
in the New World

"Generations come and generations go,
but the earth remains forever."
Ecclesiastes 1:4

Contents

Preface

When the Vision 2020 survey project was launched, more than 1,000 second-generation Korean Seventh-day Adventists in North America responded by returning questionnaires. My initial intent with this impressive amount of survey data was rather simple. I planned to create a statistical report with tables and graphs, and then discuss the findings with their implications for the future of the Korean Adventist church in North America. Such a report would be intended primarily for second-generation Korean Adventists and some first-generation immigrants who could read English. Beyond the small circle of the Korean Adventist community, I imagined that some church administrators in the North American Division might be interested in such a report as they dealt with the issues and concerns of the Korean churches in their territories.

In the course of examining the survey data and mulling over the contents of the report, I decided to broaden the scope of the project. I wanted to provide a full picture of the Korean Adventist church in North America by tracing its historical roots. I also wanted to report on the present state of the Korean church in North America.

Moreover, I wanted this report to be suitable for more than just the limited Korean Adventist lay audience. It was my hope that this report would be read by the students of Asian religions in general and Asian immigrant churches in particular. I believed this work would make a significant contribution to the growing body of knowledge on the subject of Asian American religions. Thus any student interested in the subject of second-generation members in ethnic churches should find this work relevant and insightful. Later, its value was affirmed by the reviewers who read the preliminary draft of this work at the request of Andrews University Press. As far as I know, this is the first extensive sociological study on second-generation Korean Adventists in North America. Only in recent years have social scientists begun to study Asian American churches from the perspective of second- and third-generation members.

Writing a book for both lay people and the academic community was a considerable challenge. Nevertheless, I have tried not to disappoint either in substance or approach.

Wherever applicable, I wanted to present the Korean Adventist church as part of the larger picture in both an ecclesiastical and socio-cultural sense. It was my assumption that the establishment and growth (or decline in some cases) of the church in North America were partially due to multiple social forces at national and international levels. So I tried to look at the church in a specific historical context and compared it with other groups.

As I considered different aspects of the Korean Adventist church, my manuscript kept expanding. This growth caused a considerable delay, to the dismay of the project sponsors and some survey participants. Thus a simple report originally conceived for lay people has become a more extensive work.

I begin this book with personal observations of my own Korean church near Loma Linda, California. This introduction offers first-hand accounts of life at a local Korean church. Thus, the style of this section is very different from the rest of the book. Yet readers may detect how my own experience has affected my overall perspective on the future of Korean Adventist churches in North America.

Chapter 1 provides a conceptual framework for the phenomenon of the Korean immigrant churches in North America. The prevalence of Christian churches in the Korean immigrant communities requires some historical and sociological explanation.

For those not familiar with the history of the Korean Adventist church, I offer a brief sketch in chapters 2 and 3. Appendices B and C also supply a chronological sketch of both the Korean Protestant church and the Asian American community.

Chapter 4 addresses issues and concerns related to the generational transition in immigrant churches. The effects of the demographic and cultural shifts from the first to the second generation are discussed.

To shed light on the findings of the Vision 2020 survey, recent social science studies on the children of Asian immigrants are reviewed in chapter 5. The assumption is that the Korean Adventist subgroup shares much in common with their peers elsewhere. In this way we can compare the life experiences of second-generation Korean Adventists with others.

The remaining chapters report the findings of the Vision 2020 survey project. When necessary, interpretation is offered. Besides the original survey group, two other groups were added later: 1) the Korean pastors in English ministry, both present and former ones at the time of the survey, and 2) some of the Internet participants on the Empower Ministry website. Their animated on-line exchanges on the future of the Korean American Adventist church provide different perspectives.

The appendices include brief summaries on selected subjects.

I hope readers find this book helpful in understanding the Korean Adventist church in North America. It may serve as a useful reference on Asian Americans in general and Korean American Adventists in particular. Furthermore, this case study may provide insights about other ethnic minority churches in North America.

USAGE OF KEY TERMS

The usage of some key terms is explained to avoid misunderstanding and confusion.

Church/Congregation: A church refers to an administrative unit that deals with personnel and budgets according to the rules of a denominational organization, whereas a congregation may be a group of people worshiping together with or without an administrative structure. So one local church may have two or three congregations with different age groups or languages represented. At some Korean churches, the small English-speaking groups may merely exist as congregations without much decision-making power on important matters of their churches.

Immigrant/Ethnic church: An immigrant church is composed of foreign-born immigrants while an ethnic church is a congregation that is different from the mainstream group in demographic or cultural make-up. All immigrant churches may be called ethnic churches, but not all ethnic churches are immigrant churches.

Korean American: Any person of Korean heritage who is a permanent resident or citizen in North America may be called a Korean American. Since the Korean Adventists in Canada are a small portion of the total group, a distinction of separate identity for Korean Canadians is not attempted.

Korean name: To maintain consistency in listing Korean names in this book, given names are placed before surnames or family names. Koreans currently tend to list their names in the original way by placing surnames before given names even without a comma after the surnames. A good example is Ban Ki-Moon, Secretary General of the United Nations.

North America: North America refers to the United States and Canada only. At the time of this report, no established Korean Adventist church existed in Mexico or in other small countries on the rest of the continent. Because of a very low representation in the survey by the Korean Adventist churches in Canada, North America is almost synonymous with the United States. At the same time, North America is to be understood as the sphere of the English-speaking Anglo culture, as opposed to the Spanish-speaking Latin American culture.

Second-generation members: These members include children of Korean immigrants who were born either in Korea or North America. In this study, the term includes the Korean-born "1.5 generation" members who followed their parents in their teen years.

White church: For lack of a better term, "white church" refers to mainstream Adventist churches in North America. The English-speaking white churches may not be fully Caucasian in terms of membership composition, but they are ethnically non-descriptive (or generic).

Youth ministry: Youth ministry is synonymous with second-generation ministry in Korean churches. In some cases, it refers to young-adult or English ministry.

Youth pastor: This term is used for any pastor who engages in second-generation ministry by communicating primarily in English. Some such pastors hold the title of "associate pastor" at their local churches, and their congregations may include young adults in their twenties, thirties, and even forties. The title is often determined by the composition of attending members in a congregation.

Acknowledgments

The future of most immigrant churches in North America becomes somewhat uncertain as the first immigrant generation fades away. Priorities and concerns of immigrant parents and their children are often different. Among others, maintaining ethnic identity with these churches can be a point of difference and even dispute. Members of the Korean Adventist church in North America, both the first and later generations, are no exception.

The leaders of the Korean Adventist churches in both first and second generations were anxious about the future direction and development of their faith community. To gauge the uncertain future, they expressed the need to gather information on the second-generation Korean Adventists. Since I shared the same concern, I agreed to lead a survey project. Thus, Vision 2020 was conceived.

Many have contributed to the project and the birth of this book. The efforts of the second-generation Korean Adventists and their leaders yielded more than 1,000 returned questionnaires. Special thanks goes to Pastor Peter Ahn, coordinator of the Korean Adventist youth ministry at the time of the survey, who spent many hours advancing this project. Without his enthusiasm and tenacity, the project would not have been completed. His colleagues in the second-generation ministry also rendered support to the survey project.

The Seventh-day Adventist Korean Church Council of North America endorsed the project, and the Korean Adventist Press provided funds to launch the survey.

I am grateful to Ronald Knott, director of Andrews University Press, who was interested in my book proposal and put it through various decision-making processes with patience and enthusiasm. Special thanks also goes to Deborah Everhart, editor of the Press, for her sharp eyes in spotting errors and for making valuable suggestions for manuscript improvement. I benefited considerably from the comments and suggestions of the anonymous reviewers of my manuscript as arranged by Andrews University Press. I am also thankful to Jeffrey Hammer, who read the preliminary draft of the manuscript with critical questions and who made many valid comments.

The financial support of some institutions and individuals made this book project a reality. Administrators of the Southern California Conference, the Southeastern California Conference, and the Korean Adventist Press promised to order books upon publication. Some of my friends contributed a considerable amount of money toward the book project, and I deeply appreciate their friendship and help.

I am also indebted to La Sierra University for granting me a sabbatical leave for this project and the research track that has allowed me to devote more time and energy to research projects and writing.

Lastly, I always appreciate my wife's sustaining support and help that provide strength and courage for life endeavors. This book project is no exception.

Introduction: My Church

I came to the United States in 1973 and joined the fledgling Loma Linda Korean Adventist Church in August 1976 when I moved to Riverside, California. It was one of the few early established Korean Adventist churches in North America.

The group claims to have started in the La Sierra area of Riverside with about fifteen Korean members in 1966. At that time, the Riverside campus of Loma Linda University[1] and the Loma Linda Food Factory[2] were attractions to the Korean members. Then they moved their gathering to Loma Linda two years later. The group was officially recognized as a company (a transitional status prior to becoming a full-fledged church) in 1972 by the Southeastern California Conference of Seventh-day Adventists. The conference hired its first Korean pastor, Elder Sung Nae Kim, for the Loma Linda group. He began his ministry in January 1973.

Although the small church building purchased by the group is located in the city of Grand Terrace, less than three miles from the western boundary of Loma Linda, the founding members wanted to identify with Loma Linda University and its world-famous medical center where most of the adult members either worked or studied. For years I have been a steady member of this church except for a few occasions when temporary responsibilities took me to other churches. At the Loma Linda Korean Church, I have served as deacon, Sabbath School teacher, choir member, elder, and head elder. I am still involved in choir, Sabbath School teaching, and eldership.

My two children attended the church until they graduated from the Adventist university near our home in La Sierra. While attending the church, neither of them asked us to move to another church for programs or personal reasons. They seemed to feel at home there. As a result, their church friends were mainly Korean Adventists.

Every Saturday my wife and I drive about twenty miles east to the church. We may pass about half a dozen Adventist churches on our way, but we have never thought about transferring our membership to another church either for convenience or a different church atmosphere. We may visit other churches on special occasions, but we are regulars at the Korean church. Having lived in the United States more than thirty years, we could be quite comfortable attending any English-speaking church in the area, including the La Sierra University Church which is within walking distance from our place. But staying with the Korean church has been almost as natural as eating rice and kimchi. Some of my colleagues at the university teasingly call my steady affiliation with the Korean church a "tribal loyalty."

When we began attending the church thirty years ago, there were fewer than one hundred attendees, including children. The old two-story building had no formal sanctuary for worship. Instead, it had two large rooms with rows of metal folding chairs. The adults worshiped in the room downstairs and the youth used the one upstairs for regular worship services. For a joint service, we met in the large room for adults. In the course of time, the church membership kept growing, and we decided to build a new sanctuary close to the old building. Today the original adult worship room is used for a toddlers' Sabbath School program.

Some members refused to participate in the pledge drive for the new sanctuary project. They argued that it would be a waste of hard-earned money and effort as future generations of Koreans would assimilate and leave their Korean church. We heard similar remarks from the church administrators at the time. Often they referred to the experiences of European immigrant churches in America and anticipated the same pattern among the children of Korean immigrants. They seemed to take the wait-and-see attitude. In spite of the uncertain future, we were pinched for space and pressed forward on the building project. In a few years, we completed a sanctuary in 1980 that could seat around

300. In the same year, the church hired its first full-time youth pastor for the English-speaking members.

Not long after the sanctuary project was completed, we decided to build another facility for multi-purpose activities and called it the "education hall." The number of immigrant families, undergraduate students, and professional school students was steadily growing. At the same time, young married couples added children at a considerable rate. Originally the third building was intended for the youth. But contrary to the initial intent, the main floor of the split-level third building became another sanctuary when it was completed in 1988. It provides a place for adult worship and a fellowship space in the basement, mainly for Sabbath potlucks. In retrospect, we should have hired an experienced architect and a general contractor to consider a long-term master plan. Even in the eyes of lay people, the non-descriptive third building with a seating capacity of about 500 has many awkward design elements.

About five years ago, the church studied the possibility of remodeling the existing facilities, especially the first (oldest) and third (newest) buildings. We were seeking to meet the needs of the growing church of about 500 members with diverse age and language groups. The more the building committee looked at the remodeling option, the more they were convinced that a brand new complex was needed somewhere in the area. The task of remodeling, without changing the original structures of the buildings and their physical arrangement, did not justify the anticipated cost and prolonged inconvenience.

Around this time, a church member who was successful in a medical venture offered to contribute three million dollars on the condition that other church members match that amount. Encouraged by the unexpected offer, the church decided to move to a new location. The building committee found a sizable empty lot of about eight acres near the eastern edge of Loma Linda.[3] Technical people have tried to determine the best option for the more than ten-million-dollar complex through numerous open hearings with the church members. With the matching fund from the members and the proceeds from the future sale of the existing complex, the targeted goal of ten million dollars appears to be within reach. And there is a possibility for a large sum of individual contributions to the building project from some well-to-do members of the church. According to a few preliminary architectural renderings submitted, the eight-acre church campus includes two worship sanctuaries for the two language groups, a fellowship hall, a gymnasium, a daycare center, and numerous classrooms and offices. The center piece of the campus is the main sanctuary that may seat around 1,000. The total size of the interconnected buildings is projected to approach nearly 100,000 square feet. The church projects its membership to be far more than 1,000 by the year 2020. The latest pledge for the new complex is the fourth among the original charter members of the church.

This time no one seems to be questioning the idea of building such an expensive facility on the grounds of an uncertain future prospect of the Korean church in America. Yet, a few have raised questions on the priority of the church. For instance, some members wonder why the church put so much money and effort into a building project while it has lost some young members to other churches in southern California. Others have pointed out that the church has spent much of its energy, time, and money on physical facilities during much of its existence. They insist that we should put our priority on people building through nurturing, training, and mission outreach. The prevailing sentiment, however, is that we should put an emphasis on both.

Every Sabbath, worshipers receive a bulletin printed in both Korean and English. The large sheet (11" x 16") with four folds informs members about the programs and events of each language group. At least once or twice a quarter, joint bilingual worship services are conducted. We also jointly celebrate special occasions such as Thanksgiving and Christmas. To accommodate the two language groups, we use translation. For congregational songs, the program prints the words in English. In the early years, we tried simultaneous translation using electronic earphones. But the reception of the method was less than satisfactory among the English-speakers. In a joint worship service, the key to success is the quality of the translation of the sermon either from Korean into English or the other way around. English-speakers are far less enthusiastic about the joint service than their parents who are willing to trade the inconvenience for the sense of one big family gathering under the same roof.

The congregation gathers at the church every Friday evening for an hour and on Saturdays from 9:30 until noon. A regular prayer meeting is also scheduled for 6:00 on Sunday mornings. During the week, the pastoral staff conducts a discipleship class each Thursday. The new senior pastor plans to have a church-wide vespers every Saturday evening. He wants to see all church members spend the entire Sabbath at church engaged in church-sponsored activities. Outside the church, most members attend small group meetings at private homes on Tuesdays. The whole church is divided into about twenty small groups, including some English-speaking groups.

Every Sabbath, the church feeds anywhere between 300 and 500 people by inviting everyone present to the potluck. This tradition has endured as long as the church has existed. In the early years, the potluck was especially intended for the students away from home. There were times that the church considered a scaled-down potluck just for visitors or no potluck at all. But no alternative lasted even a month. In spite of its cost, logistics, and labor for cooking, serving, and cleaning, the church members have maintained the weekly tradition of a communal meal. Regardless of the size of the congregation, faith and food seem to be inseparable elements at most Korean immigrant churches. The church is an extended family sharing the same meal once a week. Some out-of-town students have moved to other Korean churches for a "better" potluck, but I doubt that the quality of food is the main reason for their transfer.

The next closest Korean Adventist church is in Riverside. Located about fifteen miles to the west, it started as a branch group of the Loma Linda Korean Church in 1985. It was mainly for the members residing in the Riverside area until they moved to a new location in 2006. Not far from the La Sierra University campus, the church serves the Korean students attending the Adventist university. As the smaller Riverside church puts emphasis on campus ministry with great personal attention, many students, including some professional program students of Loma Linda University, have been attracted to that church. In my opinion, the presence of more than one Korean church in the same area has posed a healthy competition, reminding us not to take any member for granted.

Concerning the loss of students and young adults to other Korean churches in the area, the new pastoral and lay leadership have decided to reverse the trend and are groping for a better way to respond to the needs of students. For instance, a separate Sabbath worship service for students at a different time and place is being seriously considered. A regular Friday evening gathering of students has already been established with a special dinner provided by the ladies of the church. The board decided to hire a qualified person for campus ministry beginning in the 2007 school year. At a given time, around two hundred Korean Adventists are being trained in different programs of Loma Linda University and its medical center.

The loss of some students happened when the English group shifted its emphasis and focus from student (or campus) ministry to family ministry. The rationale was that students are temporary guests attending the Loma Linda Korean Church while pursuing their education or training in the area. This change of perspective reflects the demographic change in the English group. A steady increase of young adults and their growing children have presented new concerns and demands. To take care of the teen group, the church hired a full-time youth pastor mainly for the junior and senior high school students. Realizing the importance of caring for the needs of students of all ages regardless of their home base, the church is determined to pursue both tracks—family and campus ministries—without sacrificing one for the other.

Over the years of my membership at the Loma Linda Korean Church, I have seen many young people come and go following their educational and life cycle changes. Among those who moved away from southern California, some chose the Pacific Northwest for their permanent settlement, primarily the states of Washington and Oregon centered around the Seattle and Portland metropolitan areas. Others moved to the Southeast, mainly Georgia, Tennessee, and the Carolinas.

Not many seem to move back to their hometown states in the Midwest or Northeast or the Canadian provinces. The majority tend to settle down in southern California after their education and training. As a result, there are more than one hundred health-care professionals, both active and retired, at the Loma Linda Korean Church.

It is my impression that most Korean Adventists who stay in the Adventist faith tend to remain at the Korean Adventist church. This seems to be more so among married couples with children. However, if they feel that their children may benefit from a better children's program at other churches, they may leave the Korean church even for an extended period of time. In response to the demands and complaints of the parents with younger children, the church will add a full-time staff member exclusively for children's ministry. This specialist will help the church retain and attract young couples with children.

Mobile single students or young professionals without their own family ties are more likely to attend other churches if they are not satisfied with the church programs at Korean churches. Some of them roam from church to church. Young couples from Korea sometimes choose to attend white churches to immerse themselves in English and American culture and observe the workings of American churches.

Less than three miles from the Korean church are high-profile white churches in size, facility, and programs. This includes one of the largest Adventist churches in the world, the Loma Linda University church. But these churches have not been a strong magnet pulling away a large number of Korean Adventists. In addition, a half dozen other Asian churches (e.g., Chinese, Japanese, Indonesian, and Filipino) coexist in the same general area. It is my feeling that not many Korean church members have visited the nearby Asian churches even once out of curiosity.

The conference church directory shows that there are twenty-nine Asian-Pacific Adventist churches, including companies, in the Southeastern California Conference territory.[4] Counting only the number of congregations, the Asian-Pacific group comprises 18 percent of the total (154) for the conference. These Asian-Pacific churches are under the direction of the coordinator for Asian-Pacific ministry. Some other conferences in the Pacific Union have a similar administrative arrangement for Asian American members.

The English group at the Loma Linda Korean Church has a few intermarried couples. The non-Koreans include four white husbands, a Filipino husband, an African American husband, and a Chinese wife. The intermarried couples have children still at home. Most of them have been very active in leading the youth activities, such as the Pathfinder club and mission trips to Mexico. At the time of this writing, the head elder for the English group is a white member. I have not heard any major concerns about racial prejudice from either side. The integration seems seamless. Sometimes white or Hispanic Adventists, usually in their fifties or sixties, attend the English congregation for awhile. Since the group uses English, it is open to anyone.

So far the target of the church's mission outreach has been mainly Koreans, either community residents or students, in the area. In the Korean-speaking group, this is very apparent. The members of the church regard this as one of the main reasons for their existence as a distinctive ethnic church.

Yet the Loma Linda Korean Church is not consciously promoting the Korean culture among its members. Although its mission states that "our mission is to maintain the characteristics of a bicultural-church based on balanced Adventist beliefs," there is no systematic cultural program for either group. The church members seem to be open to the best of both cultures. The only visible ethnic marks at the church are the dominance of people of Korean ancestry, the use of the Korean language in the Korean congregation, Korean dishes[5] at the potluck, and some members wearing Korean costumes on special occasions, especially on the first day of a new year by both solar and lunar calendars. In the Korean congregation, the children's story is told in Korean, and children's special music is often sung in Korean. The parents conduct Sabbath programs in Korean for pre-school age children, but most classes for school-age children are conducted in English.

For nearly thirty years, the church has supported the operation of a Korean school for its children and others in the community on

Sundays during the school year. There the children, usually in the elementary grades, learn the Korean language and Korean culture. The part-time teaching staff are all Koreans. That is the only systematic effort of the church to transmit the mother tongue and culture to members of future generations. Undoubtedly, the family life is far more powerful in imbuing the Korean culture. Both the Korean language and customs are daily reinforced by parents and grandparents at home. For this reason, the church is not using the time of public gathering for cultural reinforcement.

Young married couples who grew up either in the United States or Korea now seem eager to establish the Korean identity in their children. They are proud of their Korean identity and heritage. Those from major metropolitan areas of Korea are cosmopolitan in their outlook and lifestyle, yet remain rooted in the Korean core. These young Koreans are different from the immigrants of my generation who came from an underdeveloped third-world country thirty or forty years ago.

The new senior pastor from Korea has an ambitious vision for the church. Having begun his American ministry at the church in January 2007, he wants to see the Loma Linda Korean Church become a model church in training young people for future leadership at their local churches but also for world mission. Stirred by his enthusiasm and vision, the church is willing to allocate the necessary means to support many new programs.

Three international cities have already established some kind of mission connection with the Loma Linda Korean Church Osaka, Japan; Lima, Peru; and Tijuana, Mexico. A former senior pastor of the church was supported for his mission work among the Korean residents in Osaka years ago. As a result of his pioneer work, there is now an organized Korean Adventist group in Osaka. A retired Korean pastor who became a member of the church started mission work among the Korean residents in the capital city of Peru, Lima. The church has sent evangelistic teams to the city and has worked to establish a dental clinic. From time to time, the church responds to financial needs of the church in Lima. The border city of Tijuana, Mexico, has been a place for frequent mission trips organized by the English group of the church. Their work includes a focus on the church building and dental care. A more coordinated systematic foreign mission work is attempted as part of the spiritual training of the church members, especially the second-generation members.

The growth potential of the Loma Linda Korean Church has a lot to do with its location. Within a thirty-mile radius, there are two Adventist universities, three high-profile private universities,[6] two state universities (including the fast-growing University of California, Riverside), and three community college systems. Hundreds of Korean and Korean American students attend these institutions. However, the major attraction of Adventist young people from North America and Korea has been Loma Linda University with its health-related programs, especially the programs in medicine and dentistry.

Attending either Loma Linda University or La Sierra University is more than receiving advanced Christian education. The two universities provide a large pool of prospective marital partners for Korean Adventist students. Many meet their spouses while pursuing education and training at one of the two schools. In spite of the high cost of private education, the area is favored by both parents and students for its advantages.

In recent years, many Korean Adventists who earned undergraduate degrees in Korea have moved to the Loma Linda area to pursue advanced health-related professional degrees. Also some healthcare professionals from Korea receive their post-doctoral training for one or two years at Loma Linda University and its medical center. Other young Korean professionals, such as nurses, move to the area for hospital employment. As a result, the Korean-speaking young adult group in their twenties and thirties has been steadily growing. This has changed the dynamics of the church as this group can easily interface with the older adult group and the English-speaking young adult group as well. In many ways, they have revitalized the Korean group as they fill the lower and middle section of age distribution.

Another benefit of Loma Linda's geographic location is the arid desert climate of southern California. Some of the Korean Adventists in the Midwest, Northeast, and Canada move to southern California when they retire. Often it is the case of parents joining their children who have established themselves in the area. Besides the balmy weather, Koreans want to spend their retirement years in a large Korean community. There are all kinds of meetings and activities for retired people in the area. Another reason for the influx, although it might be a remote one, could be the easy access to the cultural life of the bourgeoning Korean community in southern California and the home country.

In the history of the Loma Linda Korean Church, about a dozen full-time pastors have served, excluding the full-time pastors[7] currently serving at the time of this writing. All but one were hired either by the local church or the conference. In the past, each full-time pastor served four and a half years on average. The longest record was fourteen years and the shortest one was two years. In general, the senior pastors lasted about six years and the associate/youth pastors endured about three years. When they finished their years at the Loma Linda Korean Church, some transferred to other Korean churches, one retired, and some associate/youth pastors changed their careers. In fact, after their time at the Loma Linda Korean Church, none of the associate/youth pastors[8] have served at another Korean church as full-time pastors. This has been a disturbing trend, and the church has been suffering from the negative reputation.

The last associate pastor (2003–2006) was a Filipino minister who transferred to a white church after three years at the Loma Linda Korean Church. He was one of two serious candidates when the position was open. The other applicant was an African American pastor, and the search committee recommended the Filipino pastor. The fact that no Korean pastor applied for the position might have something to do with the way the previous two Korean pastors ended their English ministry at the church. Both left the church in a less than honorable way, and this was known among the limited number of Korean pastors in English ministry. As a result, no qualified Korean pastor applied at that time. Fortunately, a Korean-American pastor with years of experience accepted the invitation to lead the English ministry at the church effective July 2007.

In spite of its increase in membership and the new ambitious building project, the church has had its share of growing pains, especially between the Korean-speaking and English-speaking groups. Besides the communication, cultural, and generational gaps, different perspectives, value systems, and priorities have caused disagreements on certain issues. Sometimes the disagreements have led to tension. There were informal private talks about separation of the two language groups for mutual benefits and convenience. But such opinion was confined to a few individuals in response to certain circumstances. Separate worship services, elections, and social activities are offered out of necessity, but the two groups are closely interrelated on major issues in the church. Under the new pastoral leadership, the church as a whole has pushed for unity and cooperation across the different language and age groups. The new leadership is determined to overcome any human obstacles with patience and understanding. Once the spirit of unity is firmly instilled in the minds of the church members, they will do many great things. For many, potential success through joint effort outweighs the potential problems of two different language groups. This is the source of holding power for the groups.

While I have been attending the Loma Linda Korean Church, major changes have reshaped life in remarkable ways. In the technological world, the worldwide web (www), email, cell phones, satellite relays, and the like have significantly affected the way we think and live. In the realm of social life, two terms may represent the new reality of North America and the world: diversity (or cultural pluralism)[9] and globalization.[10] And the technological and social worlds are closely interwoven, constantly affecting each other.

As the United States has pushed for integration and acceptance of different groups, diversity has become a catch word. It is looked upon as the source of strength, not weakness. Uniqueness and difference are signs of distinction, not shame. Uniformity is not regarded as a necessary condition for unity. Thus valuing diversity has profoundly affected the self perception of ethnic members.

At the international level, globalization has transformed almost every aspect of life since the late twentieth century. More than anything else, globalization has turned the whole world into a village. Distance is not an impediment to communication among people. In the virtual cyber world, people engage in instant interaction across a continent or an ocean. Thus immigrants in North America are continuously reminded of their roots and identities. No more is the sense of isolation or separation from home felt among foreign immigrants. They are not compelled to give up their root identity.

Also while I have attended the Loma Linda Korean Church, South Korea has been transformed into a different nation. The once poverty-stricken agrarian third-world country has become a wonder of economic development. In information technology, Korea is on the cutting edge in many areas. Now ranked about tenth in the world in terms of gross national product,[11] the country is highly visible. Some Korean brand names—such as Samsung, LG, and Hyundai—are as ubiquitous as wireless cellular phones and passenger cars. In the world of sports, Korea hosted two major events: the summer Olympic Games in 1988 and the World Cup (soccer) in 2002. The city of Daegu was chosen to host the World Athletic Championship Game in track and field in 2011. The high-profile international events have exposed Korea to the world and the world to Korea as well. Many Koreans now have their names recognized internationally. The new UN Secretary General (Ban Ki-Moon), prominent scientists, art performers, women golfers, and male athletes have made Koreans proud of their nationality. Among the Koreans living in North America, especially younger ones, these people reinforce their ethnic identity and pride in measurable ways.

Even in the Christian world, Korea stands out. The largest Protestant churches in the world are in Korea. These mega churches have served as a model of church growth. Furthermore, Korea is ranked second in sending out missionaries. Only the United States has sent out more missionaries than Korea, but many predict that Korea will soon outnumber America (Moll 2006).

Likewise, the Adventist church in Korea has been the major force in the Northeast Asian region, especially in financial contributions and membership. The Northern Pacific-Asia Division created in

1997 has been headquartered in Seoul, and its presidents have been Korean. The division includes China, Japan, Korea, and Taiwan. Korea's Sahmyook University located in Seoul is the largest Adventist institution of higher learning in terms of student enrollment.

Some Korean Christians come to North America with mission objectives in mind. The new senior pastor of the Loma Linda Korean Church reflects the global mission perspective of the Korean Christian church in general. Often on Sabbath, about half a dozen visitors from Korea worship at the Loma Linda Korean Church, occasionally outnumbering visitors from nearby Korean churches.

Directly affecting the Korean churches in North America is the continuous flow of Korean immigrants. More Korean nationals are likely to travel to America and stay there temporally or permanently. Soon Korean tourists may freely enter the United States without a visa once the U.S. government exempts South Korea from the visa requirements.[13] South Korea has the largest foreign student population in the United States, approaching the 100,000 mark.[14] In addition, the recent Free Trade Agreement between the United States and Korea has opened the gates of the two countries wider. Although the agreement needs to be approved by the lawmakers of both countries, the impact on human migration is going to be significant when the agreement is ratified and implemented.[15]

Some may wonder why I stress the national and international changes when writing about my own experience at a local church in southern California. Major changes at the national and global levels provide psychological grounds for people's identity and outlook. The promotion of diversity in America, the intimate connection of North America with Korea through globalization, the increasing international profile of Korea, and Korea's active leadership role in world mission are powerful reminders of national or ethnic origins of Korean people in North America. These may partially explain why the members of the Loma Linda Korean Church want to posit themselves as a model church in North America and in the world. The external changes briefly described here may feed a different outlook, confidence, and pride in the people.

I decided to share my own personal observations of the Loma Linda Korean Church so as to provide a concrete glimpse of the Korean Adventist church in North America. Undoubtedly, my church is unique and different in many ways. Perhaps no other Korean Adventist church on either side of the Pacific Ocean resembles it in terms of its unique location and membership composition. But as an ethnic church, it is quite similar to many other Korean Adventist churches in North America. As I revealed, my own church has its share of challenges and promises as well. There are challenges to overcome the generational differences aggravated by cultural differences. I hope my personal observations may offer unique insights for understanding the Korean church in North America. This is the only place in the book where the experiences of a local Korean American church are described from a personal perspective.

Throughout the book, I attempt to discover patterns among Korean Adventist churches in general. To that end, I have to treat the subject matter in a more general, collective, and objective manner. If one can sense optimism in my perspective on the future of the Korean Adventist church in North America, perhaps that optimism may be partially attributed to my own experience at the large, growing church in southern California.

Whenever one is willing to share personal experience in public, that person takes a risk of personalizing a group experience. So I was mindful not to be too subjective. Nonetheless, any misrepresentation and distortion in describing my home church is entirely my own fault.

NOTES

1. The Riverside campus of Loma Linda University became a separate independent institution, La Sierra University, in 1991.

2. The Loma Linda Food Factory near the present-day La Sierra University gradually phased out in the 1980s for financial reasons.

3. The city of Loma Linda has been negotiating with the San Bernadino county to annex the small area to the city.

4. The Southeastern California Conference does not include the Los Angeles and Ventura counties. The Los Angeles county has a high concentration of Asian/ Pacific residents.

5. The typical Korean potluck menu includes steamed rice, kimchi, vegetarian tofu stew, seaweed, a variety of vegetables, and fruit. Seldom are carbonated beverages or sweet desserts served.

6. These three are Claremont University, University of Redlands, and California Baptist University.

7. There are two full-time pastors for each language group.

8. Four made career changes and one now pastors at a white church.

9. The passage of the Civil Rights Act by the US Congress in 1964 may be considered the beginning of cultural pluralism. The act prohibits discrimination on the basis of gender, race, nationality, and religion, among other attributes. Consequently, equal treatment engenders equal respect for everyone.

10. According to Guillen (2001), scholarly writing on globalization began to appear around 1965. The volume of publication on the subject showed a noticeable increase around 1985.

11. In 2005, South Korea was ranked the eleventh-largest economy in the world in terms of its Gross National Product (GNP): $787,624,000,000, according to the World Development Indicators Database compiled by the World Bank in July 2006. In that year, the GNP of South Korea was greater than that of India, Mexico, or Russia, among other countries.

12. It was announced in March 2007 that the 2011 World Athletic Championship games in track and field would be held in Daegu, South Korea.

13. Citizens of twenty-seven nations can enter the United States and stay up to ninety days without a visa. The South Korean government has tried to obtain the status of the visa waiver program (VWP), but South Korea has failed to meet the VWP standard mainly in the area of a visa refusal rate of 3 percent. See http://www.state.gov/r/pa/prs/ps/2006/71974.htm and http://www.americanchronicle.com/articles/viewArticle.asp?articleID=3621.

14. According to the Immigration and Customs Enforcement (ICE) of the Homeland Security Department, 93,728 Korean students enrolled in 2006, an increase of 14.8 percent from 2005. Korean students compose 14.9 percent of the total number of non-immigrant foreign students in the United States. See http://wolk.multiply.com/reviews/item/69.

15. The Free Trade Agreement was made between Korea and the United States on April 2, 2007. The agreement will be implemented when it is ratified by the legislators of both nations.

CHAPTER 1

Ethnic Church and the Korean American Community

In North America, the term "ethnic church" is used mainly to refer to the membership composition of a congregation. The ethnic reference tends to be made for a racial or national identity of a church group. A black church or Japanese church are examples. It may also refer to a language spoken by a congregation which is something other than the mainstream language of the surrounding culture. This may include a single national group or multiple nationalities. An example of a single national group is a Vietnamese church, while multiple nationalities may be represented by a Hispanic church for various Spanish-speaking Latin American nationalities. These racial, national, or linguistic aspects of the ethnic churches distinguish them from the mainstream churches of the larger society.[1] Thus, often the term "ethnic church" may imply a minority status of subgroups.

In most immigrant communities, the churches are ethnic as they serve people from other countries or regions speaking languages other than English. Language is the key demarcation among groups of different origins. For that reason, there are no separate churches in the United States for immigrants from Australia, Great Britain, or Canada. For the same reason, immigrants from India rarely establish their own churches in America as they speak English. This proves that English is a key ingredient for integration.

1

Whether the congregations are Protestant, Catholic, or some other branch of Judeo-Christianity, these churches are highly visible in their communities. They draw the attention of immigrants, especially new arrivals. In fact, these churches extend helping hands to new immigrants at their ports of entry, usually key international airports, as a way of adding new members to their churches.

In Judeo-Christian America, ethnic churches serve as a bridge between the immigrant communities and the larger society. As a result, these churches become part of much larger networks in terms of denominational or religious affiliation. Accordingly, they can better serve the immigrants in their communities.

From the perspective of immigrants, it is not hard to understand the importance of ethnic churches. Uprooted from their familiar home countries, most immigrants experience a great amount of stress. Economic uncertainty and the sense of estrangement are major sources of anxiety. So immigrants look for a place where they can receive comfort, guidance, and support. Besides one's family members, no other groups in an immigrant community can provide more intimate and sustainable help than the churches. With both internal and external networks, an ethnic church can respond to the wide range of needs of the immigrants.

In particular, the ethnic ambience these churches create with a native language and culture can be very powerful and enchanting to the newly arrived immigrants. Worshiping in one's native tongue with people from the same region or country uplifts their spirits. When the immigrants participate in the religious services, they are momentarily transported back to the land they left and re-live their home life in the host country. So most immigrant churches enjoy adherence and loyalty from their members.

In addition, interacting with fellow compatriots will help immigrants gather useful information about the life situation of their host country. The practical assistance, both formal and informal, they find in their ethnic churches is valuable. So even after they are securely settled in the host country, they continue to associate with their churches for the comfort of being among those with the same language and cultural group. Due to the challenging circumstances most immigrants experience in their host countries, religion and ethnicity become a powerful combination. Here blood and belief thickly coalesce.

SECOND GENERATION AND THE ETHNIC CHURCH

Unlike most of their parents, children of immigrants, either raised or born in North America, have an option to stay with their ethnic church or to leave it. Of course, they do not have much choice as minor dependents while attending their parents' church. But once they become old enough to drive their own cars and graduate from high school, they are almost out of parental restraint. Nevertheless, many of them may choose to continue attending their ethnic churches as adults with their own children.

Other than the common quest for spirituality that applies to all generations, children of immigrants may not attend an ethnic church for the same reasons as did their parents. Socialized and educated in America, most second-generation members are not as concerned about economic survival or establishing a social network in the larger society. To them, the language and cultural barriers are not the major issues or concerns in their social advancement. Yet, their continuous attendance at an ethnic church may be explained in terms of ethnic attachment that helps form identity among the second-generation members and their children as well.

In postmodern, multicultural America, no one is forced to lose one's ethnic identity. Unlike the majority of immigrants from Europe before the middle of the twentieth century, the new immigrants, mainly from Asia and Latin America, are not pressured to enter a melting pot. On the contrary, they are encouraged to preserve their heritage. By being bilingual and bicultural, they hope to better adapt to the globalizing world. In the increasingly interdependent world, life is becoming more transnational. Immigrants want to be more than American. The one-time enormous melting-pot image of America has been replaced with that of a gigantic salad bowl.

So if young people desire to retain their ethnic subculture,[2] they may try a variety of things. Taking a language course, visiting one's mother country,[3] or joining an ethnic club are some common approaches for learning about their ethnic heritage. To most church-goers, however, an ethnic church is perhaps the most powerful arrangement to fulfill the same purpose. There members engage in personal interactions with other coethnics on a regular, long-term basis. In such a community of faith, relationships tend to be intense and intimate. Although cultural concerns are supposed to be secondary in any religious setting, the effects of ethnic reinforcement upon the participants could be significant. If a religious group engages in deliberate "ethnicity reproduction" for its members, the outcome could be more explicit and potent (Ebaugh and Chafetz 2000). In this regard, no other ethnic organizational arrangement can match the church that provides opportunities for ethnic reinforcement for multiple generations on a weekly basis.

Another factor in measuring the significance of the influence of an ethnic church may be the proportion of community members who are affiliated with it. In other words, the higher the proportion of community members who are affiliated with a particular church, the greater the influence of the church in that community. If 80 percent of community members are churchgoers in community A, the influence of the church is much greater in A than in community B where only 30 percent of community members are affiliated with the church. It is simply the weight effect of majority.

This is the case in most Korean American communities as far as Christianity is concerned. As almost 80 percent of Korean Americans claim to belong to a church, the influence of the church in such a community can be quite substantial.[4] Accordingly, one can assume that the church may act as a purveyor and preserver of the Korean culture to its members. The intention of these churches as cultural promoters may vary by congregation. Some are deliberate while others are indifferent.

Much of this book is about ethnicity and religion in the context of the Korean Adventist community in North America. Before we look at the relationship of the two dimensions in detail among the second-generation members, we want to trace the popularity of Christianity among Koreans. This may shed light on the high percentage of church affiliation among Korean Americans. Such a phenomenon is to be understood from both historical and sociological perspectives.

CHRISTIANITY AND KOREANS

Attentive observers of the Korean American community may agree that "any consideration of Korean Americans must start with their faith and churches" (Lien and Carnes 2004:48). Indeed, the Protestant churches, mainly Presbyterian and Methodist, have played key roles in the Korean American community since its beginning in Hawaii in 1903.[5] From the Greater Los Angeles metropolitan area to any medium-size Midwestern or southern city, one may easily find a Korean church.[6] There is a saying that whenever three Koreans get together in America, they talk about starting a church. In this regard, Koreans are far more eager to establish a church than those from their Asian neighboring countries, China and Japan.[7]

To many Korean immigrants and their children, the church is a significant part of their social life. Perhaps only their family and work or school may command more of their time and energy than the church.[8] Their commitment to church is substantial in terms of time, effort, and financial contributions. Thus, in visibility and influence, no other Korean American community organization comes even close to it.

Why do many Korean immigrants turn to church and regard it as an important part of their lives in America? The prevalence of church life may be attributed to the history of the Christian church in Korea and its influence in modern Korean society. The Christian church in Korea is approaching the 125-year mark. Christianity was first introduced to Korea in 1885 by American missionaries.[9] That took place only three years after the first treaty between Korea and America forced by the gun-boat diplomacy that started in 1845. It should be noted here that the United States forced Japan to open up to the outside world with the same tactic by displaying its mighty naval force, known as Black Fleet, in 1854.

From the beginning, the Christian church had played significant roles in modernizing the one-time xenophobic hermit kingdom. The pioneer American missionaries to Korea established a western educational system and medical facilities. Their mission schools educated many future Korean leaders, including women, in different fields. As a result, Koreans looked upon the Christian church as a progressive force throughout much of the twentieth century.

The first one hundred years of the Christian church in Korea paralleled the country's constant political and social turmoil of that period. This includes the demise of the last Korean dynasty in 1910, the Japanese colonial occupation from 1910 to 1945, the Pacific War (1941–1945), and the Korean War (1950–1953) with devastating effects for decades. During this time of tremendous national suffering and confusion, many Koreans turned to Christianity for support, guidance, and strength.[10] Also, millions of Korean War refugees from the communist North Korea established and supported the Christian church in South Korea.[11] As a result, South Korea became an ardent Christian country in spite of the continuous political and economic hardships. At present, almost 25 percent of South Koreans claim to be churchgoers. In the last few decades, the country has become a model case for church growth with numerous world-class mega churches in Seoul and other large cities.

Finally, the establishment of the Christian church in Korea was largely the result of mission efforts by the mainline Protestant denominations[12] based in North America. Especially during and after the Korean War, the extensive American civil aid programs were administered through the churches. Consequently, Korean people tended to associate Christianity with America throughout much of the twentieth century. Through frequent contacts with Americans individually and collectively, the Christian community became the most exposed segment of the Korean society to America. This is an important factor in understanding the high percentage of Christians among the Korean immigrants in America.

Although the opportunity to emigrate to America has been fairly open to most Koreans, far more Korean Christians have taken advantage of the self-selective process. For instance, some studies[13] have shown that about 70 percent of Korean immigrants to America were churchgoers at home. Accordingly, the majority of Korean immigrants join a Korean church when they come to the United States. This affects even the Korean immigrants who were not churchgoers at home. The non-Christian immigrants may see the benefits of joining a church when many Koreans in their community attend a church. To them, the church is a place for social gathering and information exchange which are valuable to immigrants. A church that congregates weekly, often two or three times a week, is the best place for Korean immigrants to fellowship in the comfort of their own language and culture. In addition to meeting the needs of immigrants, Korean pastors and lay members are actively recruiting the newly arrived members to their churches in the name of soul winning and church growth. Also an excessive number of former ministers in Korea and seminary graduates in America help to account for the phenomenal growth of Korean churches in America. The above reasons may explain why most Korean immigrants affiliate with a church in North America.

SECOND-GENERATION KOREAN AMERICANS

The circumstances and needs of second- and third-generation Korean Americans are quite different from those of their immigrant parents. They do not struggle with language barriers or cultural adaptation. They may attend any church that conducts services in English, including many Korean churches that offer programs for English-speakers. But if the second-generation members and their children follow the pattern of the first-generation immigrants in church attendance, this may be due to something other than family tradition.

As previously implied, one explanation could be the effects of ethnic reinforcement in ethnic churches. American-educated, second-generation members will attend a Korean church because they have chosen to. Usually it is an indication that they wish to preserve and strengthen their Korean identity. Their weekly encounter with and exposure to other Koreans reinforce their own and their children's ethnic identity. And their interaction may be intense in the name of a common ancestry and belief. Here, religion and ethnicity are intertwined as "religion plays an ethnic function in America and ethnicity has powerful religious overtones" (Ebaugh and Chafetz 2000:94).

Another reason why second-generation Korean Americans may remain in Korean churches could be the comfort zone the ethnic church provides. Being familiar with the people and culture, Korean Americans may feel at ease in associating with their coethnics. This could be an attractive feature of the ethnic church if the minority members feel somewhat uneasy with others who may be distant due to ethnic or cultural differences.

In addition, some Asian Americans tend to see their churches as a haven in the sea of moral decline. They want to believe that church is an antidote to the undesirable influence of the secular society.[14] Such a perception is more evident among the first-generation Asian immigrant parents who want to protect their children from the moral dangers of the larger society.

A final explanation could be the spiritual overtone of the Korean churches. Each cultural or national group establishes a somewhat different spiritual tradition and overtone. This may reflect the history of a particular national church in the context of a national history. The Korean Christian church had gone through a great deal of suffering and tribulation during much of its first hundred years. Yet it overcame the national hardships and became very strong and dynamic. The church demands personal conviction and commitment to their beliefs. Faith is more of an action than reasoning. As a result, Korean Christians have become active in mission outreach worldwide. Likewise, many Korean churches in North America mirror the image of the home churches. Some of these churches bear the sense of mission to evangelize the secular American society.[15] Thus, their messages and activities might have special appeal to the Korean Americans. In fact, many Korean American churches are evangelical in theology and lifestyle. This requires a strong personal commitment.

Thus, if the Korean churches in America resonate with the personal and spiritual aspirations of their members, they will continue to attract Korean Americans. As long as members of future generations find the church meeting their personal and spiritual needs, they may retain membership in a Korean church.

In the next chapter, the establishment of Korean Adventist churches both in Korea and North America will be presented. Their beginnings and growth are to be understood against the historical backdrop of these countries.

NOTES

1. Among European immigrants, examples may include the Irish Catholic, Greek Orthodox, and Dutch Reformed churches. Recent immigrants from Asia may include the Korean Presbyterian church and the Cambodian Catholic church. On the other hand, the linguistic denotation, as with the La Sierra Spanish Church, refers to the common language spoken by the members regardless of their different national origins in Latin America.

2. In one study, close to 90 percent of Chinese and Korean high school students expressed their desire to know more about their cultural heritage. See Park (2005:56).

3. Many foreign governments and private organizations sponsor special programs for the children of their overseas compatriots. For instance, the South Korean government has supported cultural education for overseas Korean children with funds, programs, materials, and personnel. Some educational and religious organizations have arranged language and cultural tour programs for overseas Korean students during vacations.

4. Overall, Asian Americans have shown a high rate of religious affiliation. Among Korean Americans in Los Angeles and New York, for example, 87 percent reported that they belonged to a religion. Of the religiously affiliated Koreans, 80 percent belong to Christian churches. See Lien and Carnes (2004:38–51).

5. A few Korean ministers followed their countrymen to Hawaii. From the beginning they conducted worship services at different sugar plantations. On the American mainland, the first Korean church was established in San Francisco in 1905.

6. In 2001, there were 3,402 Korean Protestant churches and 154 Korean Catholic churches in the United States. This assumes that there was one church for roughly every 300 Koreans. (See Ebaugh and Chafetz 2000:48–49.) It can be estimated that there were about 4,000 Korean churches in 2007.

7. According to the same saying, when three Chinese get together, they talk about opening a restaurant, while three Japanese consider starting a business.

8. Koreans are the most actively involved in their church programs among Asian Americans. Many Korean churches hold daily prayer meetings in the early morning hours, usually starting between five and six o'clock, before members go to work or school. Besides the early morning prayer meetings, they meet two or three other times per week to worship together.

9. The first American missionaries to Korea were Horace G. Underwood, William B. Scranton, John W. Herton, and Henry G. Appenzeller.

10. During the Korean struggle against the Japanese colonial rule for thirty-six years, some American government officials and missionaries took sides with the Korean people.

11. Christianity was stronger in North Korea before the division of the nation in 1945. Christianity was first introduced to the northern region of the country. Many North Korean Christians fled to South Korea for the freedom of religion before and during the Korean War (1950–1953).

12. The major mainline Protestant denominations include Presbyterians, Methodists, and Baptists in that order. Yet the Presbyterian church is the most dominant one in Korea and the United States. According to one report, the three denominations comprised 42, 14, and 5 percent, respectively, in Los Angeles and Chicago. On the other hand, Catholics, non-denominationals, and Evangelicals made up 14, 13, and 5 percent, respectively (Hurh 1998:107).

13. About three of four Koreans (75%) in Los Angeles and Chicago reported that they were churchgoers (Hurh 1998:107; Min in Min and Kim 2002:4).

14. They see some aspects of Americanization or assimilation as destructive and undesirable (Ebaugh and Chafetz 2000:122).

15. Zeal for Christianizing America and the world is more common among evangelical Korean Americans (Ebaugh and Chafetz 2000:186–188).

CHAPTER 2

The Roots of the Korean Adventist Church

To better understand the Korean Adventist church in North America, we may want to study how the church first emerged in Korea before branching out to North America. Such historical knowledge should be helpful to those who are not familiar with the modern history of Korea, especially that country's relations with the United States which have spanned more than a century.[1]

Readers are strongly encouraged to review Appendixes B and C. The chronological description of modern Korea and the Asian American community listed there will show the historical context in which the Korean Adventist church established itself both at home and in America.

THE IMMIGRATION ROOTS OF THE KOREAN ADVENTIST CHURCH

The first Koreans to hear the Adventist message were two commoners dreaming of a better life in Hawaii. The history-making event did not take place in Korea, however, but in Japan in 1904. The two dreamers were Hung Jo Sohn and Hung Yul Lee. Recruited by the agents of Hawaii sugar plantation owners, they sailed first to the Kobe harbor in Japan for a medical examination.[2] Korean laborers who passed the physical examination were to obtain entry visas to the then American territory of Hawaii. At that time, Korea did not have adequate Western-style medical facilities to handle large numbers of people. The first Western medical doctors to Korea were American missionaries who had arrived only about twenty years earlier in 1885. The American missionary doctors had to establish their clinic from scratch. Trying to convince the Koreans of the effectiveness of their quaint Western medicine was not easy for the foreigners. So the American government used Japanese medical facilities in screening the Korean labor applicants.

One may wonder why two men, with so many of their countrymen, would want to go to far-away islands in the first place. The age-old Confucian norms would have discouraged men from leaving their families and ancestral villages. Filial piety was the core of Confucianism, and it would be shameful for a man to leave his parents and family. Neglecting one's filial duties was a cardinal sin. Such duties would include caring for his parents and performing the annual ancestor worships, among other things.

Toward the end of the 500-year-old Yi dynasty (1392–1910) at the dawn of the twentieth century, the political circumstances of Korea were very precarious. The last Korean kingdom was steeped in continuous political turmoil. As a result, the shattered nation became a pawn in the hands of the surrounding superpowers in northeast Asia.

During much of the second half of the nineteenth century, the United States, China, Japan, and Russia were involved in political manipulations seeking to control the small hermit kingdom. Separated only by a narrow strait from the Korean peninsula, Japan seemed to have an upper hand in the political jockeying of the superpower. For the island nation to the east, the Korean peninsula was a valuable land bridge connecting itself to the mainland of Asia, especially China. At that time, Japan was a rising empire since the Meiji Reform in 1868 following its acceptance of America's demand for an open trade.[3] The reform began modernizing Japan after the model of Western nations, including the United States. Soon its political ambition was to expand the empire into China and beyond.

Japan had long viewed Korea as a strategic acquisition for expansion, and in 1592 it had even invaded Korea. But Japan was defeated by the Korean navy led by Admiral Soon Shin Lee. The situation was different for the Korean kingdom at the beginning of the twentieth century, however. The worsening domestic conditions had forced many Korean men to search for better opportunities elsewhere.

Around the time Mr. Sohn and Mr. Lee left for Japan, the last Korean kingdom, Yi Dynasty, was about to become a Japanese protectorate, a prelude to the eventual colonization of the country for thirty-six years. Korea became a Japanese protectorate in 1905 and became its colony in 1910 when it was annexed to Japan.[4] Only the final victory of the United States in the Pacific War in August 1945 ended the Japanese colonial occupation of Korea.

In the meantime, the Hawaiian islands were experiencing a severe labor shortage in its booming sugar farming and sugar refinery business. The Hawaii sugar plantations relied heavily on labor recruits from Asian countries. When the U.S. Congress passed the Chinese Exclusion Act in 1882 to prohibit importing Chinese workers, the plantation owners turned to Japan first and then to Korea. As the Hawaiian islands are located almost at the half-way point between the American mainland and the Pacific rim of Asia, it was easier and cheaper for the sugar plantation owners to bring laborers from Asia by steamships than to bring Americans either from the Midwest or from the east coast.

During the labor recruitment drives in Korea, some American missionaries encouraged their church members to migrate to Hawaii. In the opinion of these missionaries, it was a sure way of escaping from the dire poverty in Korea (Patterson and Kim 1977).

On December 22, 1902, in the midst of a cold winter, the first ship left the Inchon Harbor near Seoul with 121 Korean applicants headed for Japan. But only eighty-six individuals from the first group boarded the next ship in Kobe for their final destination. Some of those left behind departed for Hawaii later, but others had to return to Korea. The Korean workers were promised sixteen dollars a month for laboring hard from dawn to dusk six days a week (Yoon 1989). The first Korean labor recruits aboard the S.S. Gaelic steamship arrived in Honolulu on January 13, 1903. It was the historic beginning of over a century of Korean immigration to America.

This is a brief sketch of the national and international circumstances when the Korean government officially approved the first overseas immigration program ever in its history of more than 4,000 years. The government was reluctant, but the people were desperate.

THE PLANTING OF ADVENTIST SEEDS

After sailing a full day from the Korean harbor, Hung Jo Sohn and Hung Yul Lee arrived in Kobe near Osaka for the physical examination and the American entry visa. While waiting for their results, they roamed the city. One day they saw a poster announcing a religious meeting. Having nothing else to do, they decided to attend. It was a crusade meeting sponsored by the Kobe Adventist church (Kim 1993:23–24).

Stirred by the speaker's explanation of the biblical prophecies about the last days, the men continued to attend the meetings. They sensed the urgency of the end times and decided to join the church. Right before they left the city, the Japanese speaker, Pastor Kuniya Hide, baptized the two transients from the neighboring country. The baptismal ceremony took place on June 12, 1904, around midnight in the pond of the Nunobiki Falls in Kobe, making the two the very first Korean Adventists. The irony was that they became Adventists in a foreign country on their way to yet another foreign country.

Mr. Sohn failed the physical examination for the entry visa and had no choice but to return to Korea. On his return ship, he met a fellow countryman, Kee Ban Yim, from Hawaii. Mr. Sohn explained what he had learned at the meeting in Kobe. Mr. Yim was so impressed with the Adventist message that he decided to join the faith as well.

When they arrived in Korea, the two began to share their new-found message with the villagers. Mr. Yim also publicly confirmed his faith through baptism in August of that same year. As a result of their joint efforts, a dozen Koreans with their family members accepted the Adventist truth. A few villages near Pyungyang (the capital city of North Korea since 1948) began to have meetings on Saturdays.

The first official Korean Adventist gathering took place in the harbor city of Jinnampo, not far from Pyungyang, on September 27, 1904. The Japanese Pastor Kuniya Hide and the president of the Japan

Mission organized the first official gathering. About forty people were present at the historic first meeting (Kim 1993:25–30).

It is interesting to note that the Korean Adventist church was born through the dream of two Koreans who wished to live happily on America's paradise island. And the one whose earthly dream was shattered became the pioneer of the Adventist movement in Korea.

FROM SMALL TO LARGE IMMIGRATION WAVES

Mr. Sohn's companion from Korea, Mr. Lee, passed the physical examination and continued to sail to Hawaii. He became the first Korean Adventist to ever step foot onto American territory. Mr. Lee's Adventist faith failed to bloom in his new life in Hawaii, however. Perhaps his new life situation was too overwhelming for the lone Adventist neophyte to follow the teachings he had hastily accepted. His knowledge about the Adventist faith was no doubt scanty and shallow. Briefly exposed to Adventist teachings during his transition in Japan, he had little chance to lay any spiritual foundation for himself. Without moral support from fellow countrymen, the sole Adventist might not have had the strength to hold onto his new faith. Both in Japan and Hawaii, he was merely a nameless labor recruit.

Indeed, the working and living conditions on the sugar plantation were harsh, leaving little energy and time for a single person to defend his new faith. Mr. Lee might not have been able to withstand pressure from other Koreans who were more likely to be either Confucian believers or Buddhists. Moreover, it is quite possible that the Adventist faith he accepted in Japan drew ridicule from other Korean Christians who were either Methodists or Presbyterians. These Protestant groups were well organized under the leadership of their ministers who accompanied the migrant workers to Hawaii. In 1905, all seven sugar plantations in Hawaii operated Christian chapels for the Korean workers and their family members (Kim in Kwon, Kim, and Warner 2001:9).

EARLY KOREAN IMMIGRATION TO AMERICA

The Korean immigration of plantation workers to Hawaii lasted only three years, from 1903 to 1905. About 8,000 Koreans came during that time. Some immigrated with wives and children, but usually men came alone. The Korean group included about 6,000 men, 1,000 women, and several hundred children. Many were residents of major harbor cities in Korea that were open to the outside world. Coming primarily from the urban middle class of Korean society, 70 percent of them were literate and 40 percent were Christians (Kim in Kwon et al. 2001:9). Most of those who came alone hoped to realize their Hawaiian dream and return home with the money they might have accumulated over the years.

The sudden halt in shipment of Korean labor recruits was ordered by the Korean king, Emperor Ko Jong, in 1905. He was deeply disturbed by the deception of a British and a Japanese recruitment contractor. The two contractors misled both the Korean government and prospective farm workers by exaggerating the work prospects in Mexico. Not knowing much about the far-away country of Mexico at the end of the vast Pacific Ocean, the Korean government approved a four-year labor contract. Thus the Korean immigration to Mexico took place in March 1905, when 1,033 Koreans were transported to the Yucatan Peninsula facing the Gulf of Mexico. The misled Koreans were treated almost like slaves by the Mexican mallow farm owners. A Korean ginseng peddler recognized this predicament and reported it to the Korean government (Hyun 1976).

At the same time, the Korean government was already under pressure from Japan to curve the competition of the Korean workers against the Japanese laborers in Hawaii. About 273,000 Japanese had come to America, mainly Hawaii, since 1890. Furthermore, the Japanese government did not want to see the formation of a sizeable Korean community in America, even in the U.S. territory of Hawaii, that could become a base for a Korean independence movement against Japan. The Korean government was helpless against such pressure when it became the Japanese protectorate in 1905.

About 60 percent of the Koreans were still in Hawaii by 1905, but only 50 percent remained by 1910. About 2,000 sugar plantation workers moved to the mainland, especially California, when their labor contracts expired. Approximately 1,000 returned to Korea (Kim in Min and Kim 2002:190). The Koreans on the American mainland were joined by a few political exiles who contemplated the independence movement against Japan. Around this time, only a small number of privileged Koreans were attending American colleges.

Most Korean men who had come to Hawaii alone did not intend to settle there permanently. Their hope was to return with sufficient money to buy a sizable rice field and a house and live happily with their families at home. But the economic reality of the sugar planta- tion labor was far from what they imagined it to be. Moreover, their desire to return home was dampened when Korea became a Japanese protectorate and then its colony in 1910. As a result, even the Koreans in Hawaii became citizens of the Japanese empire. In addition to this complication, the Korean-born residents were not eligible for American citizenship according to the Naturalization Act of 1790.[5] This was the case for all non-white immigrants until 1952 when the U.S. Congress passed the McCanan-Walter Act. Until then, foreign- born Asians could not become American citizens regardless of how long they had lived in the United States.

Unable to travel to Korea for lack of money and not wanting to show their labor-hardened dark skin under the simmering tropical sun, many of the plantation workers found Korean wives by exchanging pictures. For this service, match-making agents played the go-between role in Hawaii and Korea. If the match succeeded, the groom would pay the matching fee to the match-maker.

From 1910 to 1924, almost 1,000 Korean women sailed half-way across the Pacific Ocean to meet the men in Hawaii. Like their future husbands, many of the women took the venture to escape from the poverty in Korea. These women were called "picture brides" (Yoon 1989). Other Asian immigrant groups in Hawaii and the mainland used the same method to bring their future wives from home.

IMMIGRATION OF KOREANS TO AMERICA IN THE POST-WAR YEARS

The end of World War II brought a stop to Japan's thirty-six- year colonial occupation of Korea. The historical moment of Korean liberation came on August 15, 1945, when the Japanese emperor surrendered to the United States.

No sooner was Korea liberated than it was divided along the 38th parallel. The southern half of the Korean peninsula was under the rule of the American occupation army while the northern half was under the Russian Red Army. A secret deal was made among the superpowers to deal with post-war Korea. The divided occupation of Korea by the two western powers lasted until 1948 when each side established its own government sponsored by the United States and Russia, respectively.[6] On the surface, South Korea became a democratic country modeled after the United States, while North Korea became a socialist nation imitating the Soviet Union. This made the two Koreas hostile toward each other. Soon the flow of people and goods across the border was forbidden.

The ideological confrontation between the two superpowers, also known as the "Cold War," erupted for the first time in the Korean peninsula when North Korea invaded South Korea on June 25, 1950. The unexpected military situation forced the United States to dispatch a significant number of troops to Korea as did fifteen other nations who were members of the United Nations. Canada was one of the other nations that responded to the Korean crisis.

The intensive war lasted three years (1950–1953), and it claimed millions of military and civilian lives on both sides. According to one estimate, more bombs were dropped on that small peninsula of 82,371 square miles during the Korean War than were dropped during the Second World War. In fact, North and South Korea are about the size of Mississippi and Indiana, respectively. Nearly 50,000 American soldiers died on the battlefields of that small country.

Since the cease-fire agreement in July 1953, the United States kept a military presence of around 40,000 troops in South Korea until the 1990s.[7] America's deep involvement in Korea for more than half a century has strengthened the relationship between South Korea and the United States. Consequently, many individual lives in both countries have interfaced during this prolonged and close relationship.

The small number of Koreans who were admitted to North America in the years following the cease-fire agreement in 1953 included GI spouses (or war brides), Korean War orphans, and a few students. Most American soldiers who married Korean women brought their wives home. For example, 6,423 Korean war brides followed their American husbands when they left Korea between 1951 and 1964. In addition, many American families had adopted Korean War orphans. From 1955 to 1966, a total of 6,293 Korean orphans were brought back by American families. Of that number, 46 percent were children of white fathers and Korean mothers, 13 percent had black fathers and Korean mothers, and 41 percent were full Koreans. Thus six of ten Korean adoptees were Amerasians (Kim in Min and Kim 2002:193).

Clearly the Korean War resulted in the immigration of a significant number of Korean women and children in the post-war years. Even now, hundreds of American families adopt Korean children given up by their birth parents. Also, American soldiers continue to marry Koreans and bring them home to the United States. But the figure is hardly comparable with those in the 1950s and 1960s.

These Koreans who became American spouses and adopted children are not so visible as a distinct ethnic group. They are scattered all over the country and blend into the American family and community life. Due to the discriminative immigration policies of the U.S. government toward Asians since the passage of the National Origin Act[8] in 1921 and the eventual Oriental Exclusion Act[9] in 1924, only a small number of Koreans were allowed to obtain permanent residence.

This action was drastically reversed in 1965 when the U.S. Congress passed the Immigration Amendment Act.[10] The new immigration law was definitely in favor of the nations formerly discriminated against in the eastern hemisphere. The amendment allowed an annual quota of 20,000 immigrants from each country, not including those invited by family members already residing in the United States. With this new policy in place, waves of Korean immigrants began hitting the shoreline of the west coast in the late 1960s. In the seventies and eighties, almost 30,000 Korean immigrants came to America every year. Koreans became one of the most rapidly growing immigrant communities in America. Since the late 1980s, Korean immigration has subsided remarkably, typically numbering less than

20,000 people a year due to a number of factors both at home and in North America. Figure 2.1 illustrates the rise and fall of Korean immigration from 1965 to 2005.

Canada was open to Korean immigration a few years earlier than was the United States. That country began accepting people with skills, mainly health-related professionals like nurses and doctors, in the outset of the 1960s. Many Koreans who originally immigrated to Canada later remigrated to the United States.

The rapid influx of a large number of Koreans over many years resulted in the formation of Korean communities in the major metropolitan areas. Unlike the Koreans who came to America in the post-war years either as students, GI spouses, or adopted children, family immigration called for different needs in America. The need for social interaction, economic activities, children's education, worship, and the like necessitated community establishments. In response to the host of needs, business shops, churches, voluntary associations, clubs, and community organizations were established. Some of the Korean towns in large cities have become almost self-sufficient. These enclaves provide most services that Korean immigrants need.

This overview is a thumbnail sketch of the history of Korean immigration to America from 1903 to the present time. The arrival

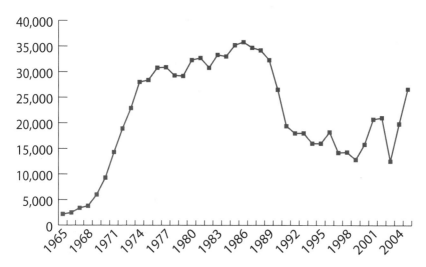

Figure 2.1 Korean Immigration to America, 1965–2005

of Korean Adventists and their establishment of immigrant churches in North America need to be understood in light of this historical and social context.

TRACES OF EARLY KOREAN ADVENTISTS IN AMERICA

Before we look at the establishment of Korean Adventist churches in North America since the early 1960s, we want to trace any evidence of Korean Adventists in America in the earlier decades of the twentieth century. For this, we have to rely on either official records or oral reports. These sources are scanty, and the anecdotal reports are hard to corroborate. Hung Jo Sohn and Hung Yul Lee, who were baptized in Japan in June 1904, were reported as the first Korean Adventists in the church's weekly magazine, *Review and Herald*, on August 25, 1904. It was the first entry of any Korean name in the denominational publication.

The third Korean convert, Kee Ban Yim, who met Mr. Sohn on the return ship from Japan in 1904, later tried to persuade his Korean friends in San Francisco about the Adventist faith. In his letter, Mr. Yim appealed to them to be concerned about spiritual matters rather than worldly things. He felt the urgency of the end time, and his two Korean friends in San Francisco appeared to have been moved by Mr. Yim's appeal. There was an unconfirmed report that the two Korean men in San Francisco met Ellen White who was living in Elmshaven in the Napa Valley around this time. One of the men was asked to return to Korea to become an aid to the first American Adventist missionary to Korea, William Robert Smith (1905–1925) (Lee 2000:27–30). There is no record of what had happened to their lives thereafter.

The Korean Adventist work in North America actually began in Mexico.[11] A Korean resident in the Yucatan Peninsula of Mexico, Sun Il Park, learned about the Adventist faith from the American missionary George W. Caviness. Park was baptized in 1910 and became the very first Korean Adventist in North America. He was a progressive community leader with a good reputation among the Koreans, and he led a number of influential Koreans to his Adventist faith. As other Korean Christians in the area realized that the biblical Sabbath was Saturday, not Sunday, many converted to the Adventist faith.

Through his efforts, the Koreans began meeting on Saturdays at a private home. This was the very first Korean Adventist gathering in North America. It took place in 1926 in Merida, the largest city of Yucatan State on the rim of the Gulf of Mexico. In the course of time, however, the Korean membership decreased as members either moved away to other cities or died. Eventually the Korean Adventist church was closed for lack of membership and it has been used by Mexican Adventist members.

Besides a few remaining descendants of the early Korean Adventists, the only physical evidence of the first generation and their activities in Mexico is a gymnasium in Merida that was named after Antonio Cong in 1997, one of the early Korean pioneers of Adventism in Mexico. Formerly a Presbyterian, Duk Yun Cong, as he was known among the Koreans, was one of the converts led by Sun Il Park. His wife was Mexican, so he spoke Spanish and was familiar with the Mexican culture. Antonio Cong was eager to share his Adventist faith with Mexicans, who were mostly Catholics. For his evangelical ventures among Catholics, he was beaten nearly to the point of death and left on the roadside. Antonio Cong would have been a martyr had he not been rescued by others.

Among other early Korean Adventists in North America, apparently a small number of Korean Adventist women came to Hawaii as picture brides, but there is no record that they got together to observe the Sabbath. On the mainland, there was a Korean Adventist who sought political refuge in America. He was pursued by the Japanese authorities for his anti-Japanese political activity. Nevertheless, he continued to seek support from others for the Korean independence movement.

Bong Ho Kang was a pioneer Adventist in Korea who moved to the United States. At home he worked closely with Kee Ban Yim to establish the fledgling church. In 1920, he was unexpectedly invited by the head of the Korean exile government, Chang Ho Ahn in Shanghai, to serve as a treasurer. Believing in the non-political involvement of Adventism, Mr. Kang sailed from Shanghai to New York via Paris in 1921. Eventually he settled down in Los Angeles. After many years of hard work, he saved enough money to operate his own business, Linsol

Paint Company, for forty years. According to him, there were only two other Korean Adventists in Los Angeles before he brought his daughter, Soon Hee Kang (Joyce Kim), from Korea in 1941.

Mr. Kang was faithful in keeping the Sabbath and paying tithe. He was a life-long member of the White Memorial Church in East Los Angeles until his death in 1985 at the age of 97. His daughter, Soon Hee, studied at La Sierra College and became a nurse. Mr. Kang and his daughter were able to reestablish a relationship with the Korean Adventist community in the 1960s when Korean immigrant churches were organized in southern California (Kang in Lee 1987:436–442).

Dr. Chang Se Kim, brother-in-law to Chang Ho Ahn, was a graduate of the Severance Medical School (now Yunsei University in Seoul) and came to the United States to further his study in medicine. While studying, he received financial help from Mr. Kang and became the first Korean Adventist to study in America.

Later, some of the Korean church leaders had a chance to visit America in the pre-World War II years either as official delegates of the denomination or as church-sponsored students. Pastor Kun Uk Lee, the first ordained Korean Adventist minister, was also the very first official delegate to the United States. He attended the forty-second General Conference Session held in San Francisco from May 29 to June 12, 1930.

Pastor Young Sup Oh was the first Korean Adventist sent by the church to study theology in the United States. He attended Pacific Union College near San Francisco and graduated in 1939. Later, he served as a conference president in South Korea.

Except for the short-lived Korean Adventist group in Mexico, the few individual Korean Adventists who came to America in the early years could not organize themselves as a Korean group as there was no support basis. They were too few and too scattered. The U.S. government admitted only a small number of Koreans each year.

ARRIVAL OF KOREAN ADVENTISTS IN LARGE NUMBERS

As mentioned earlier, Koreans began to immigrate to the United States in large numbers in the late 1960s following the passage of the watershed Immigration Amendment Act of 1965. When the gate was opened wide, many Koreans were eager to come to America. In this regard, Korean Adventists were no exception. In fact, it appears that a higher percentage of the Korean Adventist community took the new opportunity to come to America than any other segment of Korean society. Many Adventist doctors, nurses, teachers, ministers, and those of other occupations came to North America. Once the movement was set in motion, it caused a wide chain reaction among church members. Such a trend continued until the mid 1980s.

One may wonder why North America was so attractive to Korean Adventists. Did their eagerness to emigrate have something to do with their life situation in Korea? Perhaps the main reason was their difficulty in keeping the seventh-day Sabbath in Korea. The typical Korean work week used to include Saturday with only a one-day weekend (Sunday), and this severely limited both educational and occupational opportunities among Adventists in Korea. In particular, it was very difficult to pursue advanced education for a prestigious profession, such as medicine or law, without breaking Sabbath observance.

Lately, there are signs of change. Even in Korea, the notion of the six-day work week is being gradually phased out as the government and large corporations are adopting a five-day work week system. It may take a while for the entire Korean society to adopt the two-day weekend.

Compulsory military service may have been another reason why Korean Adventists considered immigration more favorably. Every able-bodied young man spends anywhere between two and three years in the armed forces, depending on the political situation of the divided Korea at a given time. In the army, many, if not all, Adventist conscripts face two major challenges: Sabbath keeping and conscientious objection. Neither of the two are assured in Korea. In the past, many Adventists were imprisoned for their objection to carry firearms. Conscientious objectors are still tried in the military court. So some Adventist parents with sons chose immigration to avoid the hardships.

In addition, the military threat posed by North Korea has caused uneasiness in the minds of many Koreans. Those who suffered at the hands of the atheist communists for personal or religious reasons during the Korean War wanted to live without the fear of war. This desire was even stronger among the refugee Christians from North Korea who were persecuted by the communists for their beliefs.

Finally, Korea is an extremely competitive society. To survive and succeed, people endure huge personal sacrifices, especially for the primary and secondary education of their children. Many parents choose to immigrate simply to avoid the enormous cost of their children's education. The financial and emotional pressures are so burdensome that moving to another country is an easy option. Many Korean Adventists face the choice between keeping their faith and worldly success in the competition of life. These might be some of the general "push factors" present in Korea.

At the same time, the perceived "pull factors" of North America include a number of favorable conditions. In other words, Korean Adventists decided to move to North America as they considered some advantages the host countries might offer. In the eyes of many Adventists outside North America, the United States is the country where the Adventist movement originated and it is still the center stage of the denomination. For this reason, it has a special appeal to overseas Adventists, including Korean Adventists. To them, the United States offers the best educational and life opportunities. And in the land of religious freedom, Adventists can pursue their goals without fear of restrictions and persecution.

Although it could be insignificant and limited to a select minority, close contact with American missionaries, especially in hospital settings, and exposure to their lives might have been a factor in the decision of some Koreans to come to North America.

Many Korean Adventists who came to North America were health-related professionals—mainly nurses, doctors, and allied-health technicians. This helped them settle down easily in the host countries as they could use their professional training and skills with few additional requirements. In fact, both the United States and Canada were eager to recruit the foreign-trained health professionals when the two countries were experiencing a shortage of doctors, nurses, and allied health professionals in the 1960s and 1970s. Even today, the nurse shortage opens up opportunities to many qualified foreign nurses. Many Korean Adventists who were not trained in healthcare fields in Korea train themselves as dental technicians in North America and run dental labs. In some small churches, their financial support has been noticeable.

THE ESTABLISHMENT OF THE KOREAN ADVENTIST CHURCH IN NORTH AMERICA

The first Korean Adventist church in North America had a humble beginning in Los Angeles. In 1962, a group of Korean Adventists, mainly health-related professionals and a few students, began to have a separate meeting in the chapel of White Memorial Hospital. As the group grew in size, it was officially organized in 1965 as the Los Angeles Central Korean Adventist Church. The first Korean Adventist church still sits on the original site next to the White Memorial Hospital in East Los Angeles. It took sixty years to organize the first Korean Adventist church in America after one of the two baptized Koreans in Kobe, Japan, arrived in Hawaii in 1904.

On the east coast, the first Korean Adventist group met between 1963 and 1965 in a dormitory at Columbia Union College in Washington, D.C. Unlike their west-coast counterpart, this Korean Adventist group was largely made up of students. The group became an organized church in 1974 with a full-time pastor hired by the conference.

In Canada, the first Korean Adventist church was established a bit later than that of their compatriots south of the border. It was in January of 1969 that Korean Adventists in Toronto, mostly immigrant families, started having their own Sabbath School in the Willowdale church. Two months later, they began to have a separate worship service in the church school gymnasium. The majority of the Toronto Korean members were working at Branson General Hospital which was operated by the denomination. The group became an organized church of about seventy baptized members in 1975.

Since the early 1970s, the Korean Adventist church has shown steady growth both in membership and number of congregations. Like other immigrant ethnic churches, the Korean Adventist churches are concentrated in the large metropolitan areas, notably Los Angeles, the San Francisco Bay area, Chicago, New York, Washington, D.C., Atlanta, and Seattle. The reason is simple. The large metropolitan areas offer better opportunities for educational and economic activities to foreign immigrants.

The pattern of establishing a new church has changed, especially after the Los Angeles riot in 1992 when Korean shops were attacked by angry mobs of African Americans following the no-guilty verdict on the white police officers who beat a black driver. The Asian immigrants are now more willing to scatter all over the country to avoid the large metropolitan areas where racial tension is high and the quality of life deteriorates. Consequently, new Korean immigrant churches have opened up in medium-size urban centers in other states. For instance, Las Vegas, Denver, Nashville, Columbus, Raleigh, Oklahoma City, and Phoenix have all seen the establishment and growth of new Korean churches.

As shown in Figure 2.2, the Korean Adventist church in North America has shown steady and healthy growth since 1965 when the Southern California Conference hired the first Korean pastor for the Los Angeles Central Korean Church.[12] The Korean Adventists have responded to the many challenges and difficulties in unity and conviction. But the tone of these churches is definitely changing as the membership composition is changing. Accordingly, the issues and concerns facing these churches are also changing.

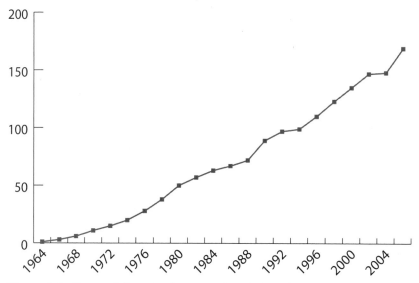

Figure 2.2 Korean Adventist Congregations in North America, 1964–2006

(Many Korean churches have two separate congregations: one for Korean-speaking members and the other for English-speaking worshipers. For this reason, there are more congregations than churches.)

NOTES

1. After a few incidents of military confrontation between the Korean army and the U.S. Navy on the western shore of Korea, the Treaty of Amity and Commerce was signed by the two countries on March 22, 1882. The treaty, commonly known as the Chemulpo Treaty or the Schfedt Treaty, was mediated by China. This was Korea's first treaty ever with a Western nation (Nahm 1988:148–154).

2. The Kobe harbor served as a transfer port for the Koreans who were on their way to Hawaii sugar plantations.

3. Commodore Matthew Perry led a fleet of four U.S. battleships in 1853 to demand open trade with Japan. The two countries signed the Treaty of Kanagawa on March 31, 1854. This was the beginning of Japan's modernization after almost 250 years of self-imposed isolation from the rest of the world (Clyde and Beers 1975:121–157).

4. The last dynasties of China and Korea came to an end only one year apart. The Yi dynasty of Korea ended in 1910 at the hands of Japan and the Ching dynasty of China ended in 1911 because of Chinese reformers who started the first republic.

5. According to the Naturalization Act passed in 1790, only free European immigrants were eligible for U.S. citizenship. This shows discrimination against non-white immigrants.

6. At the request of the United States and its allies, mainly Great Britain and China, Russia got involved in the Pacific War only three months before the surrender of Japan. The United States demanded the advancing Russian army to occupy only the northern half of Korea above the 38th parallel line (border) while the southern half was to be occupied by an American army. Such a partition was arranged by the Yalta meeting in February 1945 and the Potsdam Conference in July of the same year (Nahm 1988:329–365).

7. The U.S. government has reduced its number of troops down to about 20,000. A less than cordial relationship between the two allies and America's new global strategy that emphasizes troop mobility have resulted in the declining presence of U.S. troops in Korea.

8. A few versions of the National Origin Act passed by the U.S. Congress around 1920 were to increase the proportion of immigrants from northern and western European countries and decrease those from elsewhere, including southern and eastern European countries.

9. After 1924, only legal Asian residents (commonly called Orientals) were allowed to enter America. No new immigrants from Asia—mainly from China, Japan, and Korea—were accepted.

10. The U.S. government began to implement the Immigration Amendment Act of 1965 in 1968. The Amendment Act reflected the political atmosphere of America following the passage of the Civil Rights Act in 1964.

11. The report on the first Korean church in Mexico was based on research by the Korean Adventist historian, Pastor Young Lin Lee. Lee has been gathering material for a book project on the history of the Korean Adventist church in North America.

12. The first Korean pastor hired by the Southern California Conference was Seung Il Lee from Korea. He resigned the post within a year for personal reasons.

CHAPTER 3

The Church at Present

For the last forty years, the Korean Adventist community in North America has shown tenacity and dedication to the work of the church. Passion and hard work, the Korean national characteristics, are evident in the pursuits of the Korean Adventists even in North America. By overcoming many challenges individually and collectively in the host countries, the immigrant generation has demonstrated impressive progress. In spite of the scattered locations of more than 100 Korean churches on the vast continent of North America, the Korean Adventists have been able to mobilize their efforts for common goals. These coordinated efforts help them maintain a distinctive identity and solidarity as a community of faith.

One may wonder how committed Korean Adventists would have been to the gospel work had they not maintained their own congregations. Would they have been more or less enthusiastic? More passive or more active? As far as the first-generation Korean Adventists and some of their Korean-born children are concerned, the church has been a home away from home. In a way, the church community is an embodiment of the home country they left years ago. Thus, the ethnic church has served as a diaspora community to these uprooted people.

The second-generation members might have a different perception of their ethnic churches. They may not have as much emotional attachment as do their parents or grandparents. Their commitment to their churches is perhaps mainly due to family ties. It will be interesting to see

31

how the Korean churches fare when the second and later generations comprise the majority of the church membership.

The report on the accomplishments of the Korean Adventist church in North America, therefore, largely reflects the efforts of the pioneer generation. Whether it is publishing work, television programs, or overseas mission outreach, the first-generation members carry a burden to their compatriots everywhere, including their own children in North America.

In order to fully understand any community of faith, one has to be knowledgeable of both its tangible and intangible aspects. The tangibles include those that can be numerated and measured, such as the number of members, churches, and financial contributions. The intangibles are more subtle and abstract. Beliefs, commitment, and spirituality, for example, are not so easy to quantify. If the tangibles are the measure of quantity, then the intangibles reflect the quality of a particular community. Yet the tangibles may reflect the intangibles. Without conviction about and commitment to a set of beliefs, a faith community cannot produce tangible results. Membership growth and increased financial contributions may reflect their spiritual commitment.

In this chapter, we look at the tangibles of the Korean Adventist church in North America. The statistical figures are ones that have been officially reported, and I have tried to use the most up-to-date sources wherever possible. From these figures, we may make inferences about the spiritual commitment of the Korean Adventist community.

Wherever applicable, the Korean Adventist church is compared with the larger Adventist communities in North America and northeast Asia. Further, we will look at the Korean Adventist community as part of the larger Korean community in North America. Such comparisons may provide a proper perspective on the place of the Korean Adventist church in the larger settings.

KOREAN ADVENTISTS AND THEIR CONGREGATIONS

According to the Korean Adventist Church Directory published in December 2005,[1] there were 113 Korean Adventist churches in North America at that time. Adding the fifty-two English-speaking congregations or groups at some of these churches results in a total of 165 Korean congregations worshiping either in Korean or English every Sabbath. In rare cases, combined congregations worship in both languages using translation.[2] The Korean Adventist churches are located in twenty-nine states and four Canadian provinces. The organizational status of these congregations is varied, depending on the membership size, history, and financial state.[3]

According to the general session report of the Korean Church Council in September 2006, there were seventy-nine (68%) organized "churches," sixteen (14%) "companies," and twenty-two (19%) "groups" as of June 2006 (Korean Church Council 2006:24). Over a three-year period (July 2003 to June 2006), the number of churches had grown from 108 to 117, an increase of 8 percent. During that period, two churches were merged with other churches in the same areas, thus reducing the total number of churches by two. The year 2006 began with a total of 15,924 members registered at these churches. This total may include a small number of non-Korean members who are connected through marriage or friendship. Over the same three-year period, 3,353 people were added to the Korean churches by birth and conversion. The net increase of 27 percent in membership over the three-year period may be regarded as a sign of remarkable growth.

The size of these congregations ranges from a dozen to more than 500 members. Outside the large metropolitan areas—such as Los Angeles, New York, Chicago, Atlanta, and Washington, D.C.—the congregations tend to be small, with rarely more than 100 members due to the small base of the Korean communities they serve.

Korean Adventist congregations are found in every union conference of the North American Division of the Seventh-day Adventist Church. The eight union conferences in the United States roughly reflect the regional configuration of the country. In spite of its size, the entire country of Canada forms a single union. Table 3.1 lists the unions in North America and indicates which states and provinces include at least one Korean church.

Table 3.1 Regional Distribution of Korean Adventist Churches in the North American Division (2006)

Union Conference (United States)	States with Korean Adventist Churches	States without Korean Adventist Churches
Atlantic	Massachusetts, New York	Connecticut, Maine, New Hampshire, Rhode Island, Vermont
Columbia	Maryland, New Jersey, Ohio, Pennsylvania, Virginia	Delaware, West Virginia
Lake	Illinois, Indiana, Michigan	Wisconsin*
Mid-America	Colorado, Minnesota, Missouri	Iowa, Kansas, Nebraska, North Dakota, South Dakota, Wyoming
North Pacific	Alaska, Oregon, Washington	Idaho, Montana
Pacific	Arizona, California, Hawaii, Nevada	Utah
Southern	Florida, Georgia, Kentucky, North Carolina, South Carolina, Tennessee	Alabama, Mississippi
Southwestern	Arkansas, Oklahoma, Texas	Louisiana, New Mexico*
	Provinces with Korean Adventist Churches	Provinces without Korean Adventist Churches
Seventh-day Adventist Church in Canada	Alberta, British Columbia, Manitoba, Ontario	New Brunswick, Newfoundland, Nova Scotia, Prince Edward Island, Quebec, Saskatchewan

*Though not organized churches, there were small Korean Adventist groups meeting in New Berlin, Wisconsin, and Albuquerque, New Mexico.

Some union conferences have far more Korean congregations than others do. Nearly half of all Korean Adventist congregations are located in five major metropolitan areas and their vicinities: Los

Angeles, New York, Atlanta, Washington, D.C., and Chicago. Yet Table 3.2, which compares the number of congregations in 2002 with those in 2006, makes it clear that the Korean Adventist church has been expanding throughout North America.

Table 3.2 Korean Adventist Churches in the North American Division

Union Conference	2002	2004	2006	Difference between 2002 and 2006
Atlantic	6	9	11	5
Columbia	16	19	21	5
Lake	16	17	17	1
Mid-America	6	7	6	0
North Pacific	9	8	10	1
Pacific	46	47	56	10
Southern	20	19	28	8
Southwestern	6	8	7	1
Canada	10	10	10	0
North American Total	135	144	166	31

Sources: Membership Directory of Korean Adventist Churches in the Americas (2001, 2003, 2005)

The Pacific Union Conference had the largest number of Korean congregations in 2006. Most of those are clustered around the greater Los Angeles metropolitan area and the San Francisco Bay area. The Korean churches in California account for about one-third of the Korean congregations throughout North America. A few churches in southern California have a membership of about 500. The Southern Union Conference ranked second after the Pacific Union Conference in its number of Korean congregations. This may reflect the attraction of the Greater Atlanta metropolitan area. The Columbia Union Conference and Lake Union Conference have also seen steady establishment of Korean churches. This growth may be attributable to major metropolitan areas like Washington, D.C., and Baltimore in the Columbia Union Conference. The Lake Union Conference has likely maintained a steady number of Korean churches because it is home to the Chicago metropolitan area as well as to the Seventh-day Adventist

Theological Seminary located at Andrews University. Students from Korea who studied at the seminary may have helped to establish Korean churches in Illinois, Indiana, and Michigan.

A Korean church has yet to be planted in twenty-one states and six provinces. In many cases, these states and provinces are part of regions which are less urbanized and industrialized with low population density. The lack of a Korean Adventist church in these regions may be due to the lack of sizable Korean communities. It should be noted, however, that other Korean protestant groups have established a presence in major cities of these regions, such as in New Orleans, Louisiana, and Birmingham, Alabama.

The regional clusters of Korean Adventist churches may also reflect settlement patterns of Koreans in America. According to the U.S. Census Bureau, ten states showed a substantial increase in a Korean population from 1990 to 2000 (see Table 3.3). The increase ranges from 18 percent in Pennsylvania to 88 percent in Georgia. Accordingly, the greater Atlanta metropolitan area has witnessed considerable growth in its Korean population as many Koreans remigrate to Georgia from other parts of the United States, including California.

Table 3.3 Ten States with Large Korean Populations, 1990–2000

State	1990	2000	Increase (%) over 1990	Overall Distribution (%)
California	259,941	345,882	33.1	32.12*
New York	95,648	119,846	25.3	11.13
New Jersey	38,540	65,349	69.6	6.07
Illinois	41,506	51,453	24.0	4.78
Washington	29,697	46,880	57.9	4.35
Texas	31,775	45,571	43.4	4.23
Virginia	30,161	45,279	50.1	4.20
Maryland	30,320	39,155	29.1	3.64
Pennsylvania	26,787	31,612	18.0	2.94
Georgia	15,275	28,745	88.2	2.67
Total (50 States)	798,846	1,076,872	34.8	100.00

*In 2000, the Korean residents in California accounted for 32.12% of the total Korean population in the United States.

Source: US Census 1990 and 2000 compiled by Yu

As displayed in Figure 3.1, the Korean Adventist churches in North America experienced steady membership growth from 11,800 in 2001 to 15,900 in 2006, an increase of 35 percent. During that period, 2,904 Koreans joined Korean Adventist churches in North America through the act of baptism (see Figure 3.2). Some were the children of church members, and perhaps most baptized adults were converts from other Christian faiths. The number of baptized members who joined the Korean Adventist church as a result of family upbringing should be compared with the number who joined the church through personal conviction as adults. In this regard, how does the Korean Adventist church in North America fare in comparison with its counterpart at home?

According to the General Conference Annual Statistical Report for the year 2005, the Korean Union Conference listed a total of 697 churches and 198 companies. The total membership of these congregations was reported to be 189,673. In the same year, the Adventist churches in Korea baptized 6,931 people. There was one baptism for every 27 members in Korea but one baptism for every 15 members in North America. By looking only at the reported official figures, the soul-winning efforts of the North American Korean Adventists appeared to be much greater than their home churches in Korea. The

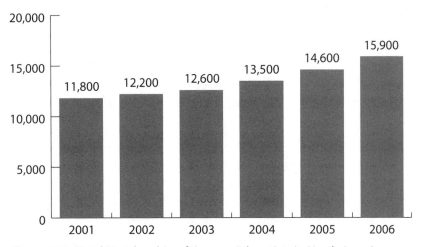

Figure 3.1 Total Membership of Korean Adventists in North America, 2001–2006

Source: General Session Reports of the Korean Church Council in 2003 and 2006

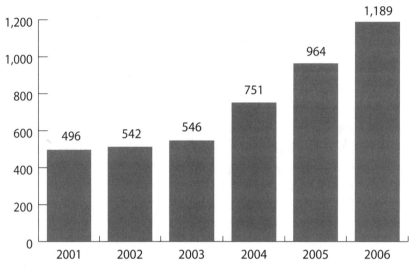

Figure 3.2 Annual Baptisms by the Korean Adventist Churches in North America, 2001–2006

Source: General Session Reports of the Korean Church Council in 2003 and 2006

membership of the North American Korean Adventist community is about 8 percent of the Adventist community at home.

KOREAN ADVENTISTS IN LARGER COMMUNITIES

Figure 3.3 presents the amount of tithe given annually by Korean Adventist churches in North America for the years 2001 to 2006. The tithe for 2005 was $12,575,725, which equates to $859.82 per Korean member, including children. Looking at the North American Division as a whole for 2005, each member contributed an average of $836.22 in tithe, with an individual annual contribution of $1,363.63 when other offerings were added. In addition to offerings and other financial contributions made through regular church channels, many Korean Adventists also engage in domestic and overseas missions projects for Korean people.

To gain an accurate perspective on the Korean Adventist community in North America, it is helpful to look at the size and proportional giving of Korean Adventists in the context of the larger Adventist community. In 2005, the Korean Adventist group made up about 1.5 percent of the total North American Division member-

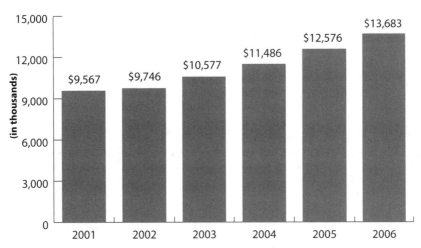

Figure 3.3 Annual Tithe of Korean Adventist Churches in North America, 2001–2006

Source: General Session Reports of the Korean Church Council in 2003 and 2006

ship of 1,006,317 and 1.5 percent of the division's tithe payment of $834,926,647.

The North American Korean Adventist group was equivalent to only about 8 percent of the total membership of the Korean Union at home, but their tithe payment was about 28 percent of the Korean Union, totaling $44,979,627. The much higher per capita tithe payment of the North American Korean Adventists might be due to the higher standard of living. Also, the high percentage of healthcare workers in North America may explain the difference. At the same time, the much lower amount of per capita tithe payment in Korea might be partially explained by a high percentage of inactive (absentee) members.

As can be seen in Table 3.4, the Korean Adventists are the third largest ethno-linguistic minority group in the North American Division. In terms of general minority classifications, however, only the African Americans, Hispanics, and Franco-phone blacks (mainly Haitians) number more than the Korean group in this division. Other Asian groups originating from the same northeast Asian region, namely Chinese and Japanese, have far fewer Adventist congregations and members than the Korean group. Their combined membership of about

2,700 with thirteen congregations is about one quarter of the size of the Korean group. This may reflect the size of the total Adventist membership in their home countries[4] and the immigration flow to America from these countries. The latter is affected by a number of conditions, including the policy of the receiving nations.

Table 3.4 Ten Large Language Groups in the North American Division, 2001

Language Group	Congregations	Membership
Hispanic	685	115,000
Haitian (French)	83	27,000
Korean	95	11,550*
Filipino	26	7,190
Portuguese	58	4,480
Native People	39	3,300
Quebecois (French)	5	3,000
Indonesian	7	1,500
Chinese	8	1,420
Japanese	5	1,277

Source: North American Division Multi-lingual Department, 2001

*The Korean Church Council reports 11,800 as of June 2001.

When comparing the Korean group with the 58 local conferences in the North American Division, the Korean group as a whole was larger than twenty-eight (48%) of the conferences in number of organized churches, excluding companies and small groups, and larger than thirty-six (62%) of the conferences in membership as reported for 2005. The Korean group as a whole contributed more in tithe than thirty-five (60%) of the conferences in the division. In proportional terms, slightly over 50 percent of the local conferences in the division had smaller operations than the Korean group. Of course, the Korean congregations are scattered throughout many conferences in North America. At one time, some Korean Adventist leaders in North America contemplated the idea of forming a Korean conference in the division. One reason for such an idea was the operational strength of the Korean churches as a whole.[5]

The Korean Adventist group in North America is quite comparable with the entire Adventist group in Japan in terms of membership size and tithe contribution. For the year 2005, the Japan Union Conference reported 15,061 members with 155 congregations, whereas Korean Adventists in North America numbered 14,626 members with 117 congregations. The Japanese Adventists contributed $11,770,776 in tithe, while Koreans in America contributed $12,575,725. Considering that the Koreans in North America are outpacing the Japan Union in membership growth rate, the Korean Adventists in North America may soon outnumber the entire Japan Union.

Beyond the Adventist boundary, how does the Korean Adventist group compare with the larger Korean Christian community in North America? Indeed, the Korean Adventist community is but a small fraction of it.

According to the *World Christian Encyclopedia* published in 2001, there were one million Korean Christians in 3,663 churches in the United States alone (Barret, Kuriar, and Johnson 2001:786). The reported figures, however, were based on the major Korean denominations, such as Presbyterian, Methodist, Baptist, and Full Gospel churches. If the figures had included independent (non-denominational) and smaller denominations, such as Adventists, the final figures would have been measurably higher. The encyclopedia also fails to report on the Korean Christians and their congregations in Canada. Taking into account these unreported sources, a conservative estimate of 500 additional Korean Christian congregations and 150,000 members can be added to the one million figure. There is roughly one Korean church for every 300 Korean residents in North America (Cha in Kwon et al. 2001:141).

In southern California alone, nearly 1,000 Christian congregations serve the growing Korean population. Coming from one of the most active Christian nations in Asia, Koreans are known for their eagerness to start churches no matter where they are situated, especially in North America. In general, one in four Koreans (25%) is a Christian in the home country, but three quarters (75%) of Koreans are believed to be churchgoers in America.

According to the U.S. Census Bureau, 1,076,872 Koreans were counted during the 2000 census. But the Overseas Korean Foundation reports that 2,123,167 Koreans resided in the United States in 2001.[6] The significant discrepancy between the U.S. official census and the foundation figures is the result of using different sources. Unlike the U.S. Census Bureau that uses a questionnaire form delivered to each household, the Overseas Korean Foundation relies on the reports of the Korean embassy, consulates, and local Korean community organizations. Other possible sources of discrepancy are individual self-identification and a large number of non-resident Koreans in America, such as students, visitors, and employees of multinational companies. Thus, the real number of Koreans should be somewhere between the official figure and the foundation figure. In addition, the same foundation reports that about 111,000 Koreans reside in Canada. Thus, about two and a quarter million Koreans might have lived in the United States and Canada in 2000.

Korean Adventists probably make up roughly one or one and a half percent of the entire Korean community in North America. The ratio is either 100 to 1 or 200 to 1, depending on which figure one uses. Yet Adventists in South Korea comprise roughly one-third of one percent (.3%) of the total population. That ratio is 300 to 1. Thus, the Korean Adventist communities on both sides of the Pacific Ocean face great challenges in reaching the larger Korean communities with their message.

THE TIPPING OF THE DEMOGRAPHIC BALANCE

The demographic scale of the Korean Adventist community in North America has already been tipped toward the American-raised or American-born second-generation members and their children (third-generation). In the foreseeable future, fourth-generation members will appear in their churches.

As of 2000, close to 6,000 (51%) Korean Adventists in North America were under thirty-five years of age, and 38 percent of the total membership were twenty-nine years old or younger.[7] This demographic tipping will accelerate as the first-generation members decline steadily by death while new members are born at a much faster rate.

Without encouraging prospects of replenishing the lost numbers with new converts or Adventist immigrants from Korea in significant numbers, the size and proportion of the first-generation group are going to steadily shrink. If such a demographic trend continues, small Korean-speaking congregations may disappear in less than thirty years. Most Korean churches may then resemble some of the old Japanese American churches with congregations made up mainly of third- (sansei) or fourth-generation (yonsei) members.

At the same time, younger members will increase through birth, marriage, and conversion. Membership increase through conversion does not seem to be a major factor in the second-generation group. Table 3.5 shows the breakdown of age groups among Korean Adventists in North America as reported in 2000.

Table 3.5 Age Distribution of Korean Adventists in North America in 2000

Age Category	Number	Percent
1–12	2,034	18%
13–19	1,089	9.5%
20–29	1,254	11%
30–35	1,534	13%
36 and older	5,434	49%
Total	11,345	100%

Source: General Session Report of the Korean Church Council in 2000

YOUTH PASTORS

According to the most recent report, a total of forty-five pastors were serving the English-speaking, second-generation members and their children at the end of 2005. The majority of Korean churches try to provide English services for their youth in one form or another. Some are full-fledged congregations and others are small informal groups. Accordingly, the quality of English programs may vary widely depending on the size of each congregation, its leadership, and its financial ability. Overall, the English programs for the second-generation groups are rather lacking in such areas as leadership, organization, program, finance, and physical space.

In 2000, only five (11%) of the forty-five pastors in English ministry were employed full time by their local conferences. With full-time status come full salaries and benefits. The rest of the Korean youth pastors, either full-time or part-time, were hired and supported by their local churches. In these cases, the churches were responsible for the payment of salaries and benefits. At some small churches, benefits may not be considered at all or are substantially compromised. In 2006, the number of full-time pastors in English ministry hired by conferences slightly improved from five to eight, according to the former English ministry coordinator.

Turnover among locally hired youth pastors has been relatively high, perhaps due to the fact that they are typically paid less and receive fewer benefits than their conference-hired peers. Dissatisfaction with lower compensation is likely heightened by the fact that many non-conference hires have the same educational credentials as their conference-hired counterparts. The difference in employment status is often a matter of timing of available positions, not necessarily the qualifications of the applicants. Table 3.6 shows the employment status of Korean youth pastors in English ministry.

Table 3.6 Employment Status of Korean Youth Pastors, 2000 and 2006*

Employment Status	Number (2000)		Number (2006)	
Conference full-time	5	(11%)	8	(20%)
Church full-time	12	(27%)	12	(30%)
Church contract	9	(20%)	0	(0%)
Church part-time	19	(42%)	20	(50%)
Total youth pastors	45	(100%)	40	(100%)

*The figures for 2006 were provided by the English ministry coordinator.

Source: General Session Report of the Korean Church Council in 2000

As previously mentioned, the majority of the youth pastors (89% in 2000 and 80% in 2006) were hired by local churches. Furthermore, almost half of the youth pastors (42% in 2000 and 50% in 2006) served part-time. The high percentage of part-time youth pastors is probably due to two reasons. Often, the local congregations are too small to afford a full-time youth pastor. These churches may not meet their conference criteria for a second pastor in terms of membership size and financial contribution. Another reason could be the lack of qualified candidates. Most second-generation members pursue other professions than ministry. This results in a tiny pool of pastoral candidates. In addition, some former theology or ministry majors change to other careers after a few years of ministry at Korean churches.

Part-time youth pastors typically can engage in substantial interaction with the youth only on weekends, perhaps just Friday evening and Saturday. Some of these part-time youth pastors have some theological training, and others have none. A few of them might have been chosen by small congregations simply because they speak English and show some leadership qualities in spiritual and interpersonal relations. In most Korean Adventist churches, high priorities tend to be set for the needs of adult members first, and the English-speaking groups do not receive as much attention as they deserve. Such a pattern needs to be changed for the long-term well-being of the second-generation congregations.

SPECIAL FEATURES OF KOREAN ADVENTIST CHURCHES

Other than the routine weekly or monthly activities centered around the local church calendar, Korean Adventists in North America have established a number of organizations and activities for all church members which are coordinated by some entities established by the Korean churches.

The Korean Adventist Church Council of North America

The hub of the Korean Adventist churches in North America is its council. The Korean churches have been able to coordinate their activities through the central organization. At present, more than 100 Korean Adventist churches in North America are members of the Korean Adventist Church Council of North America. This association coordinates the activities of Korean Adventist churches in the United States and Canada. In addition, the Korean Adventist churches in South America (one each in Brazil, Argentina, Paraguay, and Peru) are associate members and they are invited to participate in the activities. The officers of the council are elected for a three-year term by the delegates of the member churches.

The main purpose of the council is to promote mutual cooperation among the member churches in their common pursuits for internal development and community outreach. Their work includes leadership training for ministers and lay people, publishing, youth training, and foreign mission. Any issues or concerns beyond the scope of a local church are reported to the council president.

The central figure in running the council is the president who is elected every three years by the delegates. His major role is that of coordinating the member churches. In response to a request from a local church or conference, for instance, the council president mediates a dispute between two parties. Since 1998, the president has been a full-time officer devoted only to the business of the Korean churches in North America. Recently, the council president has also become the president of the Korean Adventist Press.

The second purpose of the council is to represent the concerns of the Korean churches to the local conferences, the union conferences, the Korean Union at home, and the North American Division. The president is a voting member of the North American Division Executive Council. Often the president serves as a liaison between a local Korean church and its affiliated conference on the matter of hiring or transferring ministers. Conferences may seek advice from the council president on any matter related to Korean churches in their territories.

According to the 2006 General Session report, the council received a total of $489,624 from October 2003 to August 2006. While the North American Division provided an annual subsidy of $30,000, Korean churches and individuals contributed the rest. During that same period, the Korean churches contributed $195,805 in the form of a membership fee. The annual membership fee ranges from $50 to $3,000, depending on the size of each church. The record shows that about 90 percent of the member churches had paid their membership dues. In addition, individual members contributed $23,950 and the Korean Adventist Press assisted the council with $37,500.

The council runs a website (www.kasda.com) for Korean Adventists in North America and other parts of the world, including Korea. The popular website carries valuable information and opinions. Sometimes the website becomes an open forum on a hot subject and changes the opinion of church members.

Every third year, the council holds a triennial session. The general session is held to hear and review reports from each department, to elect new officers, and to plan for the future. In the general session of 2006, the following departments presented reports: Youth, Outreach, KAYMM (Korean Adventist Youth Mission Movement), Education, Women's Ministry, Korean Adventist Development and Relief Agency, and Korean Adventist Press.

Annual Education for Ministers and Lay Leaders

Each year since 1980, the council has offered a week-long annual extension education program for Korean pastors and lay leaders. It is open to anyone who desires to attend. Anywhere between 150 and 250 people attend each year, and their travel and accommodation expenses are paid by their local churches. The educational program covers a wide range of subjects from personal ministry to hermeneutics. The annual meeting is held at a different location each year to expose attendees to different regions of North America. Maine, Alberta, and Colorado were some of the rare sites for these annual meetings.

Summer Camp Meetings

Each summer, both the Eastern states and provinces and the Western counterparts hold separate week-long camp meetings. In general, the Rocky Mountain range serves as a continental divide between the East and the West. The two camp meetings are usually one or two weeks apart during the last part of July or the early part of August. The meetings are for both Korean-speaking and English-speaking Korean church members. This has been a solid tradition that has continued since 1979 for the East and 1984 for the West. It has continued for almost thirty years without a single lapse.

A designated local church in each region (East and West) is responsible for planning and running the summer camp meeting. On average, about 2,000 people attend the regional camp meetings. The total budget for both camp meetings is about $400,000. The attendance of English-speaking members has been increasing as young adults attend with their children. Unlike the early years when the Korean program was the main concern, more balanced programs have been offered for both language groups in recent years. Soon the second-generation members and their children may outnumber their parents and grandparents. Accordingly, the church leadership is expanding and enhancing the quality of the programs for this English-speaking group.

The East region changes its summer campsite every year, usually meeting somewhere along the Atlantic coast. However, the West has held its meeting at the Pacific Union College campus every year. Some outlying regions in North America, such as the Northwest (Washington State and British Columbia), Florida, and the Southwest (Texas and Oklahoma) hold their own mini camp meeting if the summer campsites are too far for members to travel by car.

Korean Adventist Press

The most visible organization for the Korean Adventists in North America has been the Korean Adventist Press. Besides dealing with published materials, it has initiated many other activities as it has a continent-wide network reach. Located in downtown Los Angeles, it is owned and operated by the Korean Adventist group in North America. The Korean Adventist Press has been in business since April 1983, and it has been doing relatively well in terms of business volume and profit. For instance, it generated a total revenue of $2,899,276 during the three-year period from January of 2003 to December of 2005 with a profit of $203,057. As a result, the Press was able to subsidize the council $10,000 per year.

Every month, the Press duplicates over 15,600 copies of the *Signs of the Times* magazine in Korean. The original version produced in Korea is reproduced at the press with an additional insert for its readers in North America. Besides the monthly magazine, the press has begun distributing another monthly magazine, *Home and Health*, which is edited and produced in Korea. Its circulation in North America is around 4,500 copies.

In addition, the publishing house reproduces a sizable number of periodicals for its readers. The *North American Church Compass*, a monthly news magazine for church members, has a subscription of about 4,500. It also publishes *Compass* in English for English-speaking Korean Adventist members. Article contributors for the English monthly are primarily second-generation members and their pastors. Initially, the English section of *Compass* was distributed as an insert in the *Korean Compass*, but now about 1,000 copies are published and distributed separately. Also the Press duplicates and distributes about 6,350 copies of Sabbath School lessons in Korean every quarter. Before 1983, the periodicals were shipped from Korea, often causing delays. But now the Korean Adventists in North America receive the same publications on time with a special addition catering to their needs.

In addition to selling Adventist books in Korean and English, the Press carries select books by other Christian authors either written in or translated into Korean. To accommodate the two language groups in the Korean churches, the Press supplies a bilingual Bible and hymnal. While the Press sells the Korean-English Bible edited by the Korean Bible Society and other Christian publishing companies, the Korean-English hymnal was compiled by the Korean Adventist Press.

With its own facility, personnel, and communication network system, the Press coordinates other activities. These include youth training and educational programs, overseas relief programs, and even guided tours for Korean Adventists. The Press has become a nerve center for the Korean Adventists in North America. The total assets of the Press were reported to be $1,683,789 as of December 31, 2005.

Television and Radio Programs

The Korean Adventist churches in southern California have maintained a weekly thirty-minute Korean television program, "Faith for Today," since 1981. The program targets Korean viewers every Sunday morning (8:30–9:00 a.m. PST) in the greater Los Angeles metropolitan area and its vicinities, including the Inland Empire and San Diego. The program has been run with donations by Korean Adventists in the region, and has a full-time speaker/pastor. In addition, the Adventist health message reaches the Koreans in North America through a satellite channel (JSTV) twice a day. The annual operating cost of the television program, including air time fees and speakers' remuneration, is now more than a quarter million dollars. The Korean Adventists in southern California have carried heavy financial responsibilities for media outreach. Besides the weekly broadcasting, overseas mission trips are organized twice a year. In 2006, for instance, a team went to Myanmar (Burma) and China to conduct evangelistic meetings. Their efforts resulted in many baptisms.

As a result of the television program, many Korean viewers have gained a greater understanding of Adventism, and some have joined the Adventist faith. Over the years, the program has featured different ministerial speakers and a few lay professionals. Lately, another Korean Adventist group based in Tennessee started a thirty-minute religious television program once a week in southern California. The same group offered a similar program on Adventist beliefs years ago.

A small Korean Adventist lay group in southern California ran a daily thirty-minute Korean radio program (5:30–6:00 a.m. PST), "Echoes of Love." Since its beginning in 1994, the daily program had been aired with only one disruption. The program, which originated in Los Angeles (Radio Korea 1230 AM), was relayed via satellite to other major cities in the United States. These included Anchorage, Dallas, Denver, Honolulu, and Houston, among others. The program had gained a world-wide coverage by being simulcast through the Internet (www.radiokorea.com). The thirty-minute program combined the gospel message with general life concerns. In the latter portion, different speakers discussed issues related to family, health, and social issues. Like the television program, "Echoes of Love" had a full-time speaker/pastor. As an extension of the radio outreach program, a Bible study group was established for Korean listeners in Los Angeles.[8]

Outside the southern California region, some local Korean Adventist churches support either television or radio programs in Korean on a limited basis. The churches in New York City support a radio program, and a single church in Seattle runs a television program.

The Adventist church in Korea has been denied its access to mass media as the church has been regarded as heretic by the mainline denominations (Presbyterian and Methodist) and the larger society. The significance of what the Korean Adventists in North America have been doing should be appreciated in light of the negative perception of Adventism in the Korean community.

Mission Work for Overseas Koreans

A few dozen Korean Adventists in North America have engaged in overseas mission work. Their mission endeavors have been in cooperation with some local churches, the Council, or the Korean Union Conference at home for logistical and political reasons. Their target populations have been mainly Koreans living in Far East Russia, Central Asia (Uzbekistan), China, Mongolia, Japan, and Peru. When some of these countries were under the communist rule, the North American Korean Adventists took advantage of their citizenship to gain access for mission work. For instance, until the 1990s, South Korean citizens were far more restricted in China and Russia than were their counterparts in North America. The mission efforts by the North American Adventists have resulted in the establishment of a few churches and organizations in the target areas. The most successful location has been China, especially the three provinces in the northeast region of the country. The vast region (formerly Manchuria) is adjacent to North Korea and has a sizeable Korean population in each province. Today many home churches, a few organized churches, and health clinics are in operation in that part of China. For instance, the Korean Adventist church in the capital city of the Korean autonomous region, Yanji, has grown to almost 1,300 members in the three provinces. Much of the work is credited to a dedicated couple, Elder Hung Shik Kim and his wife, who spent seven years in Yanji in the 1990s. Eventually they left the mission field for health reasons. The North American Adventists established a dental technical school in Yanji with about $200,000 of donated money. Elder Haeng Sun Kim of Napa Korean Church has been responsible for running the dental technical school in the same city. Some members of the Napa Korean Church and others set up a scholarship fund to support Korean students in China.

Far East Russia is near the northeast region of China and has many Korean descents as well. From 1990 to 1997, Pastor Young Kil Yoo and his wife worked among the Korean Russians in Khabarovsk and its vicinity. During this time, he baptized almost two hundred people, both Koreans and Russians. Under his leadership, a few Korean churches and affiliated Korean language schools were established. Later, the Korean Union Conference opened an Adventist college on the island of Sakhalin.

During the Stalin era, many Koreans in Far East Russia were relocated to Central Asia, and they settled mainly in Uzbekistan. Pastor Jung Whan Jo and his wife were committed to mission work among the Koreans from 1992 to 1997. The couple started a Korean church in Tashkent, the capital city of the former Russian republic. Although Mongolia does not have a Korean community, a young Korean-American Adventist woman, Joan Park, did some pioneer mission work there. Upon graduation from Pacific Union College in 1992, she went to the mission field at the age of 21. Joan was met by a sole American Adventist missionary couple who had been there for nine months.

With the missionary couple, Mr. and Mrs. Jolly, Joan introduced the Adventist message to the country for the first time. As a result of their efforts, about twenty Mongolians were baptized and around 100 were keeping the Sabbath by the time Joan left in September 1998. She made three separate trips back to Mongolia including the last one with her newlywed husband, John Kim. Altogether she served for five years and four months in that land-locked country as a lay missionary.

Besides soul winning, Joan set out to translate the Bible into Mongolian. The New Testament in Mongolian was grossly inadequate and the Old Testament had yet to be translated. With the help of others, Joan translated and published the book of Genesis in Mongolian. Ever since leaving the country, she has continued translating the Bible. She and her dentist husband are considering going back to Mongolia someday.

Japan is Korea's next-door neighbor (only an hour's flight away) and the two countries share much in common. There are more than half a million Koreans in Japan, yet there was no Korean Adventist congregation worshiping there until Pastor Suk Woo Chung went to Osaka in January 1987. With the support of the Loma Linda Korean Church, his mission efforts resulted in a small Korean Adventist group in the second largest city of Japan. Recently, some North American Korean Adventists have gone to Japan for short-term mission work among the Korean residents.

In South America, only Argentina, Brazil, Paraguay, and Peru have a Korean congregation in their largest cities. These churches were typically established by Korean immigrants to South America. The Korean group in Lima, Peru, however, has been served by a retired Korean-American pastor with some assistance from North American Korean church members. The Loma Linda Korean Church has recently considered establishing a mission outpost there for its members.

Lastly, the Korean Adventists in North America are anxious to share their message with the people of North Korea. Once the communist country is open to mission activities, many Korean Adventists in North America, including the former North Korean refugees during the Korean War (1950–1953), may rush there. Some of the Adventist mission work in China and Far East Russia will eventually extend to North Korea.

BMW (Bicycle Mission to the World)

A group of Korean Adventists in North America has assisted with rural mission work for native people in Africa and Asia since 2004. The initial goal of Bicycle Mission to the World (BMW) was to provide bicycles to gospel workers in rural areas of some African nations. So far they have supplied over 2,000 bicycles costing $156,000. Besides providing mission bicycles, the group has supported scholarships for local students, construction projects of churches and water wells, and medical and dental treatments with the help of Korean Adventist professionals. As of 2007, almost half a million dollars has been spent on the various projects. Now the goal is to supply 5,000 bicycles a year for mission work in developing nations. The BMW mission group is unique in that its members seek to supply non-Koreans with affordable transportation.

Relief Work for North Korea

To most Koreans at home or abroad, the sad news from the northern half of Korea has been the cause of pain and sympathy. Massive starvation and malnutrition have claimed a fraction of the population in that totalitarian nation. Many have risked their lives for freedom and a better life by escaping from the oppressive regime. Many North Korean escapees wait in hiding in China for eventual admission to South Korea. If captured, they are returned to North Korea, and their fate is predictable—either imprisonment or hard labor.

In response to the pitiful situation, the Korean Church Council has coordinated relief work for the escapees, orphans in North Korea, and a few hospitals. With the help of the Korean Union and North Pacific Asia Division headquartered in Seoul, Korea, North American Korean Adventists established the Korean Adventist Development and Relief Agency (KADRA) in the United States in 2005.

KADRA assisted the agency that aids the North Korean escapees in hiding by donating $20,000. Also, with money donated by Korean Adventists, it supplies ingredients—including flour, yeast, sugar, and oil—to bake 10,000 loaves of bread to feed the North Korean orphans of an eastern city every day. This requires thirteen tons of flour and 600 kilograms of milk powder among other items every month. The baking ingredients are purchased in China and transported to North Korea. The monthly relief operation costs about $7,000. In addition, at the request of a hospital in the same city, KADRA has supplied medical equipment by acquiring used items at a cheap price. In addition, it has supplied a limited amount of pharmaceutical products. The total value of the medical supplies to North Korea has been about $160,000 as of August 2006.

In response to the terrible humanitarian disaster in North Korea, Adventists in North America donated $150,000 for the first six months of the KADRA operation. This shows the depth of sympathy expressed toward the suffering of their compatriots. The further challenge is how the Korean Adventists in North America will be able to respond to the increasing number of requests for aid coming from other North Korean cities and governmental agencies.

Youth Mission Project

The first-generation Korean parents are very concerned about spiritual growth and commitment among their children. To provide first-hand mission experience in unfamiliar settings to their children, the Korean Church Council started mission outreach programs in 1996. The Korean American Youth Adventist Missionary Movement (KAYAMM) is run mainly by Korean youth pastors, and it has trained a wide range of second-generation youth from early teens to college students and even young professionals. By the summer of 2006, a total of 349 Korean youth had received discipleship training through the programs offered by KAYAMM. Short-term overseas mission activities, teaching English to children in non-English-speaking countries, and summer vacation schools are the typical programs of KAYAMM. As of the summer of 2006, 271 young missionaries were trained and dispatched to twelve countries. Some of the mission fields include China, Colombia, Mexico, Mongolia, Peru, and the Philippines.

In addition, KAYAMM offers what they call "prophet schools" (following the old Hebrew model) for spiritual education at different local churches and regions in North America. Between September 1, 1998, and August 31, 2006, the project had received close to one million dollars from different sources. The bulk of the contributions came from individual Korean Adventists. KAYAMM needs about $150,000 per year to run its programs.

The 1,000 Missionary Movement was established near Louisville, Kentucky, by a few Korean Adventists in North America. It started in the Philippines and was aimed at Adventist youth in Pacific Asia. The Korean Adventists played key roles in promoting the movement with leadership, programs, and financial support. When the founder of the movement moved to the United States, he started the same program initially for the Korean Adventist youth in North America. After training, the young missionaries would go out to overseas mission fields for one-year terms. Over the years, the program has expanded recruitment efforts beyond the Korean Adventist community to attract diverse Adventist groups.

Also, the Korean Church Council has coordinated an annual summer cultural program for its youth. The month-long cultural exposure program in Korea is intended to help teenage Korean Americans examine and establish their own ethnic identity. This cultural enrichment program is a joint cooperation between the North American Korean Church Council and the Korean Union Conference at home.

Los Angeles Sahm-Yuk College

One unique aspect of the Korean Adventist efforts in North America is the establishment of a college for Koreans in California. Los Angeles Sahm-Yuk[9] College operates with the state approval of California, but it is not accredited by the regional educational association (Western Association of Schools and Colleges–WASC). A group of former Korean Adventist professors and administrators in Korea and presently active professionals in ministry and other fields started the adult school. It is primarily for those Korean-speaking immigrants who still work or are in retirement. So all classes are conducted in Korean on Sundays using a church building.

The Los Angeles Sahm-Yuk College offers a Bachelor of Theology degree. The main objective of the college is to train Korean lay members who are interested in advancing their theological knowledge or serving as lay pastors. In addition, those who could not finish college education during their working years can earn a bachelor's degree through the school.

In the first school year, 2003–2004, about fifteen adults enrolled to take classes on campus, and another thirty took courses by correspondence. Because some had already earned a degree in another field at the time of their enrollment, they could finish the degree program in just one year. According to the director of the school, the future of the college may lie in serving a much wider area beyond the region of southern California through distance learning programs.

Scholarship Foundations

Two scholarship foundations have been established by Korean Adventists in North America: one mainly for Korean American students and the other for Korean-Chinese Adventist youth in China.

The Korean-American Scholarship Foundation was established with $100,000 donated by Joyce Kim, daughter of Bong Ho Kang, one of the early Korean Adventists who came to America in 1921. The initial money increased substantially when two other Korean Adventists—Seong Rim Choi of the Los Angeles Central Church and James Lee of the Eugene Church in Oregon—donated $100,000 and $35,000, respectively. Mr. Choi turned in the birthday gift money from his children for the scholarship fund and Mr. Lee gave the money he had saved for his son's Harvard education after Harvard University offered him a full scholarship. The quarter-million-dollar fund has not been touched as the key donors keep contributing annually.

Each year, about twenty Korean American Adventist students in college and professional schools and five theology majors at Sahmyook University in Korea receive $1,000. As of 2007, about $100,000 has been awarded over four years.

The Bethesda Scholarship is unique in that it was established jointly by Korean Adventists in North America and Korea for Korean-Chinese Adventist youth in China. Every other year for ten years, the Korean American Adventists have helped Korean-Chinese Adventist students to develop future lay leadership for the Korean Adventist churches in China. The foundation has supported about 150 students, including two medical school graduates in 2007.

In sum, the Korean Adventist church in North America is a small scattered community. Yet what this community has attempted and accomplished is impressive. It is a growing dynamic community with zeal and commitment. Perhaps this Adventist diaspora community may reflect its progressive and dynamic home country, Korea. It should be noted that most of the accomplishments are the result of hard work and the vision of first-generation members who were educated and experienced in Korea. If the second-plus generation members continue the same spirit of their forefathers, the Korean church in North America may continue to shine. Yet the Korean church faces challenges as it stands at the trans-generational crossroad. The question is how the Korean Adventist church in North America is going to be shaped by the members of the second generation and beyond.

OTHER OVERSEAS KOREAN ADVENTIST COMMUNITIES

As a footnote to our discussion of the Korean Adventist church in North America, we want to briefly survey other overseas Korean Adventist churches. This may provide readers with a global perspective on the Korean Adventist international network.

China was the first site for the Korean Adventists' overseas ventures. In the late nineteenth and early twentieth centuries, many distressed Koreans migrated to China mainly for economic or political reasons. A large number of Koreans from the northern regions of the Korean peninsula crossed the two rivers, Tomen and Yalu, that served as the border demarcation. The Korean migrants settled down in the northeastern Chinese provinces close to Korea. That area was known as Manchuria at one time. When both Manchuria and Korea were under Japanese rule, movement between the two countries was relatively unrestricted. During this period, Korean Adventist workers established churches and administered a branch mission there.[10]

When North Korea and China became communist countries in 1948[11] and 1949,[12] respectively, the Adventist churches, like other religious institutions, were forced to close. Decades later, the communist China was open to the outside world in the early 1980s, and Korean Adventists from North America and Korea began planting churches there. As a result, numerous Korean Adventist congregations, mainly in the form of home churches, have existed in China today. Such is not the case for North Korea.[13]

As pointed out in chapter 1, Japan played a key role in introducing Adventism to Korea. But only a few Korean Adventist congregations have existed there with the help of Korean missionaries. Lately, Korean ministers have been sent to the Japan Union[14] which has experienced a shortage of trained ministers.

Besides the two neighboring countries, Korean churches were also established in central Asia (Uzbekistan), Far East Russia (once a Japanese territory, Sakhalin Island), Southeast Asia (the Philippines), Germany, South America (Argentina, Brazil, Paraguay, and Peru), and Australia. These locations on different continents are the testimony of the international mobility of Koreans in the last two centuries.[15]

In terms of size, the Korean Adventist church in North America is the largest overseas Korean Adventist community. In both scale and activities, it has surpassed every other overseas Korean Adventist community. In fact, it is much larger than all other overseas Korean Adventist communities in Asia, Australia, Europe, and South America combined. The Korean Adventist group in the United States is also situated in the most powerful nation on earth. Accordingly, this group can play significant roles in reaching out to Koreans everywhere.

NOTES

1. A complete directory of the Korean Adventist churches in North and South America has been published every other year by the Korean Adventist Press in Los Angeles. The names of church members and their contact information (address, telephone number, and email address in some cases) are listed by household. Also indicated are congregational arrangements for local churches as either Korean or English.

2. The two language groups in the Chicago Unity Church worshiped together for some time using translation. Then they switched back to separate services.

3. A group of worshipers may evolve from a "group" to a "company" and then eventually to a "church." The change of status depends on membership size and financial contributions.

4. According to the 2005 annual statistical report of the General Conference, there were 4,256 Adventists in Hong Kong/Maccao, 4,925 in Taiwan, and 15,061 in Japan. The same source reports that there were more than 330,000 Adventists on the mainland of China.

5. The idea met with opposition from church administrators at various levels of the North American Division. Some Korean leaders also showed little enthusiasm for the proposal. They were skeptical about the feasibility of operating such an entity as the Korean churches were scattered across North America. Second-generation members were far more indifferent. American-educated members regarded the idea as anachronistic.

6. This figure was reported on the website for the Overseas Koreans Foundation (http://www.korean.net/morgue/status_1.jsp?tCode=status&dCode=0101).

7. These figures are quoted from the report of the seventh General Session of the Korean Church Council in 2000. The reports of general sessions held in 2003 and 2006 did not include age breakdowns.

8. At the time of this writing, the radio program has been suspended due to a contract dispute.

9. Sahm Yuk is a common name used for Adventist educational institu-

tions at all levels in northeast Asia. Sahm Yuk in Chinese literally means "three education": education for physical, mental, and spiritual development. In English, the Sahm-Yuk College in California is called Los Angeles Adventist College.

10. There were seven churches with 570 members in Manchuria. Since the members of these churches used only Korean, they were affiliated with the Korean Union Mission in 1939 (Hyun 1976:565).

11. North and South Korea became separate states in 1948 along the two different political ideologies supported by the Soviet Union and the United States, respectively. This division happened three years after Korea's liberation from the Japanese colonial rule in 1945.

12. Technically, the organized Korean Adventist churches in China are under the administration of the Chinese government. Like any other Christian groups, they are supervised by the Bureau of Religious Affairs. Many of the congregations are home churches.

13. The Korean Union Conference has included the North Korean Mission in its annual statistical report. As last reported on North Korea in 1959, there were 26 churches with 866 members. However, the figures might reflect the state of North Korean Adventist churches around 1950 when the Korean War broke out. By 1959, North Korea had closed down all religious organizations to become a truly atheist communist country.

14. In comparison with Korea where about a quarter of its population claims to be Christians, Japanese Christians comprise less than 5 percent of the total population. The total number of Adventists (15,061) in Japan is less than 10 percent of Korean Adventists (182,936). See the online Annual Statistical Report of the General Conference (2005:20).

15. Overseas Koreans number around six million, and they are the fourth largest diaspora community in the world. Only China, Israel, and Italy have more overseas compatriots than does Korea (Um 2003:13).

CHAPTER 4

The Church in Transition

In the history of the Korean Adventist church in North America, 2006 will be remembered as a landmark year in leadership. That year the Korean church delegates selected Pastor Don Kim, a second-generation member, as its council president. That signifies a leadership change as he represents both second-generation and first-generation members.

Born in Korea, Pastor Kim came to the United States as a teenager with his parents. As he is bilingual and bicultural, he understands the issues and concerns of both generations. He served as a youth/associate pastor at a few Korean churches. Then he became a senior pastor at a major Korean church in Canada. From there he moved to a sizeable white church in Vancouver, Canada. Consequently, he is familiar with the Korean Adventist community and the larger Adventist community as well. The Korean Adventist community in North America may expect fresh perspectives and different approaches from the new leadership team.

One of the critical questions concerning the future of any immigrant church, regardless of ethnic origin, is that of continuation. It is about ethnic identity of a particular group. In this regard, the role of the second-generation members, either raised or born in North America, is crucial as they bridge the first immigrant generation and American-born third and fourth generations. Most third-plus-generation members tend to be less exposed to the culture of their grandparents unless their parents are conscious about preserving their ethnic identity. What is going to happen to Korean churches in North America once they are comprised primarily of second- and third-generation members?

A church may be compared to a fruit tree. Each tree requires a certain type of soil, nutrients, and climate. The orange tree, for instance, grows best in a climate with warm temperatures and dry air. The apple tree, on the other hand, yields best in a relatively mild temperate zone. Moreover, each tree needs different types of fertilizer and amounts of moisture. As trees are an integral part of their environs, they are constantly affected by the conditions of the soil and climate. Fertile soil and an ideal climate will make the trees grow strong and yield bountiful fruits while barren soil and an adverse climate will hinder normal growth. In worsening conditions, trees may eventually wither and die.

When a fruit tree is uprooted for transplanting, with its roots and branches severely trimmed, it takes a long time to recover from the shock. Some trees, nonetheless, are able to re-root deeply in the new soil and produce thick branches. Furthermore, the transplanted trees may develop unexpected flavors and textures in their fruits as they adapt to the new environment. In contrast, other trees may continue to struggle during the re-rooting process, and some of them may never recover from the trauma of transplantation. The new environment is too foreign for them to adapt.

In many ways, immigrant churches are like transplanted trees. Removed from their native soils and climates, they go through many internal and external readjustments. These churches experience varying degrees of difficulty during the transition in the unfamiliar soil and climate known as North America. The outcomes for these transplanted churches are mixed. Some survive and prosper, while others continue to suffer and fail.

In the course of time, some of these immigrant churches may lose their original ethnic distinctiveness while others may continue to retain much of their native flavor. In these churches, noticeable changes take place when the offspring of the first-generation immigrants increase. The transformation is inevitable, yet the nature and extent of it may depend on many unknown factors. At present, the

Korean Adventist churches in North America are in the midst of transition and readjustments. Some of these changes are obvious, while others are more subtle. Let us identify the changes that take place.

STRUCTURAL ARRANGEMENTS

Many Korean Adventist churches in North America have become two-language and two-culture congregations. The 2006 church directory, for instance, lists 113 Korean churches in the United States and Canada with 178 congregations at the end of 2005 (*Membership Directory* 2005). The division is along the generation line between Korean-speaking immigrants and English-speaking second- and third-generation members.[1] In some churches, the English-speaking members have already outnumbered the Korean-speaking adults, and the generational shift will be inevitable in the course of time. Eventually, the group speaking only Korean, a small older minority, may phase out in these churches.

The main question concerning the characteristics of Korean-American churches in the foreseeable future is how many second- and third-generation Korean Americans want to make their church ethnically distinctive. This involves both membership composition and subcultures of these churches.

As shown in Table 4.1, the obvious language and cultural differences among members make internal changes inevitable. The spiritual outlook, value system, interpersonal relations, and lifestyle of each generation are considerably different from the others. The second-generation members, either born in Korea or in North America, and their children tend to think and act like their peers in mainstream American society. They speak the English language, which in turn shapes their thinking patterns differently. Unlike English, for example, the Korean language is very much age-conscious with different levels of honorific expression. Furthermore, the second-generation members have internalized different value systems and standards through childhood socialization, formal education, and real life experiences in North America.

Table 4.1 The Church in Transition

First Generation	Second/Third Generation
Korean-Born	North American-Born/Raised
Korean-Speaking	English-Speaking
Ethnicity Bound/Compelled	Ethnicity Choice/Appreciated
Group Priority	Individual Priority
Group Affiliation	Individual Choice
Vertical Relation	Horizontal Relation
Authoritarian Leadership	Democratic Leadership
Closed/Isolated Church	Open/Interactive Church
Homogeneous Church	Heterogeneous Church
Introverted Outlook	Extroverted Outlook
Centripetal Activity	Centrifugal Activity

The collective efforts to respond to the changes resulting from the generational shift have varied. Most, if not all, Korean Adventist congregations have tried to accommodate the changes as much as their capabilities and resources allow. Only a few, usually small and isolated congregations, have ignored the internal changes, perhaps out of helplessness.

The congregations with a combined membership of 150 or more are usually able to assist their youth groups in tangible ways. Typically, these churches hire a full-time youth pastor and have the English-speaking group run their own worship program and activities. Large churches, usually with a membership of 300 or more, may have one youth pastor for children and teenagers and another minister for young adults. Also, these churches provide a separate space for youth and young adult activities. In this arrangement, the youth pastor is more likely to hold the position of associate pastor. Often these churches maintain the one-church/two-language group (or congregation) model. They operate with a single church board and single budget under the leadership of a senior pastor.

Some smaller churches realize the benefits of a larger congregation in serving their youth and have attempted to merge with other small churches to create a larger congregation. The aim is often to establish a sizable youth congregation with a full-time associate pastor for English-speaking members. In this situation, the Korean-speaking adults are willing to bear the discomfort and inconvenience that may come with the merge. Although it happens, such a move is rather rare.

In other cases, a Korean congregation merges with a non-Korean church. In this scenario, often an older white church, usually located in or near an urban center, has been losing its members through demographic and neighborhood changes over the years. It needs to merge with another group to maintain its existing congregation. Otherwise, even the maintenance of the old church building is beyond the ability of the remaining members. Occasionally the group that moves in eventually takes over the church building.

Sometimes a Korean group without their own church building becomes a subgroup of an existing American congregation by merging with it. The benefits for the Korean group are the organizational support given by the host church and the use of physical facilities. If the host church has a program for young people, that is a side benefit for the Korean group.

Another option for second-generation members is to establish an independent group. In a few metropolitan areas, graduate/professional students and young adults have started their own congregations independent of their parents' church. Initially, a few concerned first-generation adults may assist such a group with finances and organizational skills, but eventually the young people become independent. They operate these churches with their own financial and program support. So far, only the Upper Room Fellowship Church (formerly called the Upper Room Young Adult Company until 2002) in Temple City near Los Angeles has remained independent without attaching itself to any existing Korean-speaking church. In the spring of 2004, the young-adult Korean congregation invited a white minister to be their pastor. A few of the members are non-Koreans.

One may wonder why these English-speaking Korean young adults want a separate independent church. These young adults have unique spiritual needs and personal concerns. But the typical youth programs in most Korean churches are oriented more towards teenagers in worship style and social activities. The young adults, with or without spouses and children, do not feel that they fit into either the Korean-speaking adult group or the teen-dominant youth group. So they want to form their own congregation, and a sufficient number of young adults within their geographical boundary share the same concerns. Someday, however, even age-specific, second-generation congregations will have to become all-age English-speaking churches as they respond to the needs of their own growing children.

In areas where such a separate arrangement for English-speaking young adults is not possible, many of the young adults drift away from their Korean churches. Some may attend non-Korean Adventist churches, and a few may join other Korean Protestant churches with English congregations just to maintain Christian identity. The reality is that many lose interest in church life itself for a while. But when the children of these second-generation young adults begin to search for their own ethnic identity, these parents may return to a Korean church to help their children establish their own spiritual and cultural identity. The young parents will have reached a life stage where belonging to a group becomes important for their children's social well-being.

At some large churches, the second-generation members are divided into English-speaking and Korean-speaking groups. The latter group attracts those who come to America in their teen years. Also, students from Korea who attend colleges or graduate or professional schools in North America often join a Korean-speaking church group for the comfort of cultural familiarity. In some cases, those who want to learn or retain the Korean language are attracted to a Korean-speaking group. In fact, many of these people are bilingual and bicultural. Thus, the division between the primary languages results in more than two informal groups. Sometimes young people are organized separately with their own officers and leaders engaging in different group activities.

Due to circumstances at different churches in various locations, no one should expect a single prescribed path to apply to all. Each local Korean church in North America may face a different future course.

Unlike their immigrant parents who are limited by language and cultural differences, the second-generation members and their children have far more freedom and options. If they choose to ignore ethnic concerns, it is easier for them to join any English-speaking church regardless of its membership composition.

The key to predicting the ethnic make-up of future Korean Adventist churches in North America is knowing to what extent future generations desire to retain their Korean identity through church life. The Korean ethnicity of these churches may range from being distinctly Korean to being totally open to anyone. Therefore, the future ethnicity of Korean churches largely depends on the intent and efforts of the second-generation members and their children to uphold their Korean identity. As crucial as the intent in determining group ethnic identity is the size of the Korean community in a given area.

DIFFERENT SCENARIOS

Most Korean churches in North America were originally organized primarily for the needs of Korean-speaking immigrant adults. They were indeed "immigrant" churches, as they were called. These immigrant churches were very much like the ones these people had left behind at home. Their theological orientation, worship style, and organizational operation were more like the home churches than the North American churches in their new communities.

Children of these immigrants, still young and obedient, were not very much in the forefront of their concerns in the early years. This changed, however, as the English-speaking, second-generation members rapidly increased in number and social status. The first-generation members have been forced to make major adjustments for the sake of the growing needs of their children and grandchildren. For instance, providing a separate place for English worship and raising funds to hire a youth pastor have become more urgent concerns. It is true that the children were sacrificed for their parents in the past, but now the parents are expected to sacrifice for their children.

As implied before, it is less clear at present how the Korean Adventist churches in North America are going to organize themselves in the years to come. Nevertheless, it is possible to anticipate different arrangements based upon the experiments of Korean Adventist churches and the precedents of other ethnic churches in North America.

Most scenarios described here are real in that they have been tried before. A local church may experiment with different models in the course of its lifetime. The scenarios discussed below reflect an adjusting process of a transforming church both to internal and external conditions. It is somewhat precarious, therefore, to predict a uniform evolving pattern among different local churches in North America. Many variables at different levels affect the future shape and courses of these churches.

1. Korean-Speaking Church

In their beginning stage, most Korean churches offer a worship service only in Korean. Usually these fledgling congregations are too small to provide a separate service for their English-speaking members. The needs of their children are either ignored for the lack of means or relegated to a nearby English-speaking congregation. On the other hand, some groups attempt to offer services in Korean to help their children learn the mother tongue. In either case, such an arrangement tends to be temporary unless younger members insist upon continuing services in Korean only to maintain their mother tongue. Such demands are rare.

2. Bilingual-Service Church

To integrate English-speaking members into the main worship service, a bilingual service is often provided. In this case, one congregation is worshiping in two languages. The service is done either through line-by-line translation or simultaneous translation using an electronic device. The key to success in this arrangement is the quality of translation. Another factor is the willingness of each language group to tolerate the redundancy of hearing the same message in two languages. Some may enjoy the bilingual service for its sense of togetherness and offer of translation, but others want to avoid such a service because of its redundancy and longer duration.

Although such an arrangement is rare on a permanent basis, it is attempted mainly for children when there is no regular youth pastor.

Most Korean churches hold a joint worship service once a month or once a quarter and on special occasions, such as Christmas. Those who push for a bilingual service tend to be the ones who want to maintain the sense of a single church family. But the reality is that not many second-generation members are excited about the joint service as they become impatient with the translation. The nature of a joint worship service is usually determined by a sponsoring worship committee.

3. Separate-Congregation Church

As a younger English-speaking group grows older and larger, members often want their own separate program and activities. Three conditions must be met for the English-speaking group: an associate pastor, adequate lay leadership, and space for a separate worship service. Some English-speaking groups could become their own churches in terms of membership and finances, yet they choose to remain part of the mother church. They may hold a joint service on a regular basis to maintain the sense of unity. The two groups remain integrated by supporting the concept of one church board and one budget. Many share the same church compound using two different buildings, and others use two separate compounds apart from each other. In the latter case, the English-speaking group rents another church or meeting place not far from the mother church. Among the Korean Adventist churches in North America, this model seems to be the most common arrangement at present.

4. Two Independent Congregations in One Church

It is conceivable that two separate congregations as described above may become two autonomous churches by establishing a separate church board and budget for each group. In this arrangement, each congregation administers its own personnel and financial matters. They share the church compound where each group occupies its own separate space. They may also share the same local name, such as Glendale, in their church title. Since the members of some families are separated only for services, independence is actually exhibited only at the administrative level.

5. Independent English-Speaking Korean Church

As pointed out previously, only one Adventist Korean church in North America out of more than 100 has established an independent English-speaking congregation. Most members of this independent congregation, Upper Room Fellowship, are dominantly young professionals and their spouses. Programs are also conducted for their children. There was once a push to establish such a group for each major metropolitan area to respond to the needs of young adults at different local churches.

6. English-Group-Dominant Korean Church

One English-speaking Korean group attempted an independent church in Chicago for a while, but they were joined by a group of Korean-speaking adults. This is a unique case in that the English-speaking group is the dominant group and those who speak Korean are a subgroup of the church. The English worship service is held in the sanctuary of the rented church and the Korean worship service for adults is held in the gymnasium of the church. The minister responsible for the English-speaking group is the senior pastor and an associate pastor serves the Korean-speaking group. The head elder is a second-generation member. This is a reversal of the typical arrangement at many Korean Adventist churches where the first-generation members are dominant in size and control.

For a while, the Chicago group held a joint bilingual service every Sabbath. The senior pastor, who is in charge of the English group, spoke in Korean, and then each sentence was translated into English. It is possible that more such churches may emerge as the first-generation Korean adults become older and fewer in the course of time.

7. Open Church

This type of church is open to anyone from any ethnic background. No longer are the Korean ethnic marks—such as ancestry, language, family ties, and customs—regarded as important criteria for membership. In reality, every English-speaking Korean church is an open church. No one consciously promotes the Korean culture in their churches, but their openness is passive. An open church advertises and actively recruits anyone from any ethnic background.

Some Asian Americans have attempted to establish a church open to anyone, but they tend to attract mainly people of Asian ancestry. A Pan-Asian church—as such a congregation is called—is a multi-Asian ethnic church usually made up of Chinese, Japanese, Koreans, and Southeast Asians. Some Korean Christians in North America have joined Pan-Asian churches since there is no Korean congregation in their communities.

It is worth noting that some Korean youth congregations have debated on the wisdom of keeping the word "Korean" in their church names.[2] Their push for inclusiveness stems from either a theological conviction about the openness of the gospel to anyone or a desire to increase membership, or both. In either case, their efforts to be more inclusive reflect their desire to remove ethnic barriers. While no sizable English-speaking Korean congregations are 100 percent Korean but have intermarried couples and non-Korean attendants, some are more intentional and systematic than others in attracting non-Koreans.

8. End of a Korean Church

In the decades to come, some Korean congregations, either Korean-speaking or English-speaking, may face the grim reality of closing their doors for good. Already a few small congregations have ended their existence mainly due to a lack of membership. This happens usually in small cities. In such cases, the remaining members join other congregations according to their language preference or proficiency. If fewer Koreans choose to immigrate to North America, the closing of Korean-speaking churches may become more common in the future.

Overview

The above eight scenarios could be viewed as an eight-stage sequential life cycle for some Korean immigrant churches. A few of them might be destined to follow the sequential path in a linear fashion. In this scenario, the final phase is a closure of the church due to lack of members or interest in maintaining a Korean church. Other churches might be locked in stage two or three. It is not inconceivable that some churches might regress from the third type to the second type, and possibly even back to the first. A surge in interest among future-generation members to discover their national or ethnic identity could trigger a reversal in the sequence. Any drastic changes in the future may depend on both internal (congregational) and external (national or international) conditions.

At present, most Korean churches in urban areas adopt one of the three bilingual options. Of these, the most common model appears to be one church with two separate congregations sharing regular or occasional joint services. A small church based in a small Korean American community, on the other hand, may lack the resources to provide for the needs of their children. Thus it might become difficult to continue their existence beyond the first generation. In small and medium-size cities, children tend to move away for their college and professional education after high school. They seldom return to their home town for permanent settlement. In contrast, the churches in southern California and other large metropolitan areas—such as Atlanta, Chicago, and New York—may continue to exist as distinctive Korean churches for many years as they are based in sizable Korean communities. Because of the demographic composition of such regions, ethnic churches may remain distinctive instead of being absorbed by mainstream churches.

There are two major prospects for the long-term future of Korean Adventist churches in North America. Simply put, distinctive Korean churches either continue or come to an end. The outcome may largely depend on the degree of Korean identity desired by the members.

OPTIMISTIC PROSPECT: CONTINUATION

One may put the two prospects in emotional terms, perhaps from the perspective of the founding immigrant generation: optimistic and pessimistic prospects. Most Korean-born parents are far more attached to their churches than are their American-born children and grandchildren. The parents want to see the churches they established continue to exist and grow. The optimists believe that the Korean Adventist church will continue with its ethnic marks to varying degrees. The marks of these churches could be people of Korean ancestry, or also the Korean language, identity, certain value emphasis, spiritual overtone, lifestyle, customs, and the like.[3]

Their optimism might be grounded in a number of factors. First of all, the United States and Canada have switched their cultural values from assimilation to that of cultural pluralism. The cultural image of these countries has been replaced with a gigantic salad bowl or mosaic. Diversity is valued and appreciated. Incoming immigrant groups do not have to give up their cultural heritages. This has definite positive effects in preserving ethnic identity.

The second source of optimism is the change of immigration policy. More than anything else, ethnic diversity is the result of the changing composition of the population. Unlike the immigrants arriving before the 1950s who were predominantly European, the majority of recent immigrants have come from Asia and Latin America. Since the early 1970s, Asia and Latin America have sent more than 80 percent of the total immigrants to the United States.[4] As a result, seven million Asians immigrated to the United States between 1965 and 2000. The people of Asian ancestry in the United States increased from 1.5 million in 1970 to 10.5 million in 2000. The increase of the Asian population was more than six-fold over just 30 years (Min in Min and Kim 2002:3).

Most Asians are visibly different from Euro-Americans in their physical appearance. Also Asian value systems and lifestyles are quite distinctive. These visible physical and cultural differences might hinder their total blending into the mainstream society. The steady increase of a non-white population, including Koreans, may provide sociocultural conditions conducive to retaining one's ethnic identity.

Furthermore, the continuous globalization has promoted diversity in unexpected ways. Chief among the effects of globalization is the enhanced sense of uniqueness in each cultural group. This may be viewed as a reaction of many non-Western societies to the sweeping globalization led by North America and western Europe. In the face of powerful Americanization and Westernization, people want to preserve their uniqueness. It may sound contradictory, but globalization has increased population heterogeneity in open countries, like the United States.

Another aspect that may slow down the assimilation process among immigrants is modern technology. Immigrants and their children are constantly exposed to and reinforced by the home culture through a wide range of modern global technologies, including telephone, Internet, radio, television, satellite link, and print media. In addition, the ease of two-way international travel by high-speed jumbo jets has made contact with people from the home country a commonplace experience. Life in today's global village has almost erased the sense of physical distance in the minds of immigrants regardless of where they live outside their native countries. Koreans on both sides of the Pacific Ocean actively use modern technologies to communicate with each other. Those living in North American urban centers are especially bombarded by their home cultures. Each cultural contact reminds and reinforces one's ethnic roots.

Another unexpected effect of globalization is the demand for multiculturally trained persons. In the increasingly interdependent and intertwined modern world, cross-cultural knowledge and experiences are highly valued. Governments, international agencies, and multinational corporations prefer those with multilingual and multicultural capabilities. In this regard, the children of immigrants can take advantage of their bilingual and bicultural experiences. This is more so among Asian Americans as Asia as a whole is rising as a major influence in international politics and economy.[5] The enhanced international status of their mother countries—notably China, India, Japan, and Korea—can instill a sense of pride in Asian Americans. Naturally they want to associate with their proud ancestral countries. Many have predicted that the twenty-first century would be an Asian or a Pacific century.[6]

Finally, optimists on the future of the Korean church may point to the continuous existence of black churches in North America. In spite of much hardship they have long endured, black churches have enjoyed both community and national support. Although African Americans speak English and share the general American cultural traits, they have maintained separate churches for many generations. The separate existence of black churches in America reflects more than what the racial discrimination of the past has imposed upon them. At one time it was caused by racial segregation, but now it is a source of identity and pride, providing a sense of community among African Americans.

Optimists may also look at Hispanic churches with a similar perspective. The sheer number of Hispanic Americans and their concentration patterns have produced sizable Hispanic communities in the large urban centers of North America. Many Hispanic Americans see their churches in their communities as a source of identity and ethnic pride.

Although the position and experiences of Native Americans are very different from the two major minority groups, it could be noted that they are another example of a group preserving cultural identity. In fact, at one time the U.S. government tried to assimilate the Native Americans by weakening tribal identity under the General Allotment Act passed in 1887, but it failed. As a result, the government made a turnabout and encouraged the tribes to retain their cultural heritage.[7]

Those who want to see their Korean churches continue to exist, not just for years but for decades and generations, may find enough precedents, examples, and reasons to be optimistic. Although the probability of a continuous existence of the Korean church is much higher now in North America than ever before, the key to the optimistic prospect is still the desire of future generations to hold onto their Korean identity. The combination of ethnicity and faith should result in mutually reinforcing positive effects experienced by some Jewish and African American groups. In that case, ethnicity becomes a catalyst for one's faith.

PESSIMISTIC PROSPECT: DISCONTINUATION

Like the optimists, pessimists may find sufficient reasons to be skeptical about the long-term future of Korean churches in North America. They wonder about the continuous existence of the church beyond the first immigrant generation. The skeptics are reminded of the experiences of European immigrants who were absorbed into the mainstream American society within one or two generations. The progress of assimilation among European immigrants was in proportion to the amount of time they spent in the host country. When it came to their children, ethnicity became a mere symbolic concern (Gans 1979).

In addition, the pessimists know what happened to children of the early Asian immigrants from China, Japan, Korea, and the Philippines in the late nineteenth and early twentieth centuries. These Asian Americans, like their European counterparts, also desired to blend into the dominant society. But unlike the European immigrants and their children, the Asians could not hide their physical differences.[8] Although they were not fully accepted, they wished to be assimilated. This was the case until the 1960s when the civil rights movement led by the blacks made other minority groups take their ethnic heritage and identity seriously.

Although today's Asian Americans are remarkably different from their counterparts of the preceding generations in terms of ethnic identity and pride, the increasing out-marriage in an open tolerant society may generate a gap between them and the ethnic community. When one's spouse is a non-Korean, his or her interest in and commitment to ethnic community can be substantially affected by the marriage situation.[9]

The most direct and imminent cause of the pessimistic future of Korean churches is the departure of some members who are dissatisfied with their parents' Korean churches. This is more common among the second-generation members of college age or older. The reasons for their leaving could be either personal or spiritual discontent or both. Simply put, the existing Korean churches dominated by the first-generation immigrants have failed to satisfy the aspirations of their second-generation members. Some of the second generation may attend non-Korean churches and others may stop attending church altogether. This phenomenon has been dubbed a "silent exodus" (Lee 1996:50–53).

Another source of pessimism about the future of Korean Adventist churches in North America involves the flow of immigration from Korea. As shown before, Korean immigration to America peaked in the mid 1980s. Since then the number of annual Korean immigrants has been steadily declining by as much as two-thirds for some years. The downturn can be attributed to three reasons: improvement in the standard of living in Korea, more restrictive immigration laws in the United States, and deterioration of the quality of life in America, especially in urban areas.

By the late 1980s and early 1990s, Korea had achieved an impressive economic prosperity. Its culmination came in 1988 when the country hosted the Summer Olympic Games in Seoul, only the second Asian nation to do so after Japan. The almost blind rush to America in the 1960s and 1970s ceased, and Koreans have become more cautious about leaving their established lives at home. At the same time, U.S. immigration laws became more restrictive in the 1980s and 1990s. In addition, the numerous racial incidents that led to the Los Angeles riot in 1992, especially targeting the Koreans and their small businesses in the south central district of Los Angeles, had chilling effects upon the prospective immigrants at home. Many of them had serious second thoughts about their plans to move to America.

Not only did the migration rate significantly decline from the late 1980s to the mid 1990s, but a measurable reverse migration was an emerging trend for a while as some Koreans decided to return home for economic and personal reasons. To them, life in prosperous Korea became more attractive. At the same time, the deterioration of the quality of life in the United States—marred by crime, drugs, youth problems, and the like—had shattered their American dreams. In the early 1990s, on average 5,000 to 6,000 people returned to Korea each year (Kim and Kim in Kwon et al. 2001:74).

Then a major economic hardship unexpectedly hit Korea when the country found itself in insolvency in 1997. The country could not pay foreign debt as the central bank did not have sufficient foreign reserves. That shock, known as the IMF (International Monetary Fund) crisis, threw the country off balance. The Korean dream was shattered and reverse migration came to a sudden halt. Recently, interest in migrating to North America has surged again as many Koreans are discouraged about the lack of economic opportunities at home. Yet the current immigration laws are far more restrictive than they were twenty to thirty years ago.

As for now, assimilation, the exodus of dissatisfied second-generation members, increasing intermarriage, and a decrease in Korean immigration to North America could be major factors that may stall the continuing existence of Korean churches. Whether one is optimistic or pessimistic about the continuation of Korean churches in North America, the factors described above show how difficult it is to predict the future of the Korean-American community in general and the Korean churches in particular.

FUTURE DIRECTION OF KOREAN CHURCHES

Assimilation is inevitable among Korean-American members of the second and later generations. It is only a matter of degree. After all, they were born or grew up in North America. The question is how much they want to preserve the culture of their parents or grandparents as a basis of their own cultural identity. As long as they want to maintain their dual identity as Korean-Americans or Korean-Canadians and maintain an interest in their cultural heritage, they may want to continue to associate with the Korean-American institutions such as Korean churches. Otherwise, a lack of desire to preserve their ethnic roots will eventually lead to the end of the Korean church as an ethnically distinctive entity.

As described, many factors might shape the direction of the church. And the factors are in constant flux. Some of them are personal, and others are national or global. The economic conditions, political situations, immigration policies, and cultural expectations and policies of the host countries, for instance, may change regardless of personal desires.

In essence, the continuation of Korean Adventist churches in North America may depend on two major factors: the number of Korean people in a given geographical boundary and their desire to preserve their ethnic identity. If there is a sizable Korean community in a certain geographical area and its members have a strong desire to maintain their Korean identity, they are more likely to maintain a Korean church.

NOTES

1. Some members are bilingual in both generations, but they tend to associate with the members of their own generation. The only group somewhat ambiguous about its place in Korean churches is the young adults from

Korea who came to America to study. They belong to the same cohort as most second-generation members, but they feel more comfortable with the Korean-speaking first-generation members.

2. Some second-generation Korean Adventist congregations do not indicate the ethnicity of their groups in their church titles. A few examples are "Living Water Fellowship Group" in the Los Angeles Central Church, "Chicago Unity English Church," and "Upper Room Fellowship Church." By excluding the word "Korean," they advertise themselves as non-Korean-speaking congregations.

3. Some immigrant groups want to preserve their Asian values and lifestyle as counter measures to the undesirable aspects of American culture, especially for young people. They want to insulate their children from excessive individualism, indulgence in pleasure, and laxity of morality.

4. From 1981 to 2000, 47% and 35% of immigrants to America came from Latin America and Asia, respectively. As a result, Latin Americans and Asians comprised 52% and 26% of the total foreign-born American population in 2002. In both cases, the figures could be higher if they included the undocumented aliens from the source continents (Schaefer 2004:103–116).

5. American public interest in Asia has increased drastically. Even some kindergarten and elementary schools offer classes in the Chinese language as China is perceived to be a land of future opportunities.

6. See Borthwick (1998), Elegant (1990), and Gibney (1992).

7. The General Allotment Act was intended to Americanize the Native Indians by introducing the concept of private ownership. By allocating 160 acres of land to each Indian household, the U.S. government tried to break down ties to their tribes. Eventually the government recognized the failure of the policy and it revived the traditional tribal system (Schafer 2004:156–158).

8. American-born Asians reveal that they are often asked where they originated from and where they learned such good English. Many feel that they are perpetual foreigners no matter how many generations they have lived in America.

9. Intermarriage is more common among American-raised Asians. Between Asian men and Asian women, the latter are more likely to find spouses outside their own ethnic groups. According to a study using a 2000 U.S. census random sample, 63% of American-raised Korean men married Korean women and only 40% of American-raised Korean women married Korean men. The same figures for Chinese are 65% and 55%, and for Japanese 63% and 56%, respectively. Korean women show the highest intermarriage rate among the Asian gender groups, and 48% of them married white men as opposed to Korean men (40%). When adding the figures for marriage to other Asians, the three Asian groups show a slight increase (male and female): Korean 72% and 48%; Chinese 77% and 66%; Japanese 77% and 67%, respectively. The recent trend is that more Asian Americans look for spouses within their own group or in other Asian groups (Asian-Nation 2005).

CHAPTER 5

Studies on the Children of Immigrants

Before discussing the information offered by the second-generation Korean Adventists on the survey in this study, we want to briefly look at the experiences of European immigrants and their children in the past. Then we will review the findings of recent studies on the children of Asian immigrant groups in North America, including those of Korean immigrants. The studies reviewed here cover a wide range of topics, including ethnic identity, language acquisition, socialization, Americanization or assimilation, intergenerational relationships, and church affiliation. The findings may shed light on the attitudes and experiences of the second-generation Korean Adventists in North America, since this group is part of a much larger cultural scene. We may also be able to compare the Korean Adventist group with their Asian peers elsewhere in both church and non-church settings. Thus we may recognize both similarities and differences between the Korean Adventist group and other groups. It is especially important to note recent trends among the children of Asian immigrants.

CHANGES OF SOCIAL CONDITIONS

Robert Ezra Park, an American sociologist, studied European immigrants to America in the early decades of the twentieth century. According to Park, first-generation European immigrants typically went through four phases of adjustment: initial contact, conflict, accommodation, and assimilation.[1] The final outcome of their experiences in America was assimilation. Americanization was only a matter of time and degree.

In the initial contacts between the incoming Europeans and the local residents, the differences in language, manners, and customs displayed by the immigrants were evidences of their foreignness. If the differences were significant, uneasiness and even tension existed between the two groups. Usually, eastern and southern Europeans faced more prejudice in America than those from northern and western Europe.[2] In either case, the members of the host group expected the immigrants to abandon their old cultural traits to be Americanized. And most, if not all, European immigrant groups were eager to adopt the American culture. The hastened Americanization was a mutual expectation in the nineteenth and early-twentieth-century America.

Children of the immigrants—who were born or grew up in America—more readily blended into the host culture. Despite the noticeable distinctions of the European immigrant nationalities, there were still enough similarities, both physical and cultural, to make assimilation into American society relatively easy. Some of the second-generation children experienced "marginality" as they were caught in two different cultures. The life they experienced in the home with their immigrant parents was not the same as the world they encountered outside the home. As a result, some children felt that they belonged to neither world. Many second-generation children—especially the children of immigrants from eastern and southern European countries with Catholic, Orthodox, and Jewish backgrounds—developed a sense of ambiguity and confusion at times. Straddling the line between American and immigrant culture, they felt largely marginalized.[3]

The first generation of European immigrants could not help but show some of their original ethnic marks regardless of how long they had lived in America. Their children were somewhat uneasy about their identity and place in American society in spite of their familiarity with the mainstream culture. But when the third generation came on the scene, many of them became interested in their own ethnic roots. This was a somewhat unexpected development. In short, the third-generation members tried to remember what their parents (second-generation) tried to forget. This has been known as Hansen's principle of third-generation interest (Schaefer 2004:143–144).

The search for one's origin in the third generation was more frequently observed among eastern and southern European descendants. The search was partially in response to the various movements that emphasized ethnic pride among the minority groups following the civil rights movement in the early 1960s. For instance, the black civil rights movement, the American Indian movement, and the Chicano movement all stirred the feelings of the European descendants too. In reaction to the civil rights movement, Polish, Italian, Greek, and Slavic Americans (eastern and southern Europeans) began to express their own voice and rights in America.

Even before the 1960s, some European immigrant groups resisted assimilation. They had remained as unmelted lumps in the gigantic melting pot. The devout orthodox Jews and conservative Catholics from the eastern and southern European countries, for example, tried to maintain their own ethnic enclaves in the Anglo-Saxon Protestant-dominant America. In particular, the orthodox Jews preserved many of their traditions and customs in the new world.[4] By the same token, some Italian and Polish immigrants tried to preserve their cultural heritages.

The landscape of immigration has significantly changed since the passage of the Immigration Amendment Act in 1965, with South America and Asia replacing Europe as the major sources of immigration to America. The new immigrants are quite different from the European immigrants in many ways. One significant difference is the geographical concentration of Asians and South Americans mainly in the eastern states (e.g., New York, New Jersey, and Florida), the Southwest, and the Pacific West.[5] When the new immigrants are surrounded by a dense, large community of fellow compatriots from the same country or region, their acculturation in America can be very slow.[6]

The change of the governmental position has also played a significant role in the assimilation of new immigrants. The governments of the United States and Canada now value diversity under the banner of cultural pluralism. This has created different social atmospheres and expectations for the new arrivals. Unlike the European immigrants of previous centuries, the new immigrants and their children have different attitudes and expectations toward assimilation into their host societies. Some of them may embrace their host cultures without any question while others may hesitate for personal or social reasons. In between are immigrants who attempt to integrate the two cultures. In this social atmosphere, a bilingual and bicultural person is appreciated. What is new in both the United States and Canada is the fact that no one is pressured to assimilate at the loss of one's cultural heritage.

Besides the changes of national attitudes towards immigrants and their cultures, many other factors affect the extent of assimilation among immigrants and their children. The first is the size of one's national group and the formation of an ethnic community in the host country. In short, the larger one's national group is, the slower one's Americanization tends to be. Further, the more dense the concentration of one's ethnic community, the slower one's assimilation is. Often these large ethnic communities are self-contained and self-sufficient, thus minimizing the necessity to interact with the larger community.

Like Chinatown in San Francisco, Koreatown in Los Angeles, or Little Saigon in Orange County, California, these communities provide a wide range of services, nearly everything short of government-related services. Newly arrived immigrants can live comfortably without speaking a word of English. So if one lives in or near one's ethnic community, the assimilation process may never take place. Tied to one's ethnic community, one is constantly reminded of his or her ethnic origin.

Globalization or internationalization is another force that slows down assimilation among immigrants. People's perspectives on other cultures as well as their own have changed in favor of diversity. In the current era of the global village, countries are becoming more open, interactive, and interdependent upon each other. Increasing cross-cultural awareness and experiences have made people value their unique cultural heritage. At the same time, globalization has enhanced cultural sensitivity and respect among people, thus leading to cultural tolerance and appreciation. This transnational life experience, aided by the use of information technology, has instilled a different worldview and mindset.

CHANGES OF ETHNIC COMPOSITION IN THE UNITED STATES, 1980–2000

In this section, we will look at how the U.S. population changed between 1980 and 2000, following the implementation of the Immigration Amendment Act of 1965. As seen in Table 5.1, the U.S. census figures clearly reveal a trend in the changes of the ethnic composition over the twenty-year period.

Table 5.1 Racial Composition (%) in the U.S. and California, 1980–2000

Racial Group	United States			California		
	1980	1990	2000	1980	1990	2000
White (non-Hispanic)	83	80	77	65	57	47
Hispanic*	6	9	13	19	26	32
Asian/Pacific Islanders	1	3	5	5	9	11

*The US Census Bureau added a separate category for Hispanics in 1980.

First of all, the census reports show the shift of immigration sources from Europe to Asia and Latin America. For instance, the increase in the Hispanic population in the nation and, especially, in California has been remarkable over the last three decades. Hispanics made up 6 percent and 19 percent in the nation and in California, respectively, in 1980; 9 percent and 26 percent in 1990; and 13 percent and 32 percent in 2000. Within twenty years the total Hispanic population doubled in the United States.

In California, about one in three residents is now of Hispanic origin. In Los Angeles, for example, the largest ethnic group is Hispanics (47%) followed by non-Hispanic whites (30%), according to the 2000 census. The rapid increase of the Hispanic population may be attributed to two major sources: immigration and birth rate. In recent years, babies born of Hispanic parents account for more than 50 percent of all births in the state of California.

At the same time, Asians and Pacific Islanders have shown a steady increase both in the nation and in California over the same period: 1 percent and 5 percent in the United States and California, respectively, in 1980; 3 percent and 9 percent in 1990; and 5 percent and 11 percent in 2000. The proportion of the Asian population tripled in the nation and doubled in California over the twenty-year period. In the Golden State, roughly one in ten residents is a person of Asian ancestry. Why has California attracted so many new immigrants in spite of its share of social problems? More than anything else, California has the major ports of entry for immigrants from Asia and Mexico: San Diego, Los Angeles, and San Francisco. Also the state has become the final destination for many foreign immigrants who settle initially in other parts of the country, especially the Midwest and the East. Factors pulling Asians from the Pacific-rim countries to California may include the reduced distance to their home countries, the mild climate, sizable ethnic communities, and educational and economic opportunities. For these reasons, many countries, including Korea, have their largest overseas population in Los Angeles.

Accordingly, the proportion of the white population, excluding Americans of Hispanic origin, has steadily decreased over the same period: 83 percent and 65 percent in the nation and California, respectively, in 1980; 80 percent and 57 percent in 1990; and 77 percent and 47 percent in 2000. Thus California and Texas have joined New Mexico and Hawaii as states where non-Hispanic whites are no longer a numerical majority.[7]

In some regions, the decline of the white population is more remarkable than in others. The states on the west coast, in the Southwest, and in the Southeast have attracted far more immigrants, including undocumented aliens, simply because of their geographic proximity to the source nations. The prospect is that such a demographic trend is likely to continue. Consequently, the pressure of the white community upon the new immigrants to assimilate has been considerably weakened. In some urban areas, non-whites have become the numerical majority. The election of a Mexican American mayor for the second largest city, Los Angeles, is a case in point. And this may continue in the coming decades unless the immigration policies are changed to halt or slow down the flow of people from Asia and Latin America. Some groups have put pressure on the U.S. government to halt or curb the flow of immigrants from the two source continents.[8]

STUDIES ON THE CHILDREN OF POST–1965 IMMIGRANTS

Serious research on the children of non-European immigrants who moved to North America in the second half of the twentieth century reflects rather recent efforts. The reported studies are therefore somewhat limited.[9]

In general, newly arrived immigrants may face either success or failure in realizing their dreams in the new world. Those who succeed in realizing their dreams in economic and social terms experience upward mobility. Usually these individuals come to the United States with social capital, such as compatible character traits, education, and job skills necessary for success. Even if they have to start in the inner cities, they are soon able to bounce back by taking advantage of the opportunities available in the new country.

Some may benefit from extensive family or community networks in starting a new life. To many, the support of these networks could be vital in the early phase of settlement. Also, it is not uncommon for Asian families to arrive with a considerable sum of money from selling their property at home where real estate is highly priced.

On the other hand, many have their dreams shattered. Often they are trapped in the life of ethnic ghettos in big American cities. Those who come to America with limited education or job skills are more likely to face hardships. Their former life experiences at home as farmers or unskilled laborers do not help much in the high-tech American society. They might be surrounded by their own compatriots, often from the same town or province, but their ethnic community may not provide any significant help. Thus their new life could be one of constant struggles for survival from the beginning. Many are bound to experience downward mobility.

Often the life opportunities of second-generation children in America are largely affected by the background of their immigrant parents. In most cases, the educational background of the immigrant parents indicates how their children might fare in America. The children of immigrants with higher education have a better chance to succeed in America than those whose parents came without much educational or occupational preparation or financial means.

In their report on selective assimilation, Alejandro Portes and Min Zhou describe how the immigrant parents of Punjabi Sikhs in California pressure their children against having too much contact with white peers (Portes and Zhou 1993). The Punjabi parents tend to perceive their children's "becoming Americanized" mainly in terms of negative traits, such as forgetting one's roots, leaving home at age eighteen, dating, dancing, drinking, and using drugs. The adults believe that these traits are not helpful for their children's success in America. The parents believe that traditional Asian family values are beneficial for the well-being of their children.

Likewise, many well-to-do Cuban parents in southern Florida shelter their children from what they consider the negative influences of American society. As a result, 62 percent of the eighth- and ninth-grade children of Cuban descendants in southern Florida identify themselves primarily as Cubans, and only about one-third regard themselves as Americans (Portes and Zhou 1993).

Among the eighteen second-generation Vietnamese Americans interviewed by Hung C. Thai (1999), all equated "American-ness" with "whiteness." When they were children and adolescents, these Vietnamese tried to be American by acting white so as to be accepted by their peers. This attitude changed once they progressed into adulthood and returned to their Vietnamese roots. They came to a point where they challenged the notions of American-ness. This happened when the American-grown young adults realized their responsibilities to care for their families and friends. Some of the core American values, such as individualism, egalitarianism, and self sufficiency, were pushed aside as they tried to help family members and friends.

In a massive study of 5,000 eighth- and ninth-grade children of immigrants from Indochina, Latin America, and the Caribbean islands who resided in San Diego and Miami, Rumbaut (1994) discovered different types of ethnic identity. Over one quarter of the youth (27%) who participated in the study identified themselves by their national origins like Cambodian or Filipino. Another 40 percent of the group chose a hyphenated American identity such as Thai-American or Jamaican-American. Only 11 percent of the group identified themselves as unhyphenated Americans. Two-tenths (21%) selected a pan-ethnic identity label like Hispanic-American.

Thus almost 90 percent of the children in the study used either their own national or continental origins as part of their ethnic identity in America. Only one-third of the survey group did not use their specific national origin for their own ethnic identity. It is interesting to note that none of the youth with Asian origins chose pan-ethnic labels like Asian or Asian American. They were specific in identifying themselves according to the countries of their parents' origin.

The same study also indicates that the overall social standing of a family affects children's identity formation in America. The study revealed that children who feel embarrassed about their parents' lack of social status and cultural sophistication are significantly more likely to identify themselves as Americans. In contrast, the children of higher-status professional parents, like doctors or engineers, are more likely to accept the ethnic identity of their parents' national origin.

In his discussion on assimilation among the American-born Chinese (ABC), Yang (1999) observes that the old ABCs who had experienced strong anti-Chinese discrimination in the past sought total assimilation in American society. This was the case among the Chinese Americans up to the 1960s. But the new ABCs who live in a social environment more favorable to their ethnic culture are proud of their Chinese identity. And the new immigrants from China, Hong Kong, Taiwan, and other southeast Asian countries like Singapore and Malaysia are more assertive about their Chinese ethnicity.

In particular, the ABCs who attend Chinese Protestant churches commonly seek selective assimilation and selective preservation of their Chinese ethnicity. They want to preserve their Chinese cultural traditions that are in harmony with their Christian beliefs. Filial piety is a good example. Often these Chinese Christians reinterpret Confucian values and norms in light of Christian principles. Even some Chinese youth who try to transcend their ethnic ties bounce back as they realize the increasing importance of their ancestral country and its influence on the world stage. Yang also noticed that among the converted Chinese, Christian identity takes precedence over the ethnic or national Chinese identity. Apparently the Chinese church makes a considerable impact upon the identity formation of its attending members.

In a study of the children of highly trained Filipino professional immigrants, Espiritu noticed that the formation of their identity is not a predictable process. Rather, it is a "dynamic and complex social phenomenon" (Espiritu in Min 2002:46). The middle-class children can have multiple and simultaneous identities in response to changing life situations.

In a study of a large Chinese church in Houston, Yang (in Ebaugh and Chafetz 2000) reports that the church provides cultural programs to help second-generation members maintain their Chinese identity. The programs include a language school and lectures on Chinese virtues, especially respecting and honoring parents and elders. The cultural programs reflect the desires of parents who are concerned about the moral effects of Americanization upon their children. The church struggles to be inclusive while trying to proselytize non-Christian Chinese by remaining distinctively Chinese. Nonetheless, "the Chinese Gospel Church is successfully Sinicizing Christianity" (Yang in Ebaugh and Chafetz 2000:195).

Yang and Ebaugh (2001) make interesting observations about the transformation of immigrant religions in the United States. They refer not to America's mainstream religion, Christianity, but to such religions as Judaism, Buddhism, Islam, and Hinduism. The major change that takes place in these non-Christian religions in America is overall democratization. In America, these religions emphasize the role of laity, a return to theological foundations, and an openness of their membership to anyone beyond traditional ethnic and religious boundaries.

These are examples of how the religious institutions established by new immigrants adapt to the democratic, multiethnic, and multicultural American society. At the same time, the old Asian religions also make adjustments to the major forces of social change like globalization. It is advantageous for these Asian religions to adapt to new situations in order to expand their influences in America and beyond.

According to one survey, about half of the Chinese and Japanese American churches in the San Francisco Bay area have become pan-ethnic Asian American churches. In that area, the number of pan-ethnic Asian churches increased noticeably "from one in 1989 to five in 1993 and 22 in 1998" (Jeung in Min and Kim 2002:200). This trend is partially explained in terms of increasing intermarriage among Asian American groups. Moreover, Jeung observes that Asian Americans have been acculturated (Americanized), but they still are not well integrated into the mainstream society (Jeung in Min and Kim 2002:215–240).

Min and Kim (Min and Kim in Min 2002) analyzed autobiographical essays written by fifteen Asian American professionals regarding their ethnic identity. They were born in either Asia or America and are the children of immigrants who moved to America after 1965. The essay writers showed a strong bicultural and Pan-Asian identity. They realized that regardless of how long they have lived in America and become Americans in terms of language and cultural acquisition, they are perceived as foreigners. This sense of being perpetual strangers in the mind of the mainstream society reinforces their Asian connections. Nonetheless, northeast Asians—like the Chinese, Japanese, and Koreans—tend to associate more with whites whereas the southeast Asians—like Filipinos, Indonesians, and Vietnamese—associate more with African Americans and Latinos.

Tuan interviewed about one hundred Chinese and Japanese Americans in California. They were either third- or fourth-generation Asian Americans. In spite of their roots in America, they reported that they were often treated as "foreigners" or "strangers" by other Americans. At the same time, they were not Asian enough in the eyes of the people who were born in Asia. Thus, most of these Asian

Americans experience an "authenticity dilemma as they are perceived as neither real Americans nor real Asians" (Tuan in Min 2002:210). "How they choose to identify, however, is not a private matter. They experience pressure to identify in ethnic or racial terms (as Asian Americans) because these remain salient markers (physical) to others" (Tuan 1998:153). Their identity in America is often perceived differently by themselves and others.

Grace Community Covenant Church was established mainly for second- and third-generation Asian Americans in Silicon Valley that covers much of the southern part of the San Francisco Bay area. The intent of this Pan-Asian church is to provide a sense of belonging to a distinct community of its members. The church sees itself as grounds for constructing "a hybridized culture" by combining some aspects of both Asian and American cultures. To strengthen their pan-ethnic solidarity, the church emphasizes what they call RICE: relevant to Silicon Valley, inviting, celebrating love for God and for our world, and encouraging each other toward spiritual growth.

Although it is an Asian church, Grace Community Covenant Church puts some norms of the dominant society into practice. They are, for instance, building a common vision, open communication, freedom to innovate, and a democratic practice with equal acceptance and treatment of people. These are antithetical to the typical Asian immigrant church where authority, hierarchy of status, and male dominance are commonly accepted. Most members of the Grace Community Covenant Church who are professionals in information technology feel comfortable and secure in this Pan-Asian ethnic church (Jeung in Carnes and Yang 2004:287–312).

In studies on children of the post–1965 immigrants reviewed above, one striking difference between the old immigrants from Europe and the new immigrants from Asia is this: the old European immigrants were eager to embrace American culture in the name of assimilation, often at the loss of their own culture, while the new immigrants from Asia are circumspective. The European immigrants and their children easily blended into America while the Asian immigrants and their children have been selective in adding the traits of American culture to their own. Thus most European immigrants tended to "de-ethnicize" their old cultures while the Asian groups tend to "re-ethnicize" their heritages. Such a difference may be attributed to a number of changes, some almost revolutionary, that took place in the second half of the twentieth century in domestic, international, and technological fields.

STUDIES ON THE CHILDREN OF KOREAN IMMIGRANTS

In recent years, social scientists, including American-trained Korean social scientists, have studied the children of the post–1965 Korean immigrants. In their longitudinal study of Korean junior and high school students in the New York area from 1989 to 1996, Hong and Min (1999) found that second-generation Korean adolescents are far more fluent in English than in Korean and feel more comfortable conversing in English with their friends. They demonstrate a high level of Americanization in terms of English fluency. Yet their close friends are mostly Koreans. In spite of the high level of "cultural assimilation" such as language fluency and cultural familiarity among the Korean youth, their social assimilation appears to be very low. In other words, fluency in English does not lead to establishing a wider social network beyond their Korean peers.

Regarding Korean language acquisition, those who attend a Korean church regularly tend to have a better command of the mother tongue than those who attend church less frequently. Like other Asian youth who want to retain the national identity of their parents, the Korean youth's ethnic identity categories were heavily Korean. About 93 percent of this group identified themselves as Korean. They saw themselves as either Korean (21%) or Korean American (72%). On the other hand, only 4 percent and 3 percent of the youth identified themselves as American and Asian American, respectively.

Kelly Chong (1998) conducted a study by participating in the lives of second-generation Koreans in the Chicago area. Her main interest was to study the role of ethnic churches in forming and maintaining Korean identity among the attendants. She asked the college students and young professionals why they were attending the Korean church instead of other English-speaking churches. Their response to

the question was mainly in terms of the social and cultural importance of the church. To them, maintaining social networks with other
Korean Americans and keeping up the Korean culture and language
were as important as religious programs. They felt that such cultural
concerns were not only important for their own generation but also for
their children.

Chong discovered that churchgoers displayed a considerably
higher degree of attachment to Korean values and moral standards
than did non-churchgoers. It appears that the conservative Korean
Protestant churches in Chicago provide a solid sense of belonging and
group identity to the young people. In the mainstream society, on the
other hand, they feel a sense of social marginality.

In a nation-wide survey conducted in the early 1980s of some 500
young Korean Presbyterians, the researcher found that many of them
valued their Korean heritage, God, and religion. But some of the youth
also doubted whether they would attend a Korean church as adults.
The higher one's school grade at the time of the survey, the more
likely one was to doubt the prospect of his or her future Korean church
attendance. In the survey, only a small minority expressed attachment
to Korean churches. In short, the Korean youth were positive about
their ethnicity and spirituality, but not so positive about their church
as an institution (Pai, Pemberton, and Worley 1987).

Another survey was conducted on church preference among the
UCLA Korean undergraduates in 1994. To the question of what kind
of church they would like to attend in ten years, 46 percent of the
randomly selected 100 subjects picked a "separate English-speaking
Korean church." This option was closely followed by an "English-
speaking service of a Korean church" by 30 percent of the participants.
Only 4 percent considered an "Anglo church" and 2 percent wanted to
attend a "Korean-speaking service of a Korean church." Seven percent
would consider an "Asian American or multi-ethnic church." But 11
percent did not indicate any preference, perhaps implying no interest
in religion (Goette in Kwon, Kim, and Warner 2001:134).

In an intensive observation study of twelve Korean undergraduate students over three years (1994–1996), Cha discovered that these

students began to affirm their Korean identities and became interested in knowing more about the Korean culture when they became adolescents. This was a major change from their childhood when they tried to deny their Korean ethnicity in order to be accepted by their school friends. During their teen years, they enjoyed their church activities and were committed to their church group. However, the same young people felt uneasy about being confined to the Korean church setting, and they wanted to explore new and different aspects of life in other settings (Cha in Kwon, Kim, and Warner 2001:141–156).

Paxton Korean Church in Boston, a second-generation Korean church where non-Koreans make up 10 percent of the attendees, had experienced a phenomenal growth rate of 25 percent per year for eight years at the time of the report. Such success was attributed to three key factors: "association with evangelical Christianity, an affirmation of Korean identity, and a sense of second-generation autonomy and ownership" (Chai in Kwon, Kim, and Warner 2001:159). In short, the church "offers the second generation the best of both worlds: a trendy new-style evangelical orientation and plenty of fellow Korean Americans who share the same experiences. While the main draw is still the Koreanness of the group, their evangelical openness to non-Koreans decreases their feelings of conflict about ethnic exclusivity" (Chai in Kwon, Kim, and Warner 2001:164).

In a case study on the second-generation members of Glory Korean Presbyterian Church in New York City, Alumkal found that most of the Korean Americans in the church had maintained their membership for the comfort of being with fellow Koreans. For that reason, some of them were a bit reluctant to shift their Korean church to a multicultural ministry (Alumkal in Kwon, Kim, and Warner 2001:181–191).

The results of the studies on Korean Americans are not so different from other Asian American groups in terms of their ethnic identity and their relations to their ethnic communities. In particular, Korean churches seem to play a major role in preserving and instilling the Korean culture in its young members.

In response to the pressures from their immigrant parents and tension with the dominant society, second-generation Korean college students in a private university in New York City established a Korean American evangelical identity. In this "religio-racial-ethnic" group identity, the religious component takes the place of master status. The Korean evangelical students reason that the racial-ethnic identity is inherited whereas their religious identity is their willing choice. Being an evangelical is the result of one's conviction and efforts.

Nonetheless, the evangelical Korean students view their racial-ethnic identity as God's gift. By attaching a religious meaning and significance to their heritage, they develop a sense of mission to non-Christian Koreans and the larger American society. They see a unique role as Korean American evangelicals. They integrate the Korean and American cultures by selecting the best qualities from each culture.

In the eyes of these students, the United States is a country of white and black. These Korean students feel that they are invisible as an in-between group. As a result, they feel alienated and marginalized. But by emphasizing their evangelical Christian identity, they overcome the sense of inferiority and transcend the worldly concerns of group status in society (Park in Carnes and Yang 2004:182–204).

In a series of focus group studies in southern California, Park discovered that "the teenagers wanted to learn more about their Korean identity and cultural community and felt pride in ethnic group affiliation" (Park 2005:54). This reflects their realization that complete structural assimilation is neither possible nor desirable in America due to their physical differences.

There was a distinctively Korean American church for English-speaking Koreans in Dallas. As the church saw limited opportunities within the Dallas Korean community for membership and financial growth, it became an open multiracial church. According to Dhingra (2004), the church is open to everyone, but it offers a variety of Korean programs behind the scenes for remaining Korean members. This double-stage format poses a dilemma for the identity of the church. It remains to be seen whether such a dual arrangement is a temporary measure during the transition or a fixed feature for the original members of the church and their offspring.

SUMMARY AND IMPLICATIONS

The reviews of the historical trends and some specific studies on the children of the post–1965 immigrants may be summarized as follows:

1) Most early European immigrants, with a few exceptions, were assimilated into their North American societies without much delay and difficulty. This was easily done as the incoming and host groups shared much in common in history, culture, and religion.

2) The recent immigrants from Asia are more likely to remain distinct for the obvious physical differences. Morever, the drastic changes in immigration and cultural policies, demographic composition, and social milieu of the host countries have made diversity inevitable and valuable. As a result, these macro changes pose less pressure on the immigrants to assimilate at the loss of their own ethnic identity.

3) Communication and transportation technologies have increased the reinforcement effects of home cultures upon immigrants outside their countries of origin. The transnational life experiences that come with participating in two or more cultures through digital devices promote a multicultural perspective.

4) Acculturation is more selective among the children of new immigrants, especially those from middle-class family backgrounds. They tend to embrace the cultural traits that are favorable for their success in the new country. As a result, the acculturation of immigrants and their children is integrated by melding the best of two cultures. So their assimilation is adhesive and additive in nature.[10]

5) Among immigrants, the desire to preserve some aspects of their home culture reflects their negative perception of some aspects of Americanization.

6) In general, the children of Asian immigrants seem to value their cultural heritage when they reach adulthood with the responsibility of caring for their parents and children.

7) In most cases, immigrant churches function as cultural transmitters to the members of younger generations. For this reason, church-attending Korean Americans are more likely to identify as Koreans than non-church-attending Koreans.

8) In the course of time, most Asian American churches merge together to establish a pan-ethnic Asian congregation. Often this is out of necessity. Nonetheless, it is an attempt to make such a pan-ethnic Asian church distinctive and relevant to Asian Americans.

NOTES

1. See the stages in Berry and Tischer (1978:150).

2. Southern and eastern European immigrants were usually Catholics, Greek or Russian Orthodox, or Jews with a rural background. The religious difference was the main source of ethnic prejudice in the Protestant-dominant America.

3. See the definition of "marginal man" on p. 170 of *The Encyclopedic Dictionary of Sociology* (1991:170). Often the children of European immigrants were called "marginal men" for the ambiguity about their place in America as they were caught between the culture of their parents and the larger society. The term was coined by Robert Ezra Park.

4. Orthodox Jews were adamant about preserving not only their traditional religious practices but also their ethnic heritage. Hasidic Jews are a prime example.

5. The U.S. census of 2000 reported a total of 11,898,828 people of Asian ancestry. The five largest Asian subgroups include Chinese (2,734,000; 23%), Filipino (2,364,000; 20%), Asian Indian (1,899,000; 16%), Korean (1,228,000; 10%), and Vietnamese (1,223,000; 10%) in that order.

6. The barrios in east Los Angeles, the Koreatown near the center of Los Angeles, and the Chinatown in San Francisco are somewhat insulated ethnic enclaves. To some new immigrants trapped for lack of communication skills and transportation means, these enclaves are closed to the outside world.

7. According to the U.S. census of 2000, the population composition of Hawaii is as follows: Asians (42%), whites (24%), and native Hawaiian and other Pacific Islanders (9%) in that order. The same source for New Mexico shows Hispanics (42%), non-Hispanic whites (23%), and American Indians (10%), respectively.

8. Some of the anti-immigration organizations include the American Immigration Control Foundation (Montrey, VA), California Coalition for Immigration Reform (Huntington Beach, CA), Federation for American Immigration Reform (Washington, DC), and National Organization for European American Rights (Mandeville, LA). Invariably these organizations are xenophobic and white supremacist.

9. Major scholarly works on the children of the post–1965 immigrants began to appear early in the twenty-first century. These include *Ethnicities: Children of Immigrants in America* (Rumbaut and Portes 2001) and *Legacies: The Story of the Immigrant Second Generation* (Portes and Rumbaut 2001).

On the children of Asian immigrants, see *Second Generation: Ethnic Identity among Asian Americans* (Min 2002).

10. The adhesive and additive nature of assimilation has been described as "segmented assimiliation" (Rumbaut 1994).

CHAPTER 6

The Survey and Its Participants

Much of the second half of this book is a report on the findings of the survey project termed Vision 2020. It is a major source of information about the second-generation Korean Adventists in North America.

THE VISION 2020 SURVEY PROJECT

The survey project was named Vision 2020 for two reasons. First, it was an attempt to anticipate the approximate state of the Korean Adventist church in North America beyond a one-generation time span. The survey was distributed in 1997–1998, and thus the span of a generation should last until about the year 2020. The survey would reveal the future state of the Korean church as anticipated in the minds of second-generation members. The project title also expresses the desire to have clear vision (20/20) regarding the future of the Korean Adventist churches in North America.

Using the means of a questionnaire, personal attitudes and church life experiences of the youth members were gathered. Two separate groups were approached. The main group included second-generation members who were attending local Korean Adventist churches in North America. Anyone older than twelve in these churches, both Korean and non-Korean, was asked to participate in the survey. The other group was Korean youth pastors, including those who had left youth ministry at the time of the survey. Most questions in the survey were closed-ended, with a few open-ended questions. In the supplementary survey for youth pastors, far more open-ended questions were asked to glean in-depth information from that group.

Efforts were made to contact all who met the criteria of age and church membership. For that reason, it was a census approach, not a sample. Youth pastors or youth leaders at the local churches served as contact persons. They were the ones who administered and collected the survey instruments. In spite of repeated instructions to include all qualified members, some churches may have left out a certain group. For instance, if the leaders used a single attempt to distribute the questionnaires on one Sabbath, those absent on that particular Sabbath could have been excluded. Those who were away from their home churches for an extended period of time either for study or work may also have been unintentionally excluded. Those who were attending non-Korean churches might have missed the survey unless their leaders made a conscious effort to reach them.

Therefore, it can be assumed that those who participated in the survey were more likely to be regularly attending members of the Korean churches. The participants' attitudes and commitment to the Korean churches might have been different from those who missed the survey. For those who did not participate, their reasons for not attending their Korean churches could have yielded valuable information about their respective churches. A separate future study may need to be conducted on those who have left Korean churches.

PRESENTATION OF THE FINDINGS

The findings of the survey on a given subject are presented in two sections. The "Findings in Brief" section is a statistical summary of each subject area. To visualize the findings, graphs and tables are used. But not all discussions on specific subjects are accompanied by graphic presentations. Anecdotal statements made in response to open-ended questions in the survey are shared in the section entitled "In Their Own Words." They represent the real voices of second-generation Korean Adventists in North America answering this question: "What do you like and dislike about your Korean church?"

The individual comments are quite informative, insightful, and helpful in understanding the intricacies of the respondents' perceptions of the Korean churches and experiences in them. The selection of personal comments is based on their relevance to a given subject. No personal comment is quoted more than once. To provide human context, a few personal clues about the respondents—such as gender, birthplace, age, and location at the time of the survey—are revealed. The information is provided in general terms lest the sources of quotations be identified, especially in small churches outside the large metropolitan areas. In the case of youth pastors, personal clues are not given so as to protect the sources. At the end of the entire report, implications and applications of the survey findings are presented in the form of practical recommendations for the Korean churches.

A few remarks should be provided about reading the figures and tables. In most figures, "N" indicates the total number of valid respondents for a certain question. Accordingly, those who failed to answer a given question are excluded from the total number. For that reason, the total respondent number in each figure is less than 1,023, the total number of respondents who returned the questionnaires. Also the respondent number (N) is slightly different for each table. If a table presents composite data from different questions, the total number cannot be given as there are different total numbers for different questions. Finally, the total of some percentage figures may be more or less than 100 (either 101 or 99) due to the way some decimal figures were rounded.

DEMOGRAPHIC CHARACTERISTICS

This section describes the background of the survey participants. The selective information includes demographic characteristics, language use, ethnic identity, and other background information that may shed light on survey findings.

Findings in Brief

A total of 1,023 second-generation Korean Adventists in the United States and Canada responded to the Vision 2020 survey. At the time of the initial survey in 1998, there were 95 Korean Adventist churches and groups in North America. The breakdown by major regions (or time zones) was as follows: 44 churches in the West (Pacific time zone), 21 in the Midwest down to Texas, and 33 in the East down to Florida. Of these, 32 churches were in California (34%) and there were six churches each in New York, Georgia, and Canada.

Two out of three respondents (64%) came from the western states (Pacific time zone), 33% from the eastern states (Eastern time zone), and only 3% from the Midwestern states (Central and Mountain time zones). Fifty percent of the participants were born in Korea, 44% in the United States, 5% in Canada, and 1% in other countries.[1] In terms of citizenship status, the participant group was made up of citizens of the United States by birth or naturalization (64%),[2] Korean citizens (26%),[3] Canadian citizens (7%), and those with other citizenship at the time of the survey (3%).

The participants identified their racial identities as follows: 955 (94%) Koreans, 34 (3.3%) half-Koreans, and 25 (2.5%) persons of other categories. The last group could be non-Korean people who were attending Korean churches at the time of the survey. Nine persons did not indicate their racial identity.

The survey respondents consisted of 570 males (56%) and 448 females (44%). Five respondents did not indicate their gender. Among the participants, only one in ten was married. Of the 104 married respondents, four indicated that their spouses were non-Korean.[4]

At the time of the survey, the median age of the group was 19. As shown in Figure 6.1, at the time of the survey, 48% of the participants were attending either academy or junior high or high school, and 23% were in college. The rest of the group (29%) were college graduates, graduate or professional school students, and young adults with a career.

Eighty-four (8.2%) people reported that they were the only Adventists in their families. In contrast, as many as 84% of the respondents had Adventist mothers and 76% had Adventist fathers. Three out of four participants were baptized at the time of the survey. The majority of those baptized (71%) made their commitment to the Christian faith public before reaching the age of 19. Of those baptized, 42% were baptized in their early teen years: 15% at the age of twelve, 15% at thirteen, and 12% at fourteen.

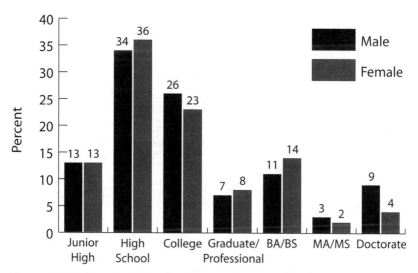

Figure 6.1 Educational Levels of Respondents by Gender (N=944)

As indicated in Figure 6.2, the children reported that only 5% of their fathers and 10% of their mothers received less than a high school education. On the other hand, 73% of the fathers and 67% of the mothers went to college. According to the children, 26% of the fathers and 11% of the mothers earned graduate or professional

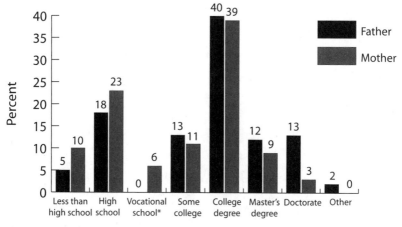

Figure 6.2 Parents' Education Reported by Children (N=928)

*Nursing education after high school could be the major form of vocational schooling. The survey question regarding educational achievement of fathers did not offer the option of "vocational school," and the question regarding educational achievement of mothers did not offer "other" as a possible answer.

degrees. Thirteen percent of the fathers and 3% of the mothers held a doctoral degree[5] at the time of the survey. Twenty-seven percent of the fathers and 18% of the mothers received education in North America. Half of the respondents thought that their parents' English was fairly good or excellent. About 58% of the fathers and 54% of the mothers received such marks from their children.

In Their Own Words: "What do you like about your Korean Church?"

- "Smallness in size (closer)." –*An American-born 17-year-old female in N. California*
- "Financially stable, talented, and intelligent people." –*An American-born 23-year-old male in S. California*

In Their Own Words: "What do you dislike about your Korean Church?"

- "Not enough old youth." –*A Korean-born 22-year-old male in S. California*
- "Not enough girls." –*An American-born 14-year-old male in S. California*
- "Not enough youths (teens). Not enough fun (no activities). Boring service." –*A Canadian-born 14-year-old female*
- "Not enough female church members. Also too old. Lack of enthusiasm. Complicated elections." –*A Korean-Canadian who came to Canada at the age of 13*
- "Unbalanced [gender ratio] of male and female. Only in Korean. Old songs." –*An American-born 14-year-old male in Maryland*
- "Disorganized. Lack of funds. Not enough English-speaking young adults." –*A Korean-born 30-year-old male in the Washington, DC area*
- "Not many college students." –*A Korean-born 18-year-old male in S. California*
- "Cliques. College students leave church after college. More activities with other Korean churches." –*A 24-year-old male who came to America at the age of 5*
- "Youth programs. Small [size] of youth. None of my age [group]. Feel stuck here." –*An American-born 19-year-old female in Maryland*
- "Not many young kids; not enough older youths." –*A 16-year-old youth in S. California*

- "Not enough youth in my age. Not enough people. Too small. Little amount of people." –*Three members of a small church in N. California expressed some part of this quotation*
- "The church members are too old....The church is not achieving its goals." –*An American-born 20-year-old female in S. California*
- "It is very small and continues to shrink." –*A Canadian-born 18-year-old female*

USE OF LANGUAGE

Perhaps no cultural mark is more prominent and significant in shaping ethnic identity than one's language. Language is more than a means of communication with others. It shapes the consciousness of the mind and speakers' worldviews. At the same time, it determines the scope and quality of social interactions. Language opens or closes the possibilities of one's relations with others. For these reasons, language is one of the key elements for ethnic grouping. People tend to identify their ethnicity according to the primary language they speak. The Korean Adventist church in North America was initially established to serve the Korean-speaking immigrants and their children. Thus, language continues to be a distinguishing factor.

To most second-generation members and their children, perhaps their mother tongue of Korean is more symbolic than practical since their primary language is English. Language division has taken place within the same church or between churches. At present, no sizable second-generation group conducts worship services in Korean. Someday the English-speaking Korean groups may outnumber the Korean-speaking congregations.

At an individual level, more Korean Americans want to learn the mother tongue as an expression of their ethnic identity. Some of those who do not speak Korean feel uneasy and even ashamed.

Findings in Brief

Roughly six in ten survey participants reported that they studied Korean in formal settings, such as regular schools in Korea or language schools run by churches or other entities in North America. On the other hand, four in ten indicated that they did not take any formal

Korean lessons. The majority (83%) of those who had studied Korean did so for the maximum of five years. The language schools were usually run on weekends,[6] and the time spent on lessons was less than four hours per week.

As shown in Figure 6.3, 31% of the second-generation members disclosed that they spoke mainly Korean at home, whereas 22% of the participants spoke mainly English. However, the largest group (47%) spoke both Korean and English at home. Less than 1% spoke an entirely different language at home. These respondents might have come from South American countries such as Argentina, Brazil, or Paraguay. Also a few were from Japan or China. Although it was a subjective self evaluation, 46% of the group indicated that they were fluent in English while only 10% said so about Korean. Surprisingly, almost half of the group (45%) claimed to be bilingual. Without an objective evaluation of their language skills, one has to regard the figure with reservation.

More than half of the participants expressed some degree of regret about not having learned the mother tongue. The source of regret lies both in themselves and with their parents who failed to force them to learn the mother tongue. As shown in Figure 6.4, which combined two separate questions on the sources of regret, 60% of the respondents attributed their inadequacy with the Korean language to the neglect of

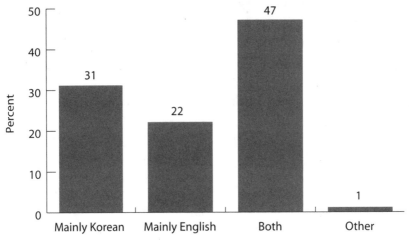

Figure 6.3 Language Spoken at Home (N=1,005)

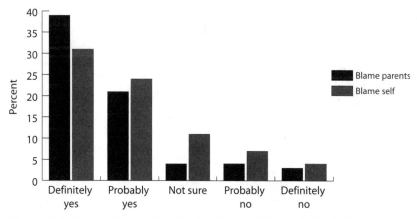

Figure 6.4 Do You Regret Not Having Learned Korean? (N=995)

their parents. At the same time, 55% blamed themselves for not having learned Korean. As expressed in Figure 6.5, regret among the participants was a forceful source of determination to make their children learn Korean, and another 20% of the participants said they would probably make their children speak Korean fluently. The two figures seem to suggest that probably only non-Korean respondents were not interested in teaching Korean to their children.

Between male and female respondents, as revealed in Figure 6.6, future mothers (96%) were more eager than their counterparts (89%) to teach Korean to their children. Birthplace seems to be a factor in teaching the mother tongue to offspring. As noted in Figure 6.7, about

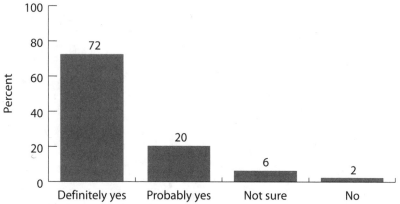

Figure 6.5 Will You Teach Your Children to Speak Korean Fluently? (N=1,006)

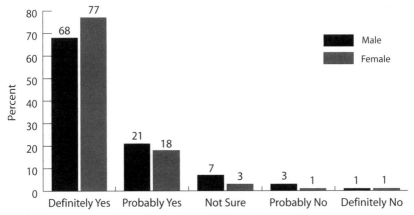

Figure 6.6 Intent to Teach Korean to Children (N=1,002)

95% of the Korean-born, 93% of the Canadian-born, and 90% of the respondents born in the United States expressed their intent to teach Korean to their children. In contrast, only 83% of those born in other countries indicated the same desire. It should be noted that Canada has been far more pluralistic in its cultural policy, including its English-French bilingual policy, than has the United States.

In Their Own Words: "What do you like about your Korean church?"

- "Able to speak both Korean and English." —*A Korean-born 23-year-old female who came to America at the age of 7*
- "Kids are close, but it's small [in number]. Parents are supportive

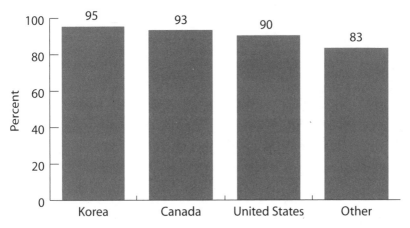

Figure 6.7 Birthplace and Intent to Teach Korean to Children (N=1,004)

of youth programs. Pastors are very understanding. I think that it's hard to say we will never need a Korean-speaking church—everyday more and more immigrants are arriving in America and some of them will never be fluent [in English]. To say that we will not need a Korean-speaking church is to say that America will not receive anymore immigrant and that the ones that are coming now will be fluent in English. We must look for all our brothers and sisters and make sure we all have a church in the future." –*An American-born 20-year-old female in Georgia*

- "Korean people. Friends. Learning Korean language and customs." –*An American-born 17-year-old female in Georgia*
- "Have the same culture; speak the same language." –*A 15-year-old female fluent in Korean and English*
- "The use of common language in both English and Korean. The common cultural communication aspect." –*An American-born 20-year-old female in S. California*

In Their Own Words: "What do you dislike about your Korean church?"

- "I dislike the fact that I receive very little spiritual benefits, because I am unable to comprehend more than 50% of the sermons." –*A Korean-born 27-year-old female in the South*
- "Korean speakers and English speakers don't hang out as much. Don't do enough for helping community." –*A Korean-born 17-year-old female in Maryland*
- "When I speak English, I feel like the other Korean elders disapprove. It's something I don't understand. I am in America and they disapprove of me speaking English. It is ironic. Weeks ago, I was at potluck and adults, including my own pastor, said that the town went bad when Xs [people] entered the community. It's wrong! The kids at X [university] should be involved in and be in diverse culture. They are not exposed enough to the real world." –*An American-born 15-year-old female in Michigan*
- "The total separation of youth and adult. Use of Korean is important." –*An American-born 21-year-old male in Illinois*

ETHNIC IDENTITY

One comes to establish an ethnic identity through a desire to be regarded as a member of a particular group. The desire then leads to interactions with others of the group when opportunity is given. Others include family members, friends, and community people. Interaction may result in accepting all or some of the ideals, values, and lifestyle choices of the people one wants to identify with. In this lifelong process, individuals develop a sense of personhood and peoplehood as well. Identity establishment is more pressing during the formative years.

An ethnic church provides opportunities to interact with members of an ethnic community. Although not many choose an ethnic church merely for establishing one's ethnic identity, the impact of an ethnic church may be significant. The amount, intensity, and regularity of collective interaction at an ethnic church is almost matchless. Given the relative ease with which second-generation members interact with the majority, the question remains: "Why do they want to associate with Korean churches?" Among the many conceivable reasons, such as parental expectations and peer pressure, perhaps their ethnic identity as Korean Americans or Korean Canadians might play a key role.

This section will examine the extent of ethnic identity among the survey participants and how this affects their desire to affiliate with the Korean churches.

Findings in Brief

Nine out of ten participants identified themselves as Korean. As reported in Figure 6.8, however, more than half (54%) considered themselves as either Korean-American or Korean-Canadian. About four in ten considered themselves as Korean with no qualifications. Only 9% of the participants identified themselves as either American or Canadian. Considering the small number of half-blooded Koreans and the non-Koreans included in the survey group, only a few full-blooded Koreans actually put themselves in this category.

As indicated in Figure 6.9, the survey revealed that most of the participants (82%) were proud of being a Korean. Their ethnic pride in being Korean is very high regardless of their birthplaces. As shown

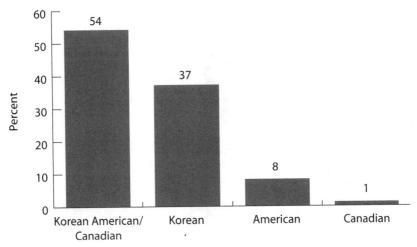

Figure 6.8 Ethnic Identity among Second-Generation Korean Adventists (N=999)

in Figure 6.10, only about 5% of those born in North America and Korea are not proud of their Korean identity.

Figure 6.11 shows that half of the second-generation members stated that each of their five closest friends was Korean. One in five indicated that their close friends were an even mixture of Koreans and non-Koreans. Only 17% of the group stated that their close friends were mostly non-Koreans. When it comes to the ethnicity of their future spouses, eight in ten wanted to marry Koreans (see Figure 6.12).

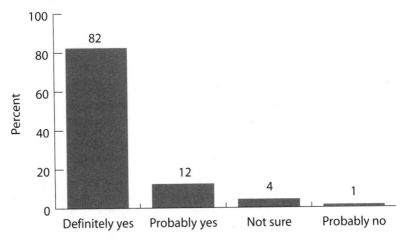

Figure 6.9 Are You Proud of Being Korean? (N=994)

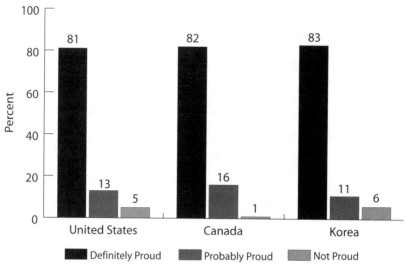

Figure 6.10 Birthplace and Korean Pride (N=1,005)

Only a minority (6.2%) thought that marrying a Korean was not an important concern. Understandably, the more proud one is about being Korean, the more important he or she believes marrying a Korean to be, as demonstrated in Figure 6.13.

In Their Own Words: "What do you like about your Korean Church?"
• "Everyone is Korean." *–A 15-year-old N. California female born in*

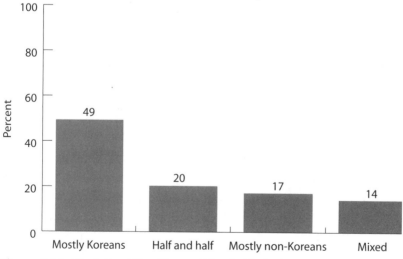

Figure 6.11 Ethnicity of Five Closest Friends (N=993)

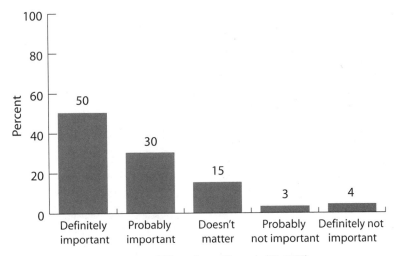

Figure 6.12 Importance of Marrying a Korean (N=873)

the United States

- "Maintaining heritage." –A *Korean-born 24-year-old female in S. California*
- "I like it because you could fellowship with your Korean friends.

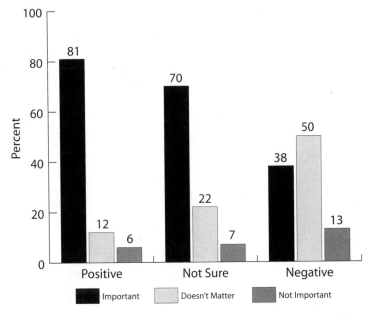

Figure 6.13 Attitude about Being Korean and Importance of Future Korean Spouse (N=865)

You are not a lot different." *–An American-born 17-year-old male in Georgia*

- "Bonding. Security of shared identity." *–A 36-year-old male in S. California*
- "Korean food, Korean friends and family. My youth pastor." *–A 32-year-old male who came to the United States at the age of 9*
- "The family feeling and community. The cultural tightness." *–An American-born 18-year-old female in S. California*
- "I like the opportunity to practice Korean. The chance to socialize with other Korean Americans. There is a tight family atmosphere." *–A Korean-born 27-year-old female in the South*
- "See friends that I don't see during the week. The social activities. I can look forward to going to church during the week." *–An American-born 15-year-old male in Florida*

In Their Own Words: "What do you dislike about your Korean Church?"

- "Focus only on Koreans. Why not other cultures?" *–An American-born 15-year-old male in New Jersey*
- "Exclusively Korean. Half white would be nice." *–A Korean-born 23-year-old female in the Northwest*
- "Judgement. Racism. Self-centered. I think [X] church people are self-centered, narrow-minded people....I also think that too many Korean SDAs are two-faced." *–A Korean-born 14-year-old female who came to the United States at the age of 7*
- "The focus of parents is on using church to retain culture. The lack of studying Jesus as to who he really is. The Korean culture pushes for career and aesthetics." *–An American-born 27-year-old male in S. California*
- "Not evangelistic (as much as it should be). Colder to non-Koreans than Koreans." *–A Korean-born 17-year-old female in Illinois*
- "I feel that a lot of Korean Americans in our country have been taught to keep the culture to themselves. We never open up to others. And we think that whites, blacks, and Hispanics are enemies. They only fear and make fun because they have not seen the beauty of our real culture. Many Koreans are racists. I believe there should be many cultures in all churches. They teach us about

loving our brothers and sisters yet they reject others because of creed and colors....We should teach them diversity and respect for others of all races, ages, or differences among peoples." *–An American-born 16-year-old male in Michigan*

- "Somewhat prejudiced against non-Koreans—kind of a superior attitude. Need a more welcoming 'welcome committee.'" *–A Korean-born 26-year-old female in S. California*
- "Too strict. Too Koreanized. Potluck except when we have subway [sandwich]." *–An American-born 14-year-old male in S. California*
- "Attitudes towards interracial couples." *–A Korean-born 26-year-old male in S. California*
- "Not genuine. Ethno-centric, biased, and prejudiced. Materialistic." *–A Korean-born 24-year-old female who came to the United States at the age of 4*
- "There is a distant separation between Korean and non-Korean." *–A 20-year-old male who came to the United States at the age of 5*

In the Words of Youth Pastors

- "Korean culture is unique and needs to be maintained. But it must be secondary to the 'Christ culture.' If there is conflict, then the culture must be sacrificed for the principles of Christianity."
- "We are different and proud of our heritage. Yet we are cliquey and more social than religious."
- "God has created and given our culture to us. Korean culture is the parents' responsibility to their children. It is definitely the responsibility of the church."
- "The unique and distinctively positive Korean cultural element could attract more non-believers to Korean SDA churches. Yet, in order to bring in more people (other than Koreans) for the survival of a small Korean-America church, the cultural aspects have to be covered. For example, Kim-chee is no longer served at potluck."
- "Korean-speaking and English-speaking will never mix together fully."
- "Too isolated from every group. Very dedicated to Korean members."

- "It creates an extra bond among the members, but sometimes it interferes with spiritual development."
- "Culture keeps people together, but it also develops a 'social club' mentality."
- "We should keep our identity to reach our kind."
- "It [maintaining a separate Korean church] can be 'racism.'"
- "Non-essential for second generation members. It can be hindrance to Christian formation for second generation."
- "It is important to keep the ethnic aspects in church but it cannot supersede over personal conversion experience. It is more important for a kid to know God personally."
- "Important, I like it [maintaining a separate Korean church]. But it will fade unless we have something distinct and important to offer to the mainstream."

SUMMARY OBSERVATIONS

The second-generation Korean Adventists in North America are quite clear about their Korean ethnic identity evidenced by multiple indicators. Their Korean churches help reinforce their ethnic identity with regular community gatherings and interactions. Yet some of the older members in the survey group are aware of the trap of being isolated and exclusive in the name of ethnic solidarity. Furthermore, they cautiously express that the church's ethnic environment may hinder spiritual growth if the cultural concerns supercede Christian principles. The challenge of the Korean American churches in North America is to keep their cultural aspects in proper Christian perspective, especially among first-generation members.

NOTES

1. Some Koreans in South America had re-migrated to the United States and Canada during the political and economic turmoil in their host countries during the 1980s and 1990s. Many of them re-migrated from Argentina, Brazil, and Paraguay.

2. Legally admitted immigrants (permanent residents) are eligible for U.S. citizenship after five years of continuous residence in the United States. The same rule applies in Canada.

3. Children of Korean immigrants who were born in Korea remain

Korean citizens until they become naturalized American citizens. In the case of minors, their citizenship status is determined by that of their parents. If their parents want to hold on to their Korean citizenship, their children have to wait until they reach the legal age of 18 to apply for U.S. citizenship.

4. The rate of intermarriage in the study group is rather low in comparison with other Asian groups. For example, the intermarriage rate among Asian Americans in Los Angeles County in 1989 was anywhere between 11 percent among Koreans and 52 percent among Japanese. Among the Koreans who married non-Koreans, female intermarriage was almost three times higher than male intermarriage, 75 percent to 25 percent. Among Chinese and Japanese, the intermarriage difference between men and women was evident although the gender difference was not as great (Kitano and Kitano 1998:329). Two factors may be attributed to such a low intermarriage rate in the Korean Adventist group. Those of marital age at the time of the survey were probably mostly Korean-born and they were more likely to find a Korean spouse for language and cultural reasons. Secondly, some, if not all, who married non-Koreans tend to marry whites and they are inclined to attend Anglo churches for the cultural ease of their spouses.

5. The survey did not ask about specific fields of doctorates. It is safe to assume that some of the doctoral-degree holders are medical doctors who were educated and trained in Korea. The rest received either medical or dental education in North America.

6. Many churches with a sizable congregation offer Korean school on weekends. In general, Adventist churches hold language classes for children on Sunday mornings, and other Protestant churches run their language schools on Saturdays. Besides Korean, these schools may also teach such things as folk music, dance, and martial arts.

CHAPTER 7

The Second Generation and Their Churches

Most Korean Adventist churches in North America are in transition. Changes have been occurring especially in membership composition, proportionality of the two language groups, administrative structure, and culture. The role of second-generation members has been steadily growing. Though they were secondary and marginal when their parents were running the churches, now they have moved closer to the center stage of their churches as they have increased in number and influence.

Nevertheless, second-generation Korean Adventists still face three major gaps between themselves and first-generation members: language, cultural, and generational gaps. Therefore, the future of their churches may largely depend upon members' abilities to adjust to changing conditions. Both the immigrant generation and the following generations need to work together through dialogue and cooperation. In most Korean churches, the next twenty years will be critical as the church leadership is transferred from the first generation to the second generation. This chapter looks at how the second-generation members relate to their Korean churches.

CHURCH CHOICE AND ATTENDANCE

In developing and maintaining a church, nothing is more crucial than worship attendance by its members. Attendance shows many vital indicators of a church, including members' commitment to their faith, support for their church as an organization, and enthusiasm for the cause of the church. Thus the level of church attendance is a barometer by which one can gauge church strength and growth potential. By looking at church choice and attendance among second-generation Korean Adventists, we may judge their commitment, support, and enthusiasm for the Korean Adventist churches in North America.

Findings in Brief

As illustrated in Figure 7.1, several main reasons were given for attending Korean churches: "feeling at home" (31%), "family church" (30%), "Korean friends" (19%), and "family expectation" (12%). For second-generation members, personal connections or relations appeared to be the key factors in their choice to attend Korean churches. Only 5% of the second-generation members attend their Korean church mainly for the quality of worship programs offered. The adult members appear to give more weight to cultural homogeneity and family connections in their choice to attend Korean churches. On the other hand, younger members (under 18) value more their Korean friendship network and family expectations in relating to the Korean churches.

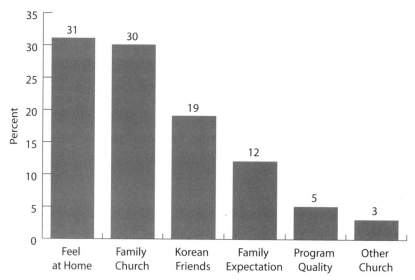

Figure 7.1 Primary Reason for Attending a Korean Church (N=960)

As revealed in Figure 7.2, the decision of second-generation members to attend a Korean church usually seems to be mainly their own (52%) or that of their parents (44%). The influence of friends (1%) or siblings (1.4%) in this important decision appears to be negligible. It should be noted that almost half of the participants were attending junior high or high school at the time of the survey.

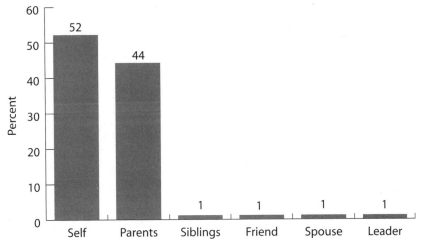

Figure 7.2 Source of Influence on Korean Church Attendance (N=1,000)

As indicated in Figure 7.3, about eight out of ten survey participants were regularly attending Korean churches, and only 3% were not attending Korean churches at all at the time of the survey. Sixteen percent of the members indicated that they were occasional attendees of a Korean church.

Figure 7.4 shows that about 80% of the survey respondents would choose a Korean church—either their present church or another Korean church—regardless of their age. Only 20% may consider the option of attending a white or other minority church. If given the freedom to choose a church to attend, the majority (80%) would still choose a Korean church (see Figure 7.5). Of those who wish to remain in the Korean church, 66% want to stay with their present church while 14% may want to switch to another Korean church. Their desire to stay with the present Korean church or another Korean church is strong in all age groups. Only 20% may choose a non-Korean church if they

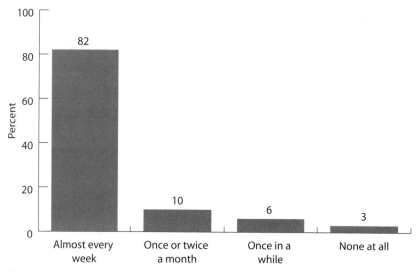

Figure 7.3 Frequency of Korean Church Attendance (N=992)

were free to do so. In this group, 13% of the participants would attend a white church, and 7% would choose another ethnic minority church.

Seven in ten regard themselves as active members at their Korean churches. Among the survey participants, only 20% consider themselves "very active" and 51% "somewhat active."

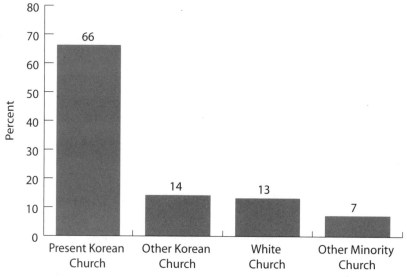

Figure 7.4 Free Choice of an Alternate Church (N=970)

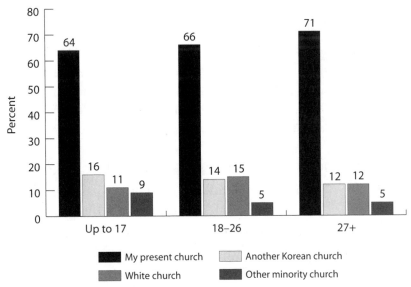

Figure 7.5 Age and Church Choice (N=964)

Church life refers to one's relationship with a congregation while spiritual life is the state of one's personal relationship with God. Figure 7.6 shows that in comparison with other segments of life, satisfaction with church life (59%) and spiritual life (44%) appeared considerably lower. In contrast, respondents were far more satisfied with their family life (80%), social life (74%), and schools (72%). The lower-level

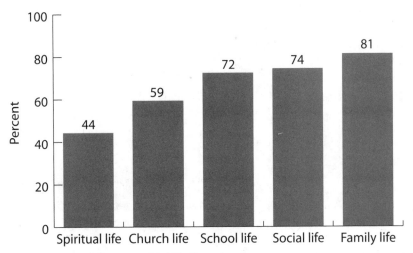

Figure 7.6 Satisfaction with Life Situations

satisfaction among the second-generation members with their church life was reflected in their perception about the needs of the Korean churches. Of the many aspects of church life that need addressing, the most urgent ones were "spiritual revival (49%), "worship program" (38%), and "youth pastor" (34%). At the same time, the second-generation members felt that physical facilities (21%), social activities (19%), and counseling (13%) posed less urgent needs at this juncture of the Korean Adventist church in North America.

There are a few independent second-generation Korean congregations. The Upper Room Fellowship Church in the Los Angeles area and another church in Chicago serve mainly English-speaking young adults. As indicated in Figure 7.7, half of the survey group supported the idea of separation, and one-third were not sure about it. Only 18% of the respondents expressed a clear opposition to the idea of an independent congregation apart from the mother church. There is no significant difference between respondents in California (49% support) and others in North America (47% support) on the issue of establishing independent English-speaking churches for second-generation Koreans. The idea of establishing a separate independent church for English-speaking members seems to be more popular among members in their twenties than with teenagers, as indicated in Figure 7.8. Yet

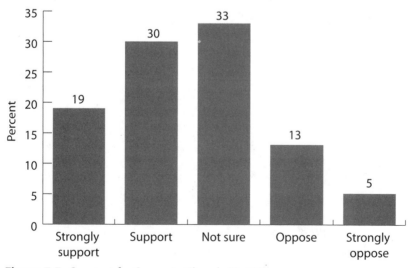

Figure 7.7 Support for Separate Church (N=960)

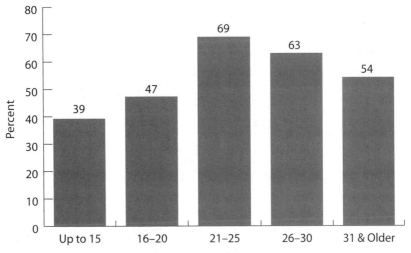

Figure 7.8 Age and Support for Separate Church (N=960)

even among those in their twenties and thirties, the idea receives less support as they grow older and start families of their own. This may suggest that members with their own families come to value maintaining community ties. It is also worthy to note that most older second-generation members (over the age of 25) were Korean-born (1.5 generation) Americans at the time of the survey.

In Their Own Words: "What do you like about your Korean church?"

- "Only Koreans." *–An American-born 14-year-old male in S. California*
- "Separate church meeting and joint potluck." *–A Korean-born 27-year-old female in S. California*
- "Very small. Church feels like family gathering. No competition among church members." *–An American-born 16-year-old female in the Southeast*
- "The growing interest for change. The energy from fellow members. Endless possibilities we are coming up with for growth." *–An American-born 23-year-old male in S. California*
- "Adult support. Youth pastor. Spiritual growth and enthusiasm of youth." *–A Korean-born 28-year-old male in N. California*
- "Relaxed atmosphere." *–An American-born 22-year-old male in Maryland*

- "Friendliness. Helpfulness of adults. Potluck." *–A Korean-born 21-year-old female in the Northeast*
- "The feeling of belonging—being comfortable with other Koreans. Getting to know the kids. Participating in helping out with the church program." *–An American-born 25-year-old female in Michigan*
- "Separate adult and youth service. Very nice worship." *–An American-born 17-year-old female in Michigan*

In Their Own Words: "What do you dislike about your Korean church?"

- "It doesn't meet the needs of Korean American generation." *–A Korean-born 24-year-old female in S. California*
- "Church has become too dull to the same activities every Sabbath." *–A Canadian-born 19-year-old female*
- "It's hard for newcomers to feel wanted and welcomed. The existing groups are too hard to break in." *–A half-Korean who left Korea at the age of 13*
- "Church politics. The segregation of ages. Separate worship—we need worship, eat, and talk together." *–A Korean-born 28-year-old female in Maryland*
- "My church is so cold. Need more graceful sermon." *–A Korean-born 20-year-old female in the South*
- "Bad neighborhood." *–An American-born half Korean*
- "Splitting of church over parental disputes. Don't have our own church." *–A Canadian-born 18-year-old male*
- "I find the fact that there are two Korean churches keep dividing. This harms our youth, outreach and church resources. It's very hypocritical." *–An American-born 18-year-old male in the South*
- "This church seems very distant and apathetic towards GOD, like other Korean American churches. There is a marked decrease in involvement in my church in the past couple of years. My church has a way of excluding people and segregating into their own cliques." *–A Korean-born 17-year-old female in the South*
- "I feel that those who really have no place in the Korean SDA community are the English-speaking young adults. We are continually treated like children. Constantly referred to as 'youth'

while in fact, many of us are married, finished with school, and ready to have children of our own. We do not have the same concerns as high school age youth. However, the majority of Korean-speaking congregations does not realize that. Many of us feel we have no church to go." *–An American-born 26-year-old female in the Northeast*

- "No spiritual emphasis. No practical Christian life is practiced. No understanding of non-Christians." *–A Korean-born 22-year-old male in Georgia*

- "Hard to get to know adults." *–An American-born 22-year-old male in N. California*

- "It is so unorganized. No dedicated youth pastor. It almost seems that the church doesn't care for the youth." *–A 16-year-old female in Colorado*

- "Need for spiritual revival. Greater concern on Korean culture than on spiritual needs." *–An American-born 35-year-old male in Illinois*

- "Gossip, gossip, gossip. People talk bad behind [your] backs. Other parents tell you what to do when they don't even do anything about their own children." *–An American-born 16-year-old female in Florida*

- "Competition among the adults on material things." *–A 17-year-old half-Korean in S. California*

- "Lack of in-depth Bible studies. Lack of training and discipleship for future leaders. Lack of committed spiritual leaders. Lack of emotion and expressiveness about our faith. Exclusiveness not reaching out to others." *–An American-born 26-year-old female in the Northeast*

- "Friction between church leaders result in power struggles, ugly fights and end up disrupting or splitting church. Egos of leaders conflict with true definition of Christian service." *–An American-born 22-year-old male in Illinois*

- "Too much politics. People seem to really be critical of others— really non-Christian attitude. The leaders of our church need have personal Bible study and prayers and more prayer." *–A Korean-born 24-year-old female in S. California*

- "There is not much interaction between youth and older church members. Very cold to visitors. Church feels old and unwelcome." *–A Korean-born half-Korean female*
- "Legalistic attitude. Hypocritical adults." *–An American-born 19-year-old female in S. California*
- "Not as spiritual as I want it to be. Too many cliques. Division between genders." *–A Korean-born 15-year-old male who came to the United States at the age of 2*
- "Parents act like kids. Too much pride and hypocrisy." *–An American-born 15-year-old male in S. California*
- "Too political. Too segregated. Cliques." *–A Korean-born 20-year-old female in S. California*
- "Small number of members for the big church. Giving rent to other churches other than SDA." *–A Korean-born 14-year-old male in Georgia*

THE IMAGE OF THE KOREAN ADVENTIST CHURCH

We live in an age of image, and young people are most conscious of that. They tend to judge a situation largely according to the image they develop of it. In general, images are formed about a person or a group based on impressions, information, observation, and interaction. While information about a person or group may come from other sources, observation and interaction are one's own real experiences. No matter how we come to know about a person or group, our perceived image becomes the basis for evaluation and judgment. Though a perceived image may not correctly reflect the reality of the person or group, its effects can be real.

The kind of image that second-generation members associate with their Korean churches develops mainly from their observations and experiences with their churches. On the whole, the mental image of their churches could be divided into two categories: favorable or unfavorable. Positive images will strengthen their relationship with their churches while negative ones will weaken their commitment to the church and even end it.

This section presents the image that survey participants associate with their Korean churches. A technique known as the "semantic differential method" was employed to extract the mental image that young people have held over the years. Twelve pairs of polar concepts were selected to describe the images they associate with their churches. For instance, the participants were asked to locate their Korean church on the "exciting–dull" continuum (a scale with seven choices) based upon their image or impression of the church. If their overall perception of their Korean church had been one of excitement, they would have marked close to the exciting end. On the other hand, if their image was more on the dull side, they would have marked near the dull end. If they perceived their churches as being neither exciting nor dull, then they would have marked the middle point on the "exciting–dull" continuum.

A word of caution is in order: The image of the Korean church is an overall general image. Although the local church an individual attends may be the major source for image formation, this is not necessarily the case with everyone. Their knowledge about and observation of other Korean churches could have contributed to their mental image of the church.

Findings in Brief

As shown in Figure 7.9, the group's overall image of the Korean church is more positive (average 45%) than negative (average 27%). At the same time, 28% of the group took a neutral position in their characterization of the Korean Adventist church in North America. Of the twelve pairs of polar concepts, there was no single area where the Korean church was considered more negative than positive. Many times the neutral position also ranked higher than all collective negative ones.

The Korean church is associated with such positive aspects as brightness (58%), kindness (55%), stability (51%), warmness (49%), and harmony (49%). These traits, except perhaps for brightness, are commonly associated with the national characteristics of Koreans. Harmony, stability, and warmness, for instance, were emphasized in the traditional teachings of Confucianism on human relations. On the other hand, the following negative aspects were registered in the minds of the second-generation members: isolation (35%), stagnation (32%), rigidity (30%), exclusiveness (30%), and dullness (30%). These are

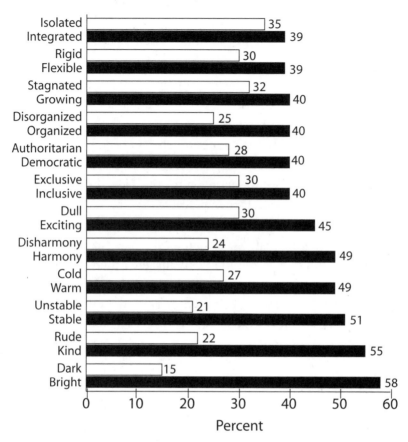

Figure 7.9 Image of the Korean Church among Second-Generation Members

traits that any immigrant minority church could easily develop because of its unique situation. Koreans in general tend to be perceived as rigid and exclusive. Some of the traits may be attributed to a combination of the following factors: the history of the small peninsular country surrounded by superpower nations, the homogeneity of the Korean people, national character, immigrants, and the Adventist lifestyle.

The "isolated–integrated" pair calls for special attention because it marks two contrasting images by only a four-point difference: 35% and 39%, respectively. In the eyes of young people, the Korean church is not well integrated into the mainstream, and therefore the church is perceived as being isolated. In the larger Korean Christian community, the Adventist faith has been regarded as heretical for its unique practices, such as Sabbath observance and adherence to dietary laws. Thus the Korean Adventist church in North America is doubly isolated from its larger communities: both the Korean community and the mainstream American community. In a similar vein, the "exclusive–inclusive" pair should be looked upon with some concern. The difference between the two polar concepts is only ten points. To second-generation members, the Korean church appears to be less inclusive. Again, language, cultural, racial, and faith differences may have erected barriers intentionally or unintentionally.

One in three second-generation members views the church as stagnating. Stagnation could result from isolation and exclusion. When the group is divided by age (up to 17 years of age versus older than 17), the perception of the Korean church becomes markedly different. As seen in Figure 7.10, without an exception, the older ones are far more negative (or critical) toward their churches while their younger counterparts are more positive (or generous). For instance, in the "isolated–integrated" pair, only 24% of the younger members feel that Korean churches are isolated. In contrast, that figure is almost doubled among the older ones (46%) who feel that their churches are isolated. In the same pair, one in two younger members views their churches as integrated, whereas fewer than one in three older members feels that their churches are integrated.

Other contrasting images of the Korean church between the two age groups are found in the "exclusive–inclusive" pair. Only one in ten younger members feels that their churches are exclusive, while as many as four in ten older ones view their churches as exclusive. On the subject of whether their churches are inclusive, 47% of the younger members agree, whereas only 35% of the older ones feel that their churches are inclusive.

Although no definite explanation for the differences between the two age groups can be given, reasonable speculations can be made. The older ones have developed a broader perspective on the social roles of their churches, and they become more critical about the inadequacy of their churches in fulfilling their social responsibilities to the larger society. In addition, they are aware of what is happening in the

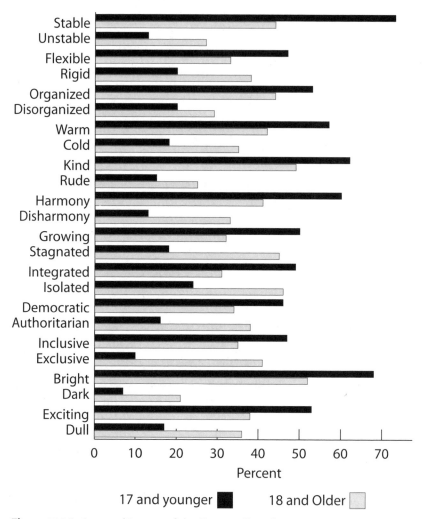

Figure 7.10 Age and Image of the Korean Church

church politicking among the leaders. On the other hand, the younger ones have a rather limited view on the roles of the church and they are comfortable with the coziness of their ethnic churches. They have not been exposed to the internal conflict and tension among first-generation members as much as the older group has. This inverse (or negative) relationship between age and church image is statistically supported as shown in Table 7.1. The older someone is, the more negative he or she becomes about the image of the Korean churches.

Table 7.1 Relationship between Age of Participants and Their Image of the Korean Adventist Church in North America

Image Traits	Correlations*
Dull–Exciting	-.237
Dark–Bright	.267
Exclusive–Inclusive	-.283
Authoritarian–Democratic	-.256
Cold–Warm	.230
Disorganized–Organized	-.179
Rigid–Flexible	-.251
Unstable–Stable	-.217
Isolated–Integrated	-.278
Stagnated–Growing	-.297
Disharmonious–Harmonious	-.308
Rude–Kind	-.238

*All correlations are statistically significant at the .001 level except the rude–kind pair which is significant at the .01 level.

In Their Own Words: "What do you like about your Korean church?"

- "Family-like atmosphere." *–A Korean-born 18-year-old female in Michigan*
- "Friendliness. Helpfulness of adults." *–A Korean-born 21-year-old female who left Korea at the age of 5*

In Their Own Words: "What do you dislike about your Korean church?"

- "The exclusiveness." *–An American-born 20-year-old female in S. California*
- "Too conservative. Concentrate on 'don't's instead of 'do's. They don't seem to take the youth group seriously." *–An American-born 16-year-old male in the Northwest*
- "Lukewarmness. Lack of outreach." *–A Korean-born 24-year-old female in S. California*
- "Rigid and old-world oriented." *–A Korean-born 34-year-old female who came to the United States at the age of 12*
- "Slow to accept new ideas. Cold attitude toward newcomers." *–An American-born 17-year-old male in Michigan*

- "Cold; isolate; non-Christian emphasis; too much cultural emphasis." –*A Korean-born 29-year-old male in S. California*
- "Rigidity, pride, stubbornness, gossip, gossip, gossip and gossip." –*A Korean-born 19-year-old male in Michigan*
- "Strictness. Dryness, sometimes coldness." –*A Korean-born 16-year-old female in N. California*
- "Spiritually dead. Lack of unity and togetherness. Everyone seems not to care." –*A Korean-born 20-year-old female in N. California*
- "The slow expansion. Slow to accept new ideas. Cold attitude toward new comers." –*An American-born 17-year-old male in Michigan*
- "Not very spiritual. Passion is gone." –*An American-born 17-year-old female in the Northwest*
- "No inspirational or intellectual stimulation." –*An American-born 25-year-old female in S. California*
- "The inability to do non-traditional things." –*An American-born 25-year-old female in Michigan*
- "Too pleasure oriented and not spiritually oriented." –*An American-born 17-year-old male in Michigan*

WORSHIP AT THE KOREAN CHURCH

In any community of faith, the worship experience is the central part of its religious life. By offering praise, praying, and listening to messages presented in a holy time and place, worshipers are uplifted and the experience transcends mundane reality. Also, the act of coming together to worship on a regular basis provides a sense of solidarity and community. Thus, worship gives the worshipers meaning for life and a sense of belonging, which are vital for a healthy life.

The spiritual satisfaction of church members is largely determined by the quality of their worship experience. If someone is satisfied with his or her worship experience, that person also tends to be happy with his or her spiritual life. In turn, this satisfaction may lead to commitment to a community of faith. And the reverse is true. For this reason, the worship service is the most important part of building a stable faith community.

In the reality of the Korean Adventist church in North America, that worship experience is often condensed into a one-hour service between eleven o'clock and twelve noon on Saturday for the majority of second-generation Adventist members. Although many churches have meetings on Friday evenings and other days of the week in or outside of church, no other meeting can be more intense than the Sabbath morning worship service. Unquestionably, Sabbath morning worship is central in its importance and impact. For this reason, much attention and care are given to that service.

In many immigrant churches in North America, however, the worship experience is somewhat fragmented because of language barriers. Whether it is a monolingual or bilingual church, it is hard to satisfy everyone. In these churches, some parents and children separate to worship in their own primary language. Even if they worship together in Korean, English, or both languages, a lack of comprehension of the language used or the translation of it tends to cause uneasiness.

Also, the message gap between generations cannot be overlooked. The linguistic and cultural gaps that accompany theological differences are wide to say the least. Sometimes the style of worship that one generation prefers may not be appreciated by the other. Of course, such a problem is not limited to only ethnic immigrant churches. But the magnitude of the problem in immigrant churches is far greater than in other churches. The challenge facing most immigrant churches is how to provide satisfactory worship experiences for the different language and age groups. The answer to this question is one of the key elements to a church's future course and shape and the well-being of its members.

Findings in Brief

Considering the proportion of Korean-born participants (50%) in the survey and those claiming to be bilingual (45%), it is quite understandable that 53% of the second-generation members prefer a mixture of separate and joint services (see Figure 7.11). This may reflect the desire of second-generation members to maintain intergenerational continuity and a sense of family and community. Fewer than one in ten (8%) respondents wants to have a complete joint

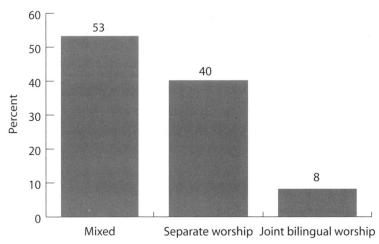

Figure 7.11 Desirable Worship Service Format (N=974)

service every Sabbath in two languages, whereas four in ten want a completely separate service every week. The ratio of those who prefer a separate service every Sabbath to those who prefer a joint service is five to one. Although the group wants to have fewer joint bilingual services, they seem to be satisfied with the content and format of the bilingual service. As can be seen in Figure 7.12, more than half (54%)

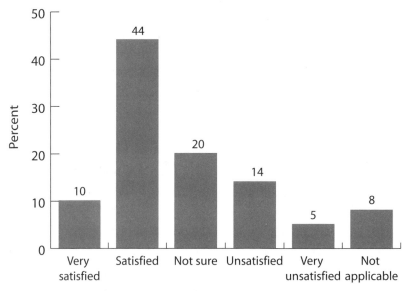

Figure 7.12 Satisfaction with Joint Bilingual Service (N=987)

indicate that they are satisfied with the way the bilingual services are conducted. This suggests that almost half of the group (46%) dislike the joint services they have participated in.

As seen in Figure 7.13, slightly more than one in three (37%) want to have a joint bilingual service once a month, and about one in four (23%) wants to see their churches conduct a bilingual service once every two or three months. Small portions of the subject group show two extremes on the subject of bilingual worship: 14% of the survey participants do not want to have a joint service at all, while 10% of the group want to have a joint service almost every Sabbath. Almost two-thirds (73%) of the survey group is in favor of separate worship services between the Korean-speaking adults and the English-speaking youth. Only 8% of the group oppose such an idea, and 16% cannot make up their minds on the subject of a separate service. It seems clear that the majority of second-generation members prefer a service in English, their own primary language.

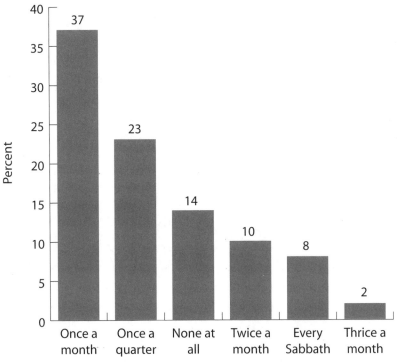

Figure 7.13 Preferred Frequency of Joint Bilingual Services

Relatively speaking, those who attend large churches with a total membership of 300 or more are less likely to be satisfied with their joint bilingual service. On the other hand, those who attend small churches with a total membership of 100 or less are more likely to be satisfied with a joint service. This is perhaps due to the more impersonal nature of a large church where people are less attached to each other. Also, large churches tend to attract young people from other churches to their programs or other special activities. Therefore, the joint service between the two language groups is thought to be less significant. In addition, large churches can offer full-fledged worship programs for English-speaking members with qualified full-time associate pastors and lay supporters, thus providing quality worship programs.

Most youth groups (89%) conduct a completely separate service without interfacing with the Korean-speaking adult service. Only a few churches begin a worship service together and then split for separate sermons in Korean and English.

YOUTH PASTORS' VIEWS ON WORSHIP

The desirability of a joint service is split among the youth pastors. Seventeen (50%) of them consider the joint service desirable and the other half are either not sure about its desirability or regard it as undesirable. As shown in Figure 7.14, the majority of youth pastors (62%) prefer a joint worship service once a month (32%) or once a quarter (29%). Only two (active at the time of the survey) of the 34 youth pastors want to see a joint service every Sabbath. On the other hand, two youth pastors do not want to have a joint service at all. Five of the youth pastors desire a joint service only when necessary, such as special occasions like Thanksgiving, Christmas, and other holidays.

In Their Own Words: "What do you like about your Korean Church?"

- "Having both English and Korean service." –A *Korean-born 24-year-old female in S. California*
- "Comfort in worshiping with people who are similar to me." –An *American-born 21-year-old female in S. California*
- "Although our church has been quite dull for the past few years, I realize that Christ's second coming is right around the corner.

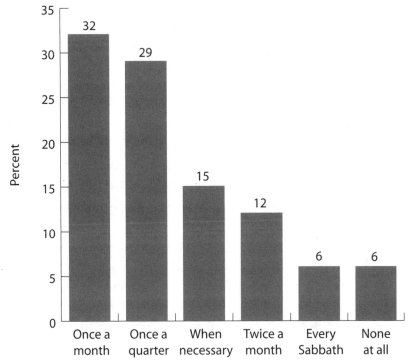

Figure 7.14 Preferred Frequency of Joint Bilingual Services among Korean Youth Pastors (N=34)

Our youth has grown spiritually and physically in the past year and we are coming together in the Lord's presence. I see and feel the spirit moving within our little youth group that has grown so much." *–A 20-year-old American-born female in California*

- "The sermon is short....Song service." *–An American-born 13-year-old female in S. California*

In Their Own Words: "What do you dislike about your Korean Church?"

- "Not allowed to play guitars for church services." *–An American-born 18-year-old male in the South*

- "I wish that we youth could have worship separated with the adults." *–A Korean-born 17-year-old male who came to the United States at the age of 10*

- "There is no program for youth. The youth group is not organized at all and there is no youth leader. The church service is really boring as there is no separate English-speaking service." *–An 18-year-old* *female born in Korea*

- "Sitting through a Korean sermon I don't understand. Petty arguments among members." *—An American-born 20-year-old in the Southeast*
- "It is very strict, stubborn, and old-fashioned. Gossip. Lack of youth involvement. They don't really care very much about the youth although they may be concerned." *—A 15-year-old female born in North America*
- "Spiritual mediocrity. Programs are too rigid and routine. Parents place too much burden of spiritual growth on youth pastors, not on themselves. Need to be more involved." *—A Korean-born 27-year-old male in S. California*
- "Worship is too outdated, too rigid. Need to adapt to changing world instead of continuing the same practice year after year." *—An American-born 27-year-old male in S. California*
- "One of the things I see in many Korean churches is that there isn't enough hard core material being presented to the present youth at our church. All we ever hear is God is good, He loves you, and etc.…it's the end of times and we are not prepared enough. I think we need our youth to be more prepared for the end of time." *—A Korean-born 17-year-old male in N. California*
- "Too many social activities. Not enough outreach. Most programs are geared to high school student[s]." *—An American-born 29-year-old person in Maryland*

In the Words of Youth Pastors
- "Korean language and culture should be expressed and influenced in our churches."
- "It takes a lot of preparation to make both groups happy."
- "Another language will not hurt anybody—keep that tradition."
- "We need to have joint bilingual service, but for how long?"
- "What a sad thing to see every week?"
- "Spiritual needs of youth and needs of adults are different."
- "What is the point? For whose benefits? Differences in language make it less likely for social, communal fellowship, as we see happening with natural segregation of adults and English-speaking

youth, and English-speaking versus Korean-speaking youth."

- "Not effective. Not too many youths and adults pay attention to it."
- "Kids don't like adults."

INTERFACE WITH OTHER ADVENTIST CHURCHES

The United States and Canada are relatively pluralistic societies. Groups of different national origins, cultures, and languages exist side by side. Yet some groups are more open to others, while others are less inclusive. There are no barriers that keep people from moving between the different groups, thus offering people a wide range of opportunities to inquire and experiment with other groups. Most second-generation Koreans have free access to any English-speaking church. They should not encounter any barriers in approaching other groups, unless they have their own psychological barriers.

Thus one may wonder: Why do Korean Adventist youth stay with their Korean churches? Have they tried other churches? If so, how do they compare their Korean churches with those other churches? Unless one takes membership in Korean churches for granted based on blood and social ties, these questions need to be raised to better understand the staying power of the second-generation members within their Korean churches. The survey had only a few questions exploring this subject. More detailed in-depth study on the subject may be required.

Findings in Brief

Among the second-generation members, one in three never attended a non-Korean church, and almost four in ten had very rarely attended a non-Korean church, as shown in Figure 7.15. Thus, three in four have hardly shown any measurable interest in visiting a non-Korean church. This finding indicates that most second-generation members are confined in their own churches as far as church attendance and activities are concerned. Only one in four respondents showed sustained interest in non-Korean churches through frequent visits.

Further analysis of the data suggests that those who attend small Korean churches are more likely to be interested in attending non-Korean churches. One may speculate that smaller Korean churches are

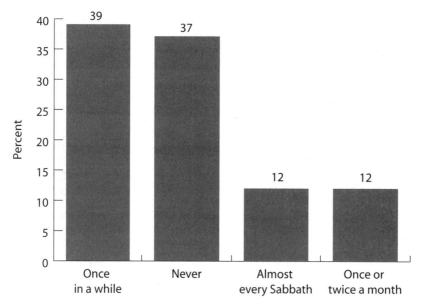

Figure 7.15 Attendance at Non-Korean Church (N=959)

less likely to have trained youth pastors and adequate facilities. Limited by human and other resources, these churches are less likely to provide wholesome, satisfactory worship and other programs. Limited social contacts in small churches could be another factor for the members' desire to explore other churches. In contrast, larger Korean churches in metropolitan areas can better meet both the spiritual and social needs of their young people, so the youth are less compelled to explore other churches.

When comparing Korean and non-Korean churches on many aspects of church activities (such as Sabbath school, music programs, and social activities—see Figure 7.16), the survey participants gave higher marks to the Korean churches with the exception of one area— mission outreach. The survey does not provide detailed explanations for the higher ratings the Korean churches received. There is no way of knowing whether the ratings are based upon personal observations and experiences or on mere impressions or hearsay. Nevertheless, the perception that a Korean church is better than non-Korean churches seems to prevail among the second-generation members. Other than family and social ties, the second-generation members may want to stay

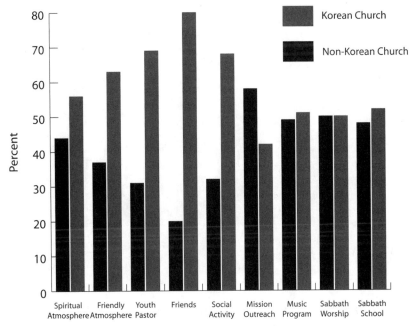

Figure 7.16 Comparison of Korean Adventist Church with Non-Korean Churches

with their Korean churches because of their belief that their church programs are more satisfying to them than those of other churches.

Younger members (under 18 years of age) are more likely to be the ones who never visited non-Korean churches. As reported in Figure 7.17, almost half of this age group (46%) never visited non-Korean churches whereas about one third of the older group (18 and older) never visited non-Korean churches.

In Their Own Words: "What do you like about your Korean church?"

- "The new church has met the needs of my spiritual growth. The main reason for attending my current church is for this reason. Church for me is to increase my spiritual growth and strengthen my relationship with God....Now I have gained new friends and I have been satisfied with my decision. Unfortunately I had to leave my home church of 20 plus years. I feel somewhat guilty for leaving my home/parent's church, but I feel I must be more loyal to God than to a church." –*A 28-year-old male in S. California*

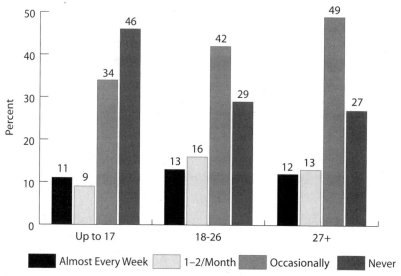

Figure 7.17 Age and Attendance at Non-Korean Church (N=953)

In Their Own Words: "What do you dislike about your Korean church?"

- "We don't know each other in a deeply personal way. Strong and trustful bonds could be better. Not enough outreach or interaction with other churches. Unresponsiveness—the opposite of black churches in expressing Amen, jubilant, songful singing. More reserved nature of Koreans." *–An American-born 21-year-old female in Illinois*

- "There is a major difference between Korean SDA churches and Korean Sunday churches. The quality of programs and the resources of Korean Sunday churches are in many ways superior to that of our churches." *–A Korean-born 21-year-old female who left Korea at the age of 5*

- "I attend mostly non-Korean SDA churches due to school programs and my own preference. My parents understand this and are not unhappy about that. Of course, they like me to attend their home Korean church." *–An American-born 16-year-old male in the Northwest*

FORMER KOREAN YOUTH PASTORS WORKING AT ANGLO CHURCHES

There are a half-dozen former Korean youth pastors who minister at other churches, mostly English-speaking white churches. A few of them were senior pastors at Korean churches by the time they accepted the calls from other churches, and they transferred to the white churches as senior pastors.

They left the Korean ministry for personal or professional reasons, including language, family, philosophy of ministry, and human relations in the Korean churches. Since most, if not all, of them are bilingual and bicultural in varying degrees, they were able to easily establish themselves either in Korean, Anglo, or any other churches.

Although the circumstances under which these pastors left their Korean churches were different, most of them seem to be happy where they are. One former Korean youth pastor reveals his satisfaction with the white church he is serving. "I feel much better about myself. I feel more competent. I feel more relaxed and less burdened. Generally I feel happier. Professionally I feel in control. I feel like I am on equally plain ground with everyone else language wise. I feel [this] ministry fits my style and personality better. My family is happier because I am happier. At first they missed the Korean church. But they have grown accustomed to the non-Korean churches."

On the other hand, one former youth pastor who left the Korean ministry has to deal with the cultural tension created in his own family, especially with his children, in spite of his own professional satisfaction. "My children miss going to a Korean church. Already in their early ages, they have become sufficiently 'Korean' to always prefer being among Koreans to others. This is a sad reality....I am so much more satisfied now than ever before in the way I relate to ministry."

Some, if not all, pastors received the calls from white churches when their relationships with their Korean congregations were less than cordial. The uneasy situations might have compelled the pastors to consider the calls from non-Korean churches more willingly. At that time, the prospect of working at another church might have looked more favorable than staying in the Korean ministry.

Some of their negative perceptions about working at the Korean churches range from personal to cultural. One pastor listed some of his negative experiences in the Korean churches: lack of respect and trust in their pastors, lack of privacy for the pastor's time and space, lack of appreciation for the pastor's service, lack of lay members' cooperation and participation, frequent transfers, relationship-oriented rather than mission-oriented, uncertainty about one's future as a minister, and pessimistic prospect about the future of Korean churches in North America. After moving to his new white church, this particular Korean pastor has experienced the opposite of the negative experiences listed above. He feels appreciated, respected, and supported by the white church members. He is given authority to direct his new church according to his vision for the church.

One pastor sees the Korean ministry as too ethnically confined when he states that "the Korean church is too exclusive and short-sighted. The Korean church badly needs new blood." Others chose the non-Korean ministry "for greater personal fulfillment in ministry." Their families seem to enjoy the greater freedom and privacy in the non-Korean churches. The pastors feel that their wives and children are under less personal and spiritual scrutiny in non-Korean churches. Such benefits may come with a price, however. From time to time, they feel less attached to their white congregations. "Sometimes, I feel as though Anglo churches are too unsociable. They have their own lives and once church is out, everyone goes in their separate ways. There is much less of a community feeling."

All of the transplanted pastors said they would not object to one of their Korean minister friends accepting a call from a non-Korean church. They would actually encourage their friends to consider such a call positively. They would advise them not to be so concerned about English. They want their friends to realize that there is a different world out there beyond the confines of Korean ethnic ministry. In contrast, no transplanted Korean pastors would seriously consider a call from a Korean church. Nevertheless, they do not totally rule out the possibility of serving at a Korean church someday in the future.

In sum, the former Korean youth pastors, including a few senior pastors at the time of transfer, appear to be content with their ministry in non-Korean churches. They feel that their ministry at other churches offers better opportunities for personal and professional growth. In comparison with the atmosphere of the Korean churches they had served and known for years, Anglo churches provide a more understanding, supportive, and cooperative atmosphere.

SUMMARY OBSERVATIONS

The Korean Adventist churches in North America display differences between the immigrant adult generation and second-generation members. The differences stem from more than just language and cultural dissimilarities. The life experiences of the two generations are quite different from each other, and these have shaped their faith differently. Most Korean-born parents endured a great deal of hardship and sacrifice in Korea and North America as well. The efforts to integrate the two generations in joint bilingual worship services and joint board meetings, for instance, have been challenging. However, this could be the source of dynamism for Korean American churches if both sides are willing to meet the challenge with openness and creativity.

For healthy growth in the Korean churches, systematic approaches to synthesize the best of the two generations are called for. From their different life experiences, each generation may offer something unique and valuable for the dynamic growth of future Korean churches.

The Korean church ought to be more open to and interact more with the larger community, lest it exist in an ethnic cocoon. Churches need to participate in and contribute to the well-being of society. Thus, their success is not merely measured in the tangible growth of church operations but in making significant contributions to the larger communities.

CHAPTER 8

Future Commitment to the Korean Church

More than four decades have passed since a few dozen Korean Adventists organized their first church in the United States. It was 1965 when the first church was established in Los Angeles. That same year was a turning point in American immigration policy when the U.S. Congress reversed the country's discriminatory policy on Asian immigration.

The early pioneers of the Korean immigrant churches have now become less visible, reaching old age and even death. At the same time, the second-generation members have been emerging to take responsibility for their own affairs in these churches. And they keep growing in number and influence. For some time to come, however, both the immigrant and second generations with their children will coexist.

As these churches go through a transition in membership composition, leadership, and culture, the following questions may be raised regarding the future: Will the Korean churches continue to exist long after the first generation is gone? If so, what are these churches going to be like? To what extent will they remain Korean in their membership make-up and cultural traits?

The future of these churches depends on a host of factors, both internal and external. A couple of external factors include the political and economic conditions of Korea and North America, and the immigration and cultural policies of the United States and Canada.

But the most critical factor is the commitment of the second-generation members and their children to the continuation of their parents' or grandparents' churches. If they have the desire and will to remain Korean, the Korean church is more likely to survive. If not, the future of the Korean church as a distinctive ethnic group is less than certain.

In an attempt to answer questions about the future, one may seek for clues from the experiences of other immigrants and their churches. Most European immigrants were fully integrated within one or two generations. As a result, their immigrant churches phased out after the immigrant generation. To most children of European immigrants, assimilation was as natural as their own physical growth.

On the other hand, the experiences of non-European immigrants and their descendants may offer some clues about the future of Korean churches. As already discussed in chapter 4, some African Americans and Hispanic Americans, for instance, have retained their ethnic identities in spite of their long history in the United States. American Indians are in the same category. To some extent, the separate existence of these groups has been the result of prejudice on the part of the white majority.

Especially when it comes to religious life, the non-European groups have maintained separate identities. Their churches are the result not so much of language and culture as it is their desire to retain a sense of peoplehood. In addition, a newfound sense of ethnic pride among minority groups in an increasingly pluralistic society is a significant factor in promoting dual identities. Known as hyphenated Americans, such as Korean-Americans, these people want to integrate both cultures in themselves. Globalization is another powerful force for people wishing to preserve their ethnic heritage in the face of sweeping power wielded by the West.

Are the Koreans in North America going to pursue the European path or the non-European path? Will they be fully absorbed to the point of complete assimilation or will they remain distinct? Based upon recent developments and trends at both national and international levels as presented in the beginning chapters, one may assume that the recent Korean immigrants are more likely to pursue the latter course.[1]

In the case of second-generation Koreans, the sense of community, family connections, and friendship networks they find in their ethnic churches could be forces strong enough to hold them as members. Also, prominent Korean values—such as filial piety, family obligation, and group conformity—could be cultural ingredients that strengthen their ties with their Korean churches.

This section attempts to understand the intentions of the second-generation members regarding their desire to remain committed to the future of their Korean churches. Undoubtedly, this is the subject of greatest concern both within and outside the Korean Adventist community. The findings may have weighty implications for future planning by the leadership of the Korean church and denominational administration.

FINDINGS IN BRIEF

As shown in Figure 8.1, only a minority (16%) of the survey participants believes that the present Korean church will continue to exist without much change. On the other extreme, fewer than 60 participants (6%) anticipate the disappearance of the Korean church in the future. One in two anticipates a great deal of change as the Korean church continues to develop, and slightly more than one in four (27%) cannot predict what might happen to the Korean church in the future. Overall, two of three (67%) second-generation members felt that their Korean church will continue, while one in three (33%) is uncertain about the future existence of the Korean church.

Among the three language-proficiency groups—English-fluent, Korean-fluent, and bilingual—there is no significant difference in anticipation regarding the future development of the Korean church. This means that command of English or Korean or both does not influence one's anticipation of the future of ethnic churches.

As shown in Figure 8.2, three in four respondents believe that they will be attending a Korean church twenty years from now. On the other hand, about one in ten (9%) admits that they are less likely to attend a Korean church twenty years from now. One in five (18%) respondents is uncertain and cannot predict future attendance.

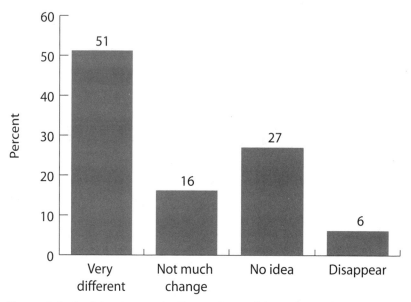

Figure 8.1 Anticipation on the Future State of the Korean Church in North America (N=964)

Between the Korean-born group and those born elsewhere (mainly the United States and Canada), members of the former are more likely to attend a Korean church in twenty years (see Figure 8.3). Regardless

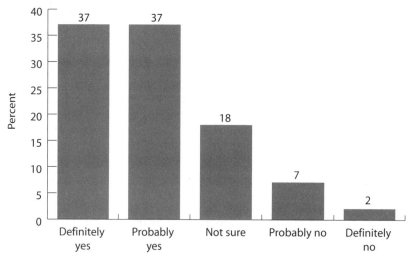

Figure 8.2 Will You Attend a Korean Church Twenty Years from Now? (N=976)

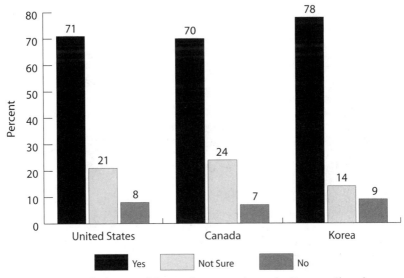

Figure 8.3 Birthplace and Future Intent to Attend a Korean Church (N=974)

of one's residence in terms of major geographical regions of North America, three quarters of the survey participants intend to attend a Korean church in the future (see Figure 8.4). As can be seen in Figure 8.5, there is no significant difference among the three age groups (up

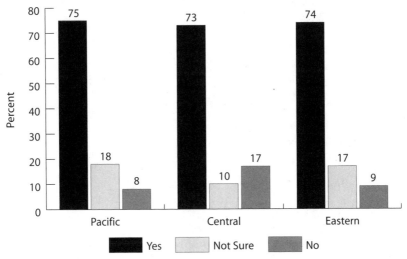

Figure 8.4 Region of Residence and Future Intent to Attend a Korean Church (N=989)

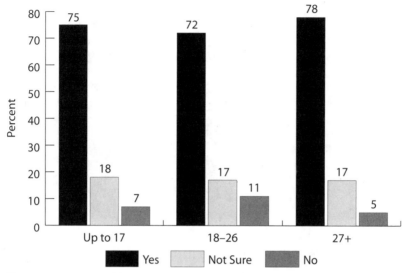

Figure 8.5 Age and Future Intent to Attend a Korean Church (N=974)

to 17, 18–26, and over 27) in the likelihood of attending a Korean church twenty years from now. Those who identify themselves primarily as Koreans (83% of this category) or Korean-Americans/Canadians (72% of this category) are more likely to attend a Korean church in the future than those who identify themselves primarily as Americans (54% of this category) or Canadians (36% of this category).[2]

As displayed in Figure 8.6, if one is fluent in Korean or both Korean and English, that person is more likely to attend a Korean church in the future than someone who is fluent only in English. Yet even two-thirds of the latter group indicated that they would attend a Korean church in the future. The same pattern holds true in the relationship between a desire to learn Korean and the probability of attending a Korean church in the future.

Friendship is a good predictor as to whether one is going to attend a Korean church in the future. As shown in Figure 8.7, someone with close Korean friends is more likely to attend a Korean church than those without close Korean friends. Yet even more than half of those without close Korean friends desire to attend a Korean church in the future. Likewise, the desire to marry a Korean is also a good predictor. Those who want to marry a Korean are far more likely to stay with the Korean

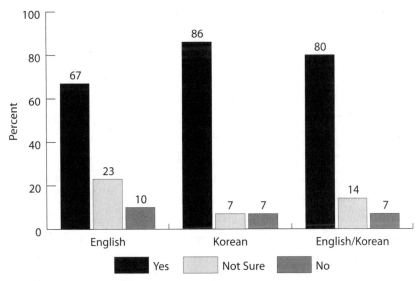

Figure 8.6 Language Fluency and Future Intent to Attend a Korean Church (N=984)

church (83%) than those who do not consider marrying a Korean to be an important matter (40%). Those who feel at home at their present Korean churches (84%) and those who identify their churches as

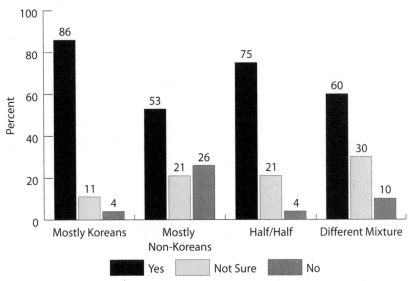

Figure 8.7 Close Friends and Future Intent to Attend a Korean Church (N=979)

part of their family tradition (81%) are more likely to attend a Korean church in the future. On the other hand, those who attend their present Korean churches mainly because they are pressured to attend are less likely to attend a Korean church in the future (46%).

Those who are satisfied with the bilingual service at their churches are more likely to say that they will still attend a Korean church in twenty years (82%) than those who are dissatisfied with the bilingual service (70%). This might have something to do with the appreciation of the Korean language that comes with the bilingual service. Those who oppose the idea of establishing a separate independent church for second-generation members are more inclined to attend a Korean church in the future. One of the reasons respondents gave for attending a Korean church in the future has to do with establishing their own identity as well as an identity for their children. Based upon the above findings, we may profile those who are more likely to be still attending a Korean church in twenty years: They are Korean-born members who value their family tradition and want to retain or learn the Korean language. They want to marry Koreans and maintain the Korean identity for themselves and their children. Their closest friends are more likely to be Koreans. Even now, they appreciate the joint bilingual service and oppose the idea of a separate independent church for English-speaking Korean members.

YOUTH PASTORS' VIEWS ON THE FUTURE OF THE KOREAN CHURCH

Two-thirds of the youth pastors (68%) believe that the Korean church will continue to exist in the future in some form. Of these, only 15% think that the church will remain as a distinctive Korean church while more than half (53%) anticipate a more Americanized English-speaking church. About 15% of the youth pastors anticipate a loss of ethnic identity in the Korean churches and the consequential transformation of the church. These assimilated churches will be open to anyone. Only four youth pastors expressed no opinion about the future of the Korean church. Two youth pastors think that the Korean church will eventually disappear.

In Their Own Words: "What do you dislike about your Korean church?"

- "No concern about the future of Korean church." –*A Korean-born 17-year-old male in S. California*
- "Not much future plan. Lack of responsibility as a group member. Lost the purpose of church." –*A Korean-born 42-year-old male who left Korea at the age of 16*
- "I am not sure how it will be in the future. And sometimes I feel there is no hope." –*A 26-year-old female who came to the United States at the age of 6*
- "One main downfall of the church is the fact that parents seem to be more liberal with their children so when they come up the ranks into high school or earlyteen, there are major behavioral problems....What I wonder is what our parents are teaching their children? Huh?? For this alone, the future of Korean-Canadian church may not exit [sic]." –*A Canadian-born 22-year-old female*
- "Lack of overall leadership. No sense of direction or vision." –*A 43-year-old male who left Korea at the age of 17*
- "Lack of enthusiasm. Lack of 'togetherness'. No direction in our church." –*An American-born 19-year-old male in Illinois*
- "Potluck food. Need bigger church. Church seems to lack vision for the future." –*An American-born 27-year-old male in Maryland*
- "I see the future of Korean churches not being able to grow or progress forward due to the lack of people (youth) who are serious about their spiritual life of their behavior to society." –*A Korean-born 18-year-old male who came to the United States at the age of 8*
- "Definite age and cultural gap. Doesn't promise spiritual growth that would interest the youth. Too rigid." –*An American-born 23-year-old female in New York*
- "No community reach out. No direction. Disorganized." –*A Korean-born 39-year-old female who left Korea at the age of 13*

In the Words of Youth Pastors

- "It's entirely up to what kind of legacy the first generation leaves."
- "It will strive and be successful by God's grace as a continued investment is made toward Korean youth ministry."

- "Don't know—but the need is there. We must move from the status quo to a new dynamic. I haven't quite put my finger on it yet."
- "The social club mentality of Korean Adventist churches are too deep rooted to allow for any real growth. I feel sincere and concerned members will begin new churches that [are] radically different from the one we have now."
- "Korean-speaking and English-speaking church are bound to grow separately. The separate growth must be encouraged and fostered."
- "We have to start churches for English-speaking Koreans. Concern for English-speaking Koreans."
- "It does not seem bright. I don't think we can expect much loyalty from second generation for the Korean church."
- "We will follow the footstep of Chinese or Japanese Church. Assimilation to American churches and the Korean church will die out."
- "Second generation Korean-Americans ought to integrate into multi-ethnic church."
- "If she wouldn't be a bilingual church, future is not bright."
- "Needs a clear sense of purpose. Needs powerful vision."
- "An emotional hurt and political segregation that have been created in the process of building and maintaining a church among the first generation Koreans formulated a suitable climate for the second generation Koreans to seek out for an independent church that is open to not just Koreans but all races which may be contrast to an unofficial expectation of the first generation Koreans. If the Koreans wish to see more church signs in Korean next to any SDA church building, two obvious movements must take place urgently in the history of Korean American SDA church: a spiritual revival among young and old generation Koreans and merging (not a takeover) local churches without any conditions attached."

INTERNET DISCUSSION

Some second-generation Korean Adventist members have engaged in animated Internet discussions[3] about their desirable church model.

Among the various topics posted, the subject of a desirable church model has drawn the most responses with nearly a ten to one ratio. With only slight editorial adjustments for the sake of general readers, the opinions posted on the Empower Ministry website are presented here in chronological order. Some writers revealed their names and others did not. To be consistent, the respondents are not identified here.

Responses to this question: "Which model of Korean-American church do you prefer?"

Currently, there are at least three different models out there.

1. Independent model: Complete separation; example: Upper Room, Cornerstone [Atlanta]; veering toward multi-ethnicity

2. "Church within a Church" model: an "English" or "youth" church within a Korean church that functions semi-independently; example: Most Korean churches have this model in varying degrees of form; maintains ties with mother church but has the shape of an independent church

3. "Church over a church" model: 2nd generation church that is the main church which has a Korean-speaking group for the parent generation; example: Chicago Unity; English church is the main church but maintains Korean cultural ties

So…among the three models that are currently out there, which one do you prefer for yourself and for your church? Where do you see yourself attending now, 5 yrs later, and 10 yrs later? Or…perhaps you see a 4th model that's not out there yet? What is it? (December 2002)

Personally I like the independent church model but gradually, like taking over the existing Korean church as we get older while bringing in whomever, whether Korean or not. I think that's the way to go, rather than suddenly breaking off. That's too much pain and difficult, I think. I can think of several examples like that. So maybe going from 2 [church within a church model] to 3 [church over a church model] to 1 [independent model].

But the problem is there's gonna be people getting lost or disillusioned about church in the meantime because there's a LOT of problems in the Korean churches today. (December 2002)

Independent church model clearly doesn't work as you see the miserable failure of upper-room and the like. The problem is that we demand independence without deserving it. We have NO idea how to run a church, or just what kind of commitment is even necessary to be part of one.

I would have to go with option 2 [church within a church] for the time being and then option 3 [church over a church] as the future model. But only in the areas where Korean-American ministry is viable, and growth can be expected. All other Korean-Americans in areas where there aren't sufficient Korean population to grow, should be recommended to find their ministry in local, English speaking churches. (December 2002)

I feel that a church veering towards multi-ethnicity is an awesome example of what Christian people should be like. I've always grown up trying to decipher between culture and religion when in reality that is something I feel that I should not have to do. Yes, it makes sense that an independent church should exist because it has worked hard and deserves it. Eventually, my generation will be the adults and almost all of us are all fluent English speakers. So what's the point of segregating ourselves?

Out of all the places that exist in this world, the church should be the least segregated. God did not create people of different ethnicities so that we can separate ourselves, but so that we can enjoy the diversity of the human race. It makes me sad and angry at the same time to see my Christian friends have excessive pride in their heritage (i.e. Korean pride) to the point where they encourage stereotypes of other ethnic groups. I am not saying that there is something wrong with being proud of one's heritage but when it stands in the way of being a Christian then perhaps it is something to review.

I am not aware of what problems exist in the Korean church but my personal concern is being who we claim to be—Christians. And a church that is multi-ethnic opens up doors that never existed before. Perhaps, these ideas are too idealistic for the near future, but I feel that it is something we should strive for. Of course, we will always have people moving to the U.S. from different countries whose first language is not English and that is another topic in itself.

Lastly, I would like to go to a multiethnic church where members leave their culture at home and bring their Bibles to worship. (December 2002)

What do you guys think of that article that Dr. Richard Choi wrote in the Compass last year? He talked about making English the official language of Korean churches as soon as possible thereby giving the young adults voice and place in the church. Basically, doing everything together (like worship and everything) with the parents in English. I thought that was pretty radical and positive. If that happened earlier, Upper Room may not have needed to happen.

In response to another post up there, there doesn't need to be ONE model. Different models can co-exist. There's a place for independent churches but they won't appeal to everybody. The same is true for other models. Different churches fulfill different roles. Nothing wrong with that. (December 2003[4])

As time passes I am beginning to realize that the format of worship, model of church, or cultural ingredients that comprise our churches are not the limiting factors of growth and transformation. It once again falls directly on my shoulders. As a member of my church—actually let me rephrase that—as a part of the body of Christ, have I experienced the Gospel (Good News) within the depths of my heart? Have I been transformed? Have I experienced the sweetness of salvation? Truly changed lives, ones that are totally committed to Christ, will shape our churches, not a new model.

We cannot look upon another church and know what is happening within the hearts and minds of those attending there for that is the work of God. Within the most inefficient model He can draw all people to Him. He does not need models, formats, and techniques to do His work. It is our utmost privilege to be united with Him in speaking of His love. I believe that God is reaching hearts in every church in ways that we may not see or perceive, and that is success. Our success is measured in our faithfulness to His calling as individuals. As we focus on this faithfulness I truly believe that He will guide each "church" and each member along the path and "model" by which He might be glorified. (December 2003)

Ultimately I feel that Model 1 [independence] sounds most promising. PROS:
1)It avoids the clash of subcultures within our churches that often exist between our parents' generation and our generation
2)It offers the quickest road to developing targeted, purposeful ministries that focus primarily and passionately on the needs of its members
3)It potentially gives its members a sense of ownership and purpose CONS:
1)Potentially painful for our relations with parents since it seems that in many cases they have looked to the church to somehow glue the seams of family and culture together
2)Requires people to step out in strong faith as they venture into the unknown and unforseeable
3)The inevitable struggles of some of the attempts can create a huge backlash against the validity of this vein of thought
Please note, I think if we, our parents AND ourselves, were more open minded and gracious in our dealing with power issues, Confucianism, and cultural ideals any model could potentially work since I don't see any single one, in and of itself, necessarily being a hindrance to the development of a targeted ministry. My resigning to the first model is because I have found in my experience that this sort of exchange is not happening en masse. (December 2002)

Multi-ethnic sounds a lot like the local American church to me. Why is there a need to create yet another church by a bunch of Korean Americans or Asians? Why not just join an existing local church? (December 2002)

I think the problem with the local "American" churches is that they may be multiethnic but so traditional that there's no room for young

*adults or others who are more contemporary in their mind-set. No won-
der their own young adults are leaving the church. So a good argument
can be made for a new young adult/genX [generation X] based church
that's multiethnic.* (December 2002)

*The fact that I am at URF [Upper Room Fellowship] though does
not necessarily demonstrate my full support for an independent church
model. We are not affiliated with any Korean-speaking adult/parent
church and so have no supervision or financial ties. Does that make us
a better church? The church I go to happens to be independent, so by
default I do support it in some fashion, but is being independent the goal
for current Korean-Americans or are there better models in the making?*

*A church is just a building. Whether a church is labeled indepen-
dent or "church within a church" does not reflect the workings of the
Holy Spirit within the hearts of each member. I'm hoping that this generation does not think that becoming independent is the best model a
church needs to achieve. Location, number of people and their demo-
graphics, and other factors often dictate what type of church you are
able to carry out.*

*Is URF a success? Our mission statement is and has been "to bring
back non-active members into our church community, train these
young people in discipleship roles, and equip them to utilize their gifts."
Because of this belief our pastor has attempted to empower the laity
through discipleship training in order to evangelize the Gospel. We
have members now that were raised in the church but had previously
left. We have non-Korean members that have joined our church. Our
church structure is laity run in some aspects. So technically, YES, we
are a success. But...*

*There is more to church than just achieving your mission statement.
If we were a company, that would be just fine, but we're not. We may
run our churches like a company and fulfill our individual tasks to run
it, but is Christianity about running a church? God is concerned about
the people within the church. He is concerned about me. I appreciate
the comments of a previous reply: "As a part of the body of Christ
have I experienced the Gospel (Good News) within the depths of my*

heart? Have I been transformed? Have I experienced the sweetness of salvation?" If this has occurred in the members of your church, then God will not care what type of church you belong to or promote. God cares about whether or not you are saved and are helping others become saved. Another question may then be: In your area, which model of church will put the Gospel into your heart and into the hearts of those around you?

In some respects URF is probably like your church. We're probably a little older, have more members that are parents, and have more multi-ethnicity. But we have struggles just the same as any other church. As we move on in faith, let's pray for the direction of our K-A churches and concentrate on what we have to do individually to impact our church collectively. (December 2002)

Responses to this title: "The English-speaking Korean American church is dead"

The Korean American SDA church as we know it is dead. Here's why: 1) There is a very limited congregation to witness to. As Korean immigration has slowed down in this country, there is a very small group to witness to. 2) The current model of most churches, which is an English-speaking church attached to the parent church, is only a temporary patchwork solution. When the youth grow up there is little space left for them except to teach the other youth and a reason many choose to just leave the church. 3) The success of the Upper Room Fellowship has been debated. I think it is irrelevant. There are only a handful of places at best that could even support a group like this anyway. Unless Korean Americans take over the country, it is irrelevant.

I think Richard Choi's ideas are intriguing, but not likely to happen. English the language of the [Korean] church? I can't see that is happening among the adults anytime soon. My personal belief is that multi-ethnicity is the answer, but there may be several solutions to this problem.

A revived church still needs people to minister to, and except in NY or LA, there aren't many English-speaking Koreans clustered in a single place. (June 2003)

In our English-speaking Korean SDA churches where family and tradition can maintain a semblance of a church while it is spiritually dead. I think these strategies (and others) contribute to the cyclical up/ down periods our churches experience. It seems the ups are often tied to when good leaders (usually a healthy college crowd) are available.

We need to reach beyond our Korean-American community if we want the gospel to impact as many people as we can. (June 2003)

He mentioned that minority cultures in North America have a certain predictable pattern of behavior until they become "indigenous." Personally I am insulted, but the point [he] makes gives me pause: Will Korean Americans continue to putter until they blend in, then be able to truly embrace multi-ethnic congregations, because we have reached a comfort level with our indigenous status? (July 2003)

You are right about the status of immigration in the US. But there is still a viable ministry in the Korean culture. Korean churches still can meet needs that make the Korean church still an important part of the future. The future is English, that is no doubt, and I think you give the older generation not enough credit. They have also seen the words on the walls, and they understand that the future is English.

I don't see the Korean Language ever being lost nor the culture, but split services and such is one way we can go...

Our church just spent $4000 on a transmitter system so I can speak the sermon in English while the Korean speaking [members] can listen to the sermon in Korean. Our church also has a 5–10 year plan, and thereby slowly changing of the main language to English, and our whole board of elders are in agreement. The future of our church is the 30s and 20s of today, and there must be a church ready for this group.

I have yet to see a mass exodus to Multi-cultural churches. Our church does have other ethnic [groups] i.e. Chinese, Filipino, and half, but we are a Korean church.

What I see as the biggest problem is not language but our system. Our old Korean SDA system. We have too many churches. We need to pool resources and create places of worship, that we can minister to a viable Korean ministry in many of our larger cities. We need to come out of the Korean social clubs of the past, and create the future church...whatever that may be. (August 2003)

Although I agree that God has used/employed many different strategies with Israel that were not his ideal, in looking at our model, God the son, while on earth—it seems that He crossed over many socioeconomic borders numerous times throughout his ministry—tax collectors, Samaritans, etc...the stories are almost endless. Although perhaps while on this earth we must work within our own boundaries, I still believe it is ideal to work within God's boundaries. Perhaps though, as it has been suggested by some, it is not the Koreanness of the church, but the fire within the church that is the limiting step.

I think it is amazing that your church board has agreed to this. Perhaps I do underestimate the adult church to some extent—but you are still one church. Do you believe that's going to happen with all churches? I still have my doubts.

I have not seen a mass exodus to any multi-cultural church yet either. Perhaps that is because the mass exodus has been out of the church altogether. At least that has been my limited experience unfortunately.

I will not dispute that there will be a need for a Korean church for many years to come, and that the Korean community has a need to be ministered to. However, I think that the English speaking population within the Korean church has a greater obligation than to itself. I also believe that with the talent that exists within our church, we could use it to further the work of Christ throughout the world on a greater level than we have been doing. Language barrier is one thing, but an only English speaking Korean church as the church of the future? I'm still not sold. Yes, there is work to be done within the Ko-Am community, but in many others as well. (August 2003)

We are not alone in converting to English. The Eugene church is already an English speaking church—they use their translators all the time. David Kim (soon to be ordained) is their senior pastor, and he does the whole service in English. The Glendale church has Pastor

Peter Ahn. He speaks Korean fluently, but he is under 40 and has a very good grasp of English and they are well under way of keeping their English speaking members....I believe this is the natural order of our Korean churches to not only survive, but thrive. I see many English speaking Adults wanting to come back to a Korean church, and when an English service and ministry is provided, I believe they will come back. So we are not throwing in the towel yet. There is still great potential.

What I see

#1 main senior pastor 40s English First

#2 2nd pastor (active or retired), 50s+ help with the Korean speaking members

#3 youth pastor 20s Fluent English language and culture; This is what I believe the future holds. (August 2003)

SUMMARY OBSERVATIONS

Among the second-generation Korean Adventists, there are three types of commitment to Korean churches. The first group is certain about their future commitment to their Korean churches while the second group is more circumspect about their future commitment. The last group has no intention of associating with the Korean churches. The survey results reveal a number of predictors as to what people are more likely to associate with the Korean churches in the future. At the time of the survey, three-fourths (75%) of the respondents stated that they would still attend a Korean church in twenty years. Therefore, if the future Korean American churches are able to meet the needs of members' personal and spiritual aspirations, they are more likely to continue to exist as distinctive ethnic churches. The challenge facing future Korean churches is that of developing capacities to convert the affirmative intent of their members into real commitment.

The extensive individual opinions expressed in the online debate may reflect their different experiences in the Korean churches, their observations, and their spiritual outlooks. The Korean Adventist community in North America has yet to engage in systematic collective debates on the future course of their churches. Once a consensus is reached, necessary plans and actions need to be implemented. The Korean Adventist churches established and maintained by the immigrant adults cannot continue as distinctive ethnic churches by default. The long-term goals and objectives of the church are to be clearly understood and pursued by members of future generations.

NOTES

1. The rising international status of the northeast Asian countries—mainly China, Japan, and Korea—will increase ethnic consciousness and pride among Asian Americans.

2. Members of Korean churches who identify themselves primarily as Americans or Canadians likely include non-Koreans who attend with their Korean spouses or friends.

3. The online discussions took place via the Empower Ministries website (www.empowerministry.com). Although Empower Ministries was created and has been maintained by the second-generation Korean Adventists, its mission is pan-ethnic. Its goal is "to support and develop Asian-American Seventh-day Adventist ministry in North America...."

4. Due to the time gap between the initial message and responses to it, the message posting is not in chronological order. Sometimes even replies to a response show a considerable time lag.

CHAPTER 9

Korean Pastors in the English Ministry

If an organization is as good as its leader, no group is more important than youth pastors for the Korean Adventist church in North America. In general, youth ministry is a challenging task at any church. But it is doubly so when pastors also have to deal with ethnic factors. The place of a youth pastor is unique in the two-language and two-culture Korean churches. They bridge the two groups by playing the role of mediator or conveyor.

In many churches, youth pastors are the peers of the group they serve. Intimately involved in the lives of the young people, they develop emotional and spiritual bonds with them. Because of communication difficulties and cultural misunderstandings with their parents, Korean youth often turn to their youth pastors with personal problems more readily than to their own family members.

Yet the Korean youth/young adult ministry faces three major problems: 1) youth occupy a marginal place in the Korean church; 2) there is lack of interest in ministry among second-generation members; and 3) many youth pastors hired by local churches do not receive full salary and benefits. Unless these problems are adequately addressed, the future of Korean churches in North America does not look encouraging. These points will be further discussed later.

The majority of youth pastors were born in Korea, and they came to North America with their parents at a young age. In this sense, they are 1.5-generation members with some bilingual and bicultural capacity. These youth pastors went through the typical life experiences of an immigrant family. For this reason, they are in a position to connect the two generations. Often, they are the conduits through which the desires and disappointments of each group are conveyed to the other. Sometimes, this go-between role may result in punishing the messenger if the message conveyed is not pleasant to the other party. Nevertheless, youth pastors help keep the cultural, language, and generation gaps from widening further. In spite of the critical position they hold in Korean churches, their work has not been appreciated as much as they deserve. The reasons are multiple and inherent in the Korean immigrant church.

First of all, the majority of Korean immigrant churches are still first-generation, adult-centered churches. Both administrative and financial matters of the church are mainly handled by the immigrant adults. This becomes a problem if the adults are not willing to share some of those responsibilities with second-generation members when they are ready. The Korean tradition to regard age as an important criterion in assigning responsibilities has something to do with this tendency. Although the age-old norm is changing rapidly at home, the immigrant church in North America seems slower to shift. Such an atmosphere results in youth pastors and lay leaders being taken less seriously by the church elders.

Secondly, youth pastors as a group are a minority in the Korean immigrant churches. A newly established church almost always hires a senior pastor for adults first. Only when the church can afford a second pastor do they consider hiring a youth pastor. As pointed out earlier, a high percentage of youth pastors are part-timers who are paid a token sum by local churches. Like anywhere else, those with part-time positions have limited clout. Furthermore, in a community where relationships tend to be vertical based on age, the young youth pastor is regarded as having less power in the organizational decision-making process.

Thirdly, youth pastors as a group have not formed a strong organizational base for their own place in the church. The Council of the Korean Adventist Church in North America created a position and allocated a budget for youth ministry after other major departments were established. The group is still somewhat marginal, and their opinions are considered as having less weight. Some church members have tried to make the concerns of youth more central in the church, thereby raising the standing of youth pastors. These efforts have not had great success thus far, but in time they may help to change the entrenched attitude of the people.

Fourthly, not many youth/young adult pastors see their ministry to youth as a lifelong commitment. Instead, youth ministry is considered a steppingstone to adult ministry. Such an attitude seems to be more evident among youth pastors who came to North America in their teens or college-age years. Their bilingual and bicultural abilities make the shift an easy option. Since the real decision-making power lies in the adult segment of the church, this becomes a tempting allurement.

Moreover, a considerable number of youth pastors revealed that they had other careers in mind when they began college. This career ambivalence generates less conviction and pride in their work for the second-generation members and their children. The Korean Adventist subculture has made health-related professions, such as medicine and dentistry, more attractive to young people. Often frustrated, some discouraged youth pastors pursue other fields, including health professions. This doesn't help attract or retain promising young people for second-generation ministry.

Finally, directly related to the above point, not many second-generation members consider ministry as their career choice. The lack of interest in ministry results in a shortage of Korean American pastors who can really understand the youth from their own perspective. Already some Korean churches have hired non-Korean pastors[1] or Korean pastors who came to North America in their twenties after finishing college in Korea. No matter how hard they work, they may not fully overcome the cultural gap between them and their congregations.

Who are the Korean pastors who serve English-speaking Korean Americans? What are their backgrounds? These and other questions were raised in a special separate survey conducted in 1998 for full-time and part-time Korean Adventist youth pastors. The survey included former youth pastors who are now in adult ministry in Korean or Anglo congregations. A few of them made career switches to other fields.

FINDINGS IN BRIEF

Of the 35 former pastors who responded to the survey, 89% were born in Korea. Only four were born in North America—two in the United States and two in Canada. Though it was a subjective self-evaluation, 63% of the youth pastors indicated that they were fluent in English whereas 43% were fluent in Korean. Seven of the 35 indicated that their ability to speak Korean is limited. All Korean youth pastors who participated in the survey were males. But this does not mean that there have never been female Korean youth pastors.

Of the 32 youth pastors who held a bachelor's degree, 26 (81%) received theirs from a college or university in North America, and six (19%) obtained their degrees in Korea. A total of 21 pastors hold a master's degree: seven hold either a Master of Arts or a Master of Science and 14 hold a Master of Divinity (most likely from the Seventh-day Adventist Theological Seminary at Andrews University). About 69% of the pastors majored in religion/theology/ministry before they started in Korean youth ministry. This means that about 30% began their ministry without proper theological and ministerial training. Only slightly over one-third (37%) of the group set out to pursue ministry without considering another career. For the majority of the youth pastors, ministry was not their first career choice.

Six (17%) pastors had started in youth ministry, perhaps as a voluntary or part-time leader, before they reached the age of 20. On the other hand, three (9%) began working in youth ministry in their thirties. The average age for starting in youth ministry was 23. More than half (57%) became involved in Korean youth ministry while attending college. Apparently, their spiritual leadership qualities were noticed during their college years, perhaps because of their major or commitment to the ministry. When there was a call for youth ministry, only 13 (38%) responded with the intent to specialize in youth ministry (or second-generation English ministry). Almost one in three (32%) used the opportunity as a steppingstone to adult ministry. The remainder

(30%) entered the Korean youth ministry without a clear conviction about their calling.

Two-thirds of the parents (66%) supported their children's decision to become ministers while six in ten youth pastors (59%) received encouragement from their siblings. Three in four youth pastors reported that they were encouraged to become ministers by the members of their church. Most of their close friends (79%) also supported their decision to enter the ministry. Of the 25 married youth pastors who responded to the survey, three out of four (76%) were encouraged to pursue ministry by their spouses. Conversely, one in four youth pastors faced some discouragement from their wives.

At the time of the survey (1998), slightly over half (54%) of the youth pastors had served five or fewer years. Those who served between six and ten years comprised about one third (34%). Four (12%) had been in Korean youth ministry for more than ten years. The longest service in the Korean youth ministry was 11 years. Only six (17%) youth pastors received a full-time salary and benefits from their conferences when they entered the Korean youth ministry. Two others were given a full salary and benefits by their local churches. The rest began with a stipend or no pay at all.

Seven in ten pastors were satisfied with the Korean youth ministry. These results differ significantly from how youth pastors view the satisfaction of their colleagues. Fewer than half (41%) of the respondents think that their fellow ministers seem to be satisfied with their profession. Seven in ten Korean youth pastors are likely to give their blessing if their children want to pursue ministry as a career. Only four in ten youth pastors, however, would approve without any reservation or hesitation. Seven in ten youth pastors would be supportive if one of their children wanted to marry a Korean pastor in North America. Eight youth pastors (25%), on the other hand, are not sure if they would encourage such a marital decision by their children.

YOUTH PASTORS' MOTIVATION TO ENTER THE MINISTRY

The majority of Korean youth pastors seem to have entered the youth ministry with a sense of conviction. A few, however, used the youth ministry as grounds for testing their fitness for ministry. After a while, some left the ministry altogether in pursuit of other careers.

Some saw youth ministry as a steppingstone to adult ministry. They accepted the call to youth ministry because they saw no opportunity for Korean-speaking adult ministry when they finished their theological training. Usually they were the ones who had completed additional theological education in North America after a few years of ministry in Korea. At the same time, some of the pastors sensed the urgency for youth at the Korean churches. A few felt a burden to preserve the virtues of the Korean culture in the coming generations. They saw their roles as cultural purveyors. Thus their motivations for entering the ministry varied.

A steady supply of high-quality, second-generation pastors is the key to the successful continuation of the Korean church in the future. This need is more critical during the transition from the first generation to the second generation as the youth pastors play the role of mediators. Their vision, commitment, and influence will determine the direction and shape of the future Korean church.

The Korean churches in North America face three major challenges in developing quality second-generation ministers. First is the lack of interest in the Korean ministry among second-generation members. The upward mobility-minded Korean youth tend to avoid ministry in favor of financially rewarding careers, such as engineering, business, and the healthcare professions. Hardly any American-raised or American-born Korean women consider pursuing theology, let alone local church ministry. Often male youth pastors experience difficulties trying to find a Korean woman who is willing to bear the burden of being a pastor's wife.

Secondly, many local churches cannot provide regular full-time employment to their youth pastors. It is not uncommon for youth pastors to work under a temporary, part-time status. Some of the youth pastors are contract pastors recognized by local conferences, and often their salaries are provided by the local churches they work for. It is quite discouraging to be less recognized and compensated than others with the same professional qualifications.

Finally, discord at Korean churches turns off some promising future pastors. Of course, this is not a unique phenomenon to Korean churches. Most immigrant churches, however, are more likely to experience internal conflicts in an early phase of establishing themselves. In addition, the intergenerational conflicts at home and in church affect the perception of some prospective second-generation ministers. A few youth pastors changed their careers after a few years of disappointing experiences at Korean churches.

The statements below reflect the youth pastors' motives for entering the ministry.

In Their Own Words: Youth Pastors' Motives for Entering the Ministry

- "To give back to people for what God has given to me. To train young people to become leaders for the future. To encourage the beauty of our Korean culture."
- "Needed to understand the Korean youth and their culture. Needed to be a bridge between both parents and youths."
- "Felt burdened on the spiritual deficiencies of Korean youth. Felt annoyed by the typical Korean adults."
- "Grew up thinking only about becoming a minister. To become an effective teacher and elucidate Christianity for the modern age."
- "I felt that God was distinctly calling me. That was the only reason other than it being a stepping stone to adult ministry."
- "Testing a calling to the ministry. Part-time side income."
- "I was mindless about the motives of entering. I felt called to be a pastor but I retaliated."

THOSE WHO LEFT THE KOREAN YOUTH MINISTRY

A separate supplementary survey was conducted among Korean youth pastors who had left the youth ministry. Special efforts were made to reach everyone, Korean and non-Korean, who had worked at a Korean church for at least six months. Fifteen former Korean youth pastors responded.

According to their reports, leaving the Korean youth ministry was primarily their own choice. In most cases, the youth pastors left to take a position as senior pastor. Ten of the former Korean youth pastors are now in adult ministry as they are comfortable with the Korean language, although their English was not an issue in youth ministry. One survey respondent is in teaching, two are in health professions, and one is in another field. Though at the time of this survey only one respondent was in teaching, as of 2007, five former Korean youth pastors were teaching at Adventist colleges and universities in North America.

The circumstances under which they left the Korean youth ministry were less than desirable, however. At the time, they were not happy in the Korean youth ministry. Some of the reasons for leaving youth ministry include "inability"; "dissatisfaction"; "economic unfairness"; "occasioned by unfavorable circumstances"; "did not see any future as my career"; "did not enjoy a small church society"; "too discouraging"; "burn-out"; "lack of sense of achievement as a pastor"; "no future"; "no financial support"; "church nepotism"; and "frustrated and angry with youth ministry with last chance."

As they look back on their decisions to leave the youth ministry, the former pastors feel a combination of relief and guilt. Here are some individual comments: "well done"; "someday I will be back into ministry when I am more motivated"; "no difference"; "guilty"; "not bad at all"; "relieved"; "feel burdened"; "very comfortable"; "I only followed God's calling in His providence"; "I am not sure."

The former youth pastors were generous in offering advice to current Korean youth pastors, parents, and church members. Their advice reflects their own experiences and provides useful insights and instructions.

In Their Own Words: Advice to Youth Pastors

- "Expect the Korean conflicts. Succeed in developing a strong church plan of youth."
- "Remember being a pastor is not so much what you do but who you are. Let your ministry be an extension of your inner life. Read at least three books on the subject before you preach…never stop studying."
- "Pursue team ministry in some form. Parents need the most amount of education; include them in your ministry."
- "Learn to speak Korean."
- "Do not be a baby-sitter or an orphan director. Don't talk about issues, but conversion and relationship with God."

- "Assuming your spiritual life is rock solid…be open minded, read widely, become more well read than anyone else in the church. Intellectual competence and superiority is important….Learn their language and their prevailing humorous perspectives. This is the language that the youth will listen to, this is the language that they speak."

- "Read widely and understand the culture and language. Practice what you preach. Mentor the one lost sheep—it is worth all the other hassle."

- "Be prepared to occupy the senior position (learn language and culture). Stay firmly now and God is in charge."

In Their Own Words: Advice to Parents and Church Members

- "Be exhaustive in support of them [youth pastors]. Give them professional freedom."

- "Don't depend on youth pastors for the spiritual growth of the children. Take a deep breath and get a big picture: sometimes realize that some are just going through the phases. Be consistent in installing Christian values and life styles. Respect youth pastor—show it to your children."

- "Get involved fully in all aspects of youth ministry. Make youth ministry the most important mission field."

- "No advice, they are not open to change."

- "Spiritual gifts are biblical: hence don't all become doctors. Managed health care will stifle your hopes. Someday you will die! So don't just prepare a good life, but prepare a good death."

- "Our youth have lots of hurts which need to be healed and can be healed by the help of their parents and churches. Then they can grow as a mature, effective Christians. Be an example to them. They need to see and feel it. Be real Christians."

- "Make time for your kids, not money."

FUTURE LAY LEADERSHIP

From its beginning, the Adventist denomination has maintained a congregational type of church. In the early Adventist church, the role of lay people was prominent. In fact, the majority of the church's

pioneers and founders were lay people without much clerical training. The development of trained pastors in church ministry came only
after the establishment of higher educational institutions. Moreover,
Adventists are told that the final work of the church will be carried out
by lay people. This prophetic message has led lay people to regard their
place as important in the church. A healthy growing church requires
combined leadership efforts of trained ministers and lay leaders.

A mutually nurturing and supportive relationship between the
two groups can create a healthy environment for church growth. In
the context of the Korean Adventist church in North America, good
lay leaders can help a young youth pastor overcome many challenges
and continue to mature personally and professionally. At the same
time, good pastors can help lay people grow in their spiritual and leadership development. At some Korean churches, there are dedicated
young professionals who render support to their youth pastors.

Most small Korean Adventist churches can only dream of finding a reliable lay youth leader. Often, these churches cannot afford
a full-time youth pastor due to financial difficulties. Even if they can
afford to hire a youth pastor, it is not easy to find a qualified Korean
youth pastor with proper training and cultural background. As a result,
cultivation of lay leadership is crucial to the development of second-
generation churches, especially for small congregations in medium-size
cities. This requires steady and systematic support for leadership training programs and implementation. In turn, such a program requires
reliable financial commitment and training of leaders. Therefore, the
development of such a program may be possible as a collaborative
effort under the coordination of the Korean Church Council.

Some youth pastors realize the importance of training lay leaders
and offer a training program. Empower Ministry is such an attempt,
targeting potential youth lay leaders. A group of youth pastors has
been training youth lay leaders through this program since 2002.
Although the main purpose of the Korean American Youth Adventist
Missionary Movement (KAYAMM) is to offer spiritual awakening
through short-term overseas mission service experiences, it may also
be viewed as a training program.

A brief overview of the subject as expressed in the survey is presented here.

Findings in Brief

As shown in Figures 9.1 and 9.2, more than half of the second-generation Korean youth (51% male, 59% female) want a career in a healthcare profession. Only three in 100 males consider ministry as a possible future career.

Although it is self evaluation, seven in ten respondents consider themselves active in church life. As Figure 9.3 displays, about one third of the group is indifferent to church activities. As shown in Figure 9.4, six in ten are interested in assuming some kind of lay leadership role in the Korean church. On the other hand, three in ten are not interested in any church leadership role at all. Six percent of the participants show an interest in the idea of part-time ministry while pursuing a different profession.

In Their Own Words:"What do you like about your Korean church?"

*   "I love my youth pastor. I like the worship programs." –*A Korean-born 17-year-old youth in New Jersey*

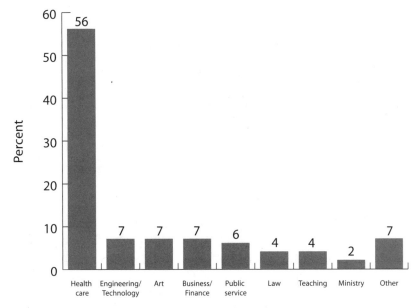

Figure 9.1 Present and Future Career Choice (N=966)

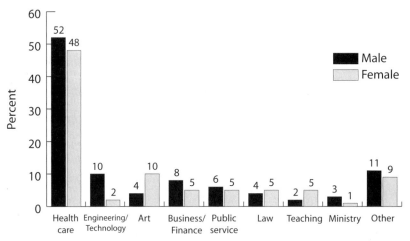

Figure 9.2 Career Choice by Gender (N=966)

- "Young people are sincere and friendly. Good lay leader who loves the Lord." –*A Korean-born 31-year-old male in Illinois*
- "The new pastor—he is fluent in English and really makes an effort to know everybody and get us involved." –*An American-born 20-year-old female in the Southeast*

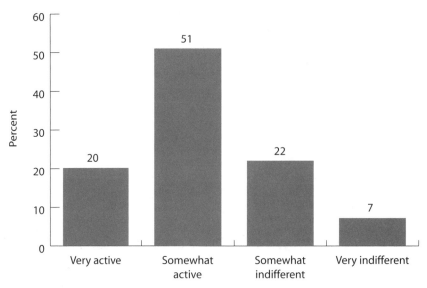

Figure 9.3 Present Commitment to Church Activities (N=987)

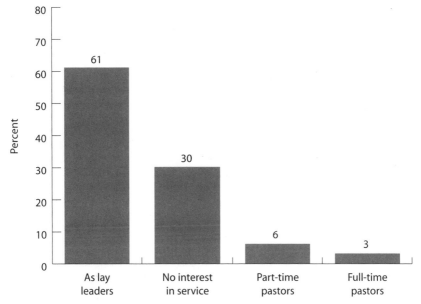

Figure 9.4 Future Service to Korean Church (N=974)

In Their Own Words: "What do you dislike about your Korean church?"

- "No youth pastor. Apathy." *–An American-born 20-year-old male in Illinois*

- "I wish we had a youth pastor, but our church cannot afford one right now." *–An American-born 21-year-old female in the South*

- "The youth pastor is not American enough." *–An American-born 27-year-old female in S. California*

- "Too much changing (turn-over) in youth pastor." *–A Korean-born male in the Northwest*

- "...intellectual stagnation is a product of spiritual stagnation. Lack of quality leadership—there are not enough qualified youth pastors." *–An American-born 17-year-old female in Florida*

- "The way they often treat their pastors. Head-strong stubborn Korean elders." *–A Korean-born 34-year-old male in S. California*

- "Would like to see more outreach. Would like to see more in reach. Would like a youth pastor or lay leader." *–A Korean-born 25-year-old female in the Southeast*

SUMMARY OBSERVATIONS

The group most crucial to the successful continuation of Korean Adventist churches in North America is those in second-generation ministry. Their role is critical as they provide a bridge between the immigrant generation and ensuing generations. No faith community can prosper without committed competent ministerial leadership. Yet prospective second-generation Korean Adventists considering ministry at Korean churches encounter a number of challenges. Unless they overcome the attraction of other professions (particularly the health-related ones), the conflicting demands of different generations, and inadequate compensation for their chosen work, not many will venture into ministry in Korean churches. Until the challenges are properly addressed at the community level, recruiting and retaining qualified pastoral candidates will continue to be a problem. It is ironic that the Korean churches at home face an oversupply of theology graduates while their counterparts in North America struggle to meet their demands. A dozen Korean churches in North America have non-Korean pastors for their second-generation members. As much as possible, the Korean churches need pastors who can help establish both the ethnic and spiritual identity of their members. At the same time, a centralized systematic training of lay leaders appears to be urgent in view of the shortage of second-generation pastors.

NOTE

1. The membership directory compiled in 2005 reports that ten non-Korean pastors were serving in English ministry at Korean churches.

CHAPTER 10

Summary, Prospect, and Suggestions

We have looked at the Korean Adventist Church in North America from both historical and empirical perspectives. The main concern of this study was the relationship between ethnicity and religion in the context of Korean American Adventist churches. A more specific concern was the continuation of the Korean ethnic church in the second and later generations. The underlying assumption is that the viability of an ethnic church may depend on its ability to meet the needs of church members, and their needs are primarily spiritual and cultural. Whether deliberate or not, ethnic churches address the cultural aspect in a pluralistic society.

More than 1,000 second-generation Korean Adventists in the United States and Canada provided the empirical data for this study. They shared their views on the Korean Adventist church by responding to survey questions. In this summary, we look mainly at the two dimensions of ethnicity and spirituality.

Some of the Korean Adventist churches in North America have already reached the crossroads of the generation shift, and others have been approaching it steadily. The demographic and cultural changes are reshaping the landscape of these churches. In some churches, the size of the Korean-born, Korean-speaking members is decreasing in relation to their children and grandchildren who keep growing in number and influence. The future of the Korean Adventist church in

North America may largely depend on the desires of upcoming generations of members in remaining and retaining their Korean identity. Even if they do, the extent and shape of their Korean identity is uncertain.

Many elements and forces will affect the demographic and cultural components of these Korean churches in the future. This survey project has yielded valuable information and insights about the attitudes and experiences of church life among second-generation Korean Adventists. Since the Korean church is basically an "ethno-religious group," this summary is divided into ethnic and spiritual dimensions.

ETHNICITY

According to the survey, Korean Adventist youth strongly desire to maintain their Korean identity. This is measured by a number of indicators, including self ethnic identity, ethnic pride, a desire to learn Korean for themselves and teach Korean to their children, a wish to marry Koreans, the scope of the Korean friendship network, their present relationship with the Korean church, and their intent to associate with the Korean church in the future. About 80 percent of the survey respondents showed a desire to maintain their Korean identity, as evidenced by the above indicators.

This phenomenon is not unique only to second-generation Korean Adventists but also reflects the general trend among the other Asian American youth groups reviewed in chapter 5. This is a relatively new phenomenon among the children of the post–1965 Asian immigrants, resulting from numerous developments at both national and international levels.

In these increasingly pluralistic societies where ethnic diversity is looked upon as a source of strength rather than a disadvantage, the members of minority communities are more inclined to preserve their ethnic heritages. The former melting-pot image of America has been replaced with the salad bowl (or mosaic) image where each piece retains its unique shape, color, and texture. This has resulted primarily from the shift in cultural policy from that of assimilation to cultural pluralism.

In addition, the development of the global village effectively reinforces home cultures upon overseas diasporas wherever they are. Regardless of physical locations, immigrants are now able to simultaneously participate in both their home and host cultures. Satellite-link, Internet, email, fax, telephone, newspapers, and jumbo jets are powerful agents of cultural reinforcement upon overseas compatriots. The Koreans in North America are no exception in this powerful transnational life experience. In fact, Koreans are one of the most savvy peoples utilizing information-age technology.

The international status of one's "mother country" also plays a key role in instilling a sense of national or ethnic pride among its overseas nationals. In the case of overseas Koreans, their mother country has enjoyed international prestige for its impressive economic growth, known as the miracle of Han River.[1] Although it had a serious setback in 1997 when the country suddenly found itself in a grave economic condition due to the IMF crisis,[2] South Korea today is the world's eleventh largest economy. The country was also the site of the highly successful 1988 summer Olympics, and a co-sponsor[3] of the World Cup (soccer) tournament in 2002. These two famous worldwide events have enhanced South Korea's national image. Thus, one can easily imagine the psychological impact of the sports events upon the overseas Koreans, especially the young Koreans. Undoubtedly, the rising influence of East Asian nations beginning in the late twentieth century—notably China, Japan, and Korea—in both economic and political arenas has changed the self-perception of many East Asians residing in the United States and Canada.

Finally, there are approximately 4,000 Korean Christian churches in North America that serve as powerful cultural preservers and transmitters. Although the primary function of these churches is to meet the spiritual needs of the members, the sociocultural impact of these churches is unmistakably strong. Every time one worships with a Korean congregation, that person is reminded of his or her Korean origins. In addition, many Korean churches engage in "ethnicity reproduction" in their worship and activities. It can be assumed, therefore, that the desire to retain the Korean identity among second-generation members will remain strong unless the above-mentioned trends are drastically reversed in the foreseeable future.

The findings of this study confirm what social scientists call the phenomenon of "adhesive assimilation" by integrating the elements of two cultures. Like other Asian American groups, most of the Korean Adventist youth in this study may want to be Korean Americans by integrating some aspects of the two cultures. Emphasis on family, education, and hard work, for instance, are a few of the trademark Korean values. At the same time, Korean Americans should be careful lest they incline to be ethnocentric, which may breed a sense of exclusivity, only in-group loyalty, and a tendency to be inward-looking. "Ethnic particularism" may impede healthy development of individuals and their community as a whole (Chai in Kwon, Kim, and Warner 2001:157–180).

SPIRITUALITY

Among the second-generation members, support for their Korean churches appeared to be solid at the time of the survey. This was measured by a number of indicators, including regularity of church attendance, positive evaluation of their Korean church, probability of choosing a Korean church over other churches under hypothetical circumstances, desire to associate with a Korean church in the future, and other factors that are indicative of church support.

It is not clear, however, whether their support for the Korean church is unconditional. In other words, no one can assume that individuals of Korean ancestry will automatically attach themselves to Korean churches. Ethnicity can push one only so far. If the conditions of their churches change, their support for those churches could also change. Simply put, the fact that they regard themselves as Koreans may not assure their support for their childhood churches in the future.

Their long-term support may depend on their church's abilities to meet their spiritual needs on a continual basis. If they are not satisfied with what their Korean church offers, they may consider searching for another church that can better meet their spiritual needs. Unlike their parents who were handicapped with language barriers and social unfamiliarity, the second-generation members and their children may be more willing to look for a church beyond their ethnic boundary. To any sincere Christian, the choice between authentic spiritual growth and ethnic attachment should be clear.

In spite of the solid indications that second-generation members desire to retain their Korean identity, statistics and anecdotal information from the survey show a rather low satisfaction with their church life. This is more evident among the older participants as they tend to be more analytical and critical about the programs and operations of their churches. Dissatisfaction with church life seems to stem from a host of sources: the communication gap aggravated by language and cultural barriers, their negative view of the overall spiritual condition of the Korean Adventist churches, the exclusive and isolating tendencies of their ethnic churches, disharmony and conflict caused by church politics, uninspiring worship programs, and the absence or inadequacy of pastoral leadership for English ministry.

The way members have reacted to their dissatisfaction with church life has been varied. Some have tried non-Korean churches while others have sought changes in their own churches. A few groups have resorted to establishing their own independent churches apart from their parents' churches. An unknown number of second-generation members have stopped attending church altogether. This usually happens after high school.

It is a great challenge for the Korean churches to keep both language groups satisfied with their church life. The future of these churches, however, largely depends upon the satisfaction of second-generation members and their children with their spiritual life at home and church. Satisfaction begets commitment.

APPLICATIONS OF THE FINDINGS

One may wonder how the Korean church should respond to the contrary tendencies among the second-generation members. The desire to retain their ethnic identity is strong while they are not so content with their church life. Most participants identify themselves as Korean and associate with their Korean churches as an expression of their ethnic identity. Yet they are not satisfied with what the church offers for their spiritual growth and development. This may not be a unique challenge facing only the Korean Adventist church in North America, but a universal problem facing most churches as far as youth and young adults are concerned. Their desire to maintain Korean identity may pull them to the Korean church, but their discontent may push them from the church. This may cause tension and uneasiness among the members. This tension can be eased only by improving the church environment and its programs to satisfy the spiritual longing of the members.

Using the two dimensions of the Korean church—ethnicity and spirituality—different types of ethnic churches are described in Table 10.1. Such a scheme may help to describe different characteristics of ethnic churches. The four types described here are a mere approximation. In other words, no church may perfectly fit in a specific type described. Nevertheless, such a conceptual model may help us to picture a local ethnic church and the effects of each type.

Table 10.1 Types of Ethnic Churches

Types	Ethnicity	Spirituality
Authentic Ethnic Church	Strong	Strong
Lopsided Ethnic Church	Strong	Weak
Open Church	Weak	Strong
Failing Church	Weak	Weak

It needs to be made clear that ethnicity and spirituality are not to be equated. The two are not equals in weight and importance by any means. Ethnicity is merely an adjective that characterizes the demographic composition of a congregation. The spiritual dimension is central to a church, and the cultural dimension is secondary, even peripheral. The ethnicity of a church may change depending on membership composition or people's preference, but not the spirituality. The relationship of the two may be compared to that of body and clothes. Clothes may be likened to a culture that may change to reflect wearers' taste.

To help understand each type of ethnic church better, historical examples are used.

Authentic Ethnic Church

If a group of people wants to maintain a community of faith along with their nationality or ethnicity either because of a language barrier, imposed segregation by a dominant group, or a desire to preserve their cultural heritage, then the ethnicity of the church members becomes an important element. An authentic ethnic church is one in which its members affirm both their spiritual and cultural identities. The members appreciate their churches because the churches enrich and reinforce members' cultural heritage in the context of spiritual life. Here the spiritual message may be presented and interpreted in specific cultural terms, thus making the church relevant to the ethnic experiences of its members. They clearly see their unique place and contribution in the multiethnic society. Thus the two dimensions are mutually enhancing and reinforcing.

Many African American churches have maintained both their ethnic and spiritual heritages. These churches have tried to be relevant to the spiritual and social needs of their people. Often, they have become spokespersons for their communities to the larger society. The civil rights movement, black theology, and Negro spirituals are some of their contributions to American spiritual and social life.

Historically, the Jewish diaspora, especially the orthodox and conservative branches, have used their synagogues as both spiritual and cultural preservers. The rabbi has become the central figure in these efforts. In this type of church, both spirituality and ethnicity are incorporated. The spirituality of these faith communities is contained in their cultural wrap.

Lopsided Ethnic Church

The lopsided ethnic church maintains its ethnicity often at the expense of the spiritual growth and development of its members. This may not be intentional, but emphasis on ethnicity can stifle spiritual growth by limiting access to more rewarding religious experiences elsewhere. The language barrier with the larger society results in social isolation which may block the flow of people and ideas. Usually, a lack of resources to promote spiritual growth is the major cause of the ethnicity-heavy/spirituality-light problems. A small immigrant church in a small ethnic community is more likely to be in this situation due to resource limitations.

This type of church is also more common among the first-generation immigrant churches in which second- and third-generation members have no choice but to stay with their parents' churches. The children and grandchildren of the foreign-born parents are pressured to stay within their ethnic community. Either out of obedience, face-saving, or guilt, some of the children may feel obliged to maintain their memberships in the ethnic churches. Some may even feel trapped in ethnic ghettos. They maintain their fidelity to their ethnic church at the expense of their own spiritual growth. This type of church may continue, but only so long as its members tolerate the isolation and inadequacy of their ethnic church for personal or family reasons.

Open Church

When the membership of an ethnic church shrinks in the course of time, the formerly language-specific or culture-specific church becomes open to anyone regardless of national or cultural identity. In this church, the importance of ethnicity as a membership criterion diminishes as it becomes more like any other mainstream church.

This usually happens in second- or third-generation ethnic churches where English is the common language and the members are comfortable blending with others. As there is no emphasis or preference on a specific national or language group, the formation of such a congregation is the result of a natural flow of people in a given area. In a limited sense, the Pan-Asian churches in California are examples of the open church. The descendants of various Asian groups compose the majority of such a church.

Others are more intentional in making their once ethnic-specific church an open church for theological reasons. They believe that the great gospel commission reaches to all people, not a specific group, and they remove all forms of artificial barriers. The church embodying Christ transcends all human cultures.

Failing Church

A failing ethnic church neither preserves the cultural heritage of its members nor nurtures their spirituality. Originally the members joined the church due to their ethnicity, but they do not find any satisfaction in such a church. Eventually they move their membership to other churches. In the end, the church is forced to either merge with another church and lose its original ethnic marks or close its doors for good.

It is possible for a church to change from one type of ethnic church to another. A shift may be triggered by membership changes, external conditions, theological emphasis, or other factors. The change may take place in a linear fashion from an authentic ethnic church to an open church, or the change may happen in an unpredictable manner. In some cases, a church may be locked into one type for a long time.

The four ethnic church types portrayed here are somewhat similar to the options Jeung (2002:216) used in describing a church choice. According to him, an Asian American may choose one of the following options: remain in an ethnic church, join either a pan-ethnic Asian church or a mainstream church, or quit attending church. In a somewhat different vein, the commonly accepted Asian American identity types may shed light on the same subject: "traditionalists," "assimilationists," "bi-cultural," and "marginal" (Cha 2001:152).

The four types of ethnic churches proposed above help to evaluate the conditions of ethnic churches in terms of spiritual and cultural dimensions.

TYPES OF KOREAN ADVENTIST CHURCHES

If a group of Korean Adventists starts a new church and chooses to call themselves a Korean church (e.g., Cleveland Korean Adventist Church), then they are identifying themselves as an ethnic church. Whether they are first-generation immigrants or second-generation Korean-Americans speaking English, they take ethnic identity, their Korean-ness, seriously. The identity mark announces who they are and even what they may want to be in cultural terms. Therefore, an authentic Korean Adventist church in North America wants to meet both the spiritual and ethnic aspirations of its members. The desire to meet both needs is more apparent among second-generation members and their children because they deliberately choose the Korean component in their church identity.

The findings of the Vision 2020 project seem to suggest that the majority of second-generation members are looking for a church that can meet their personal, cultural, social, and spiritual needs. In other words, they want to see their Korean church as a place where they can be enriched culturally, socially, as well as spiritually.

Unfortunately, some Korean Adventist churches fall in the category of the lopsided ethnic church as they fail to spiritually nurture their members. Such imbalance may be due to the small size of the church, heavy adult membership, an emphasis on cultural issues over spiritual issues, a lack of youth leadership and quality programs, and isolation from other churches. Small and isolated churches are more likely to face this situation. The ethnicity of the congregation may attract some Koreans, but the church fails to measure up to their spiritual expectations.

In reality, very few second-generation Korean groups or congregations are exclusively Korean. Many second-generation Korean groups show the presence of non-Koreans through the use of English in their worship and other activities. At present, the percentage of non-Koreans in most churches is very low, but their presence is bound to increase in the course of time. Intermarriage is presently the main source for bringing in non-Korean members.

Some leaders are actively promoting the concept of open church by de-emphasizing (or de-ethnicizing) the Korean aspects in membership and programs. A few English-speaking Korean congregations have attempted to be open churches. Some of them have removed the name "Korean" from their church title. Such an act is more than symbolic. In some quarters, the move to stay away from Koreanness has met resistance. Those who oppose a removal of the Korean name long to preserve the Korean identity for their church as well as for themselves. As reported with other groups, this tendency is more common among married couples who have children. They are looking for cultural ground in a religious context on which they can build their children's cultural (or ethnic) identity. If they have a choice to move to another Korean church in the same town, the problem can be solved. If not, the issue can be a source of contention within the church.

The open church concept is less likely to take hold if an English-speaking congregation is affiliated with its mother church. Studies have shown that most Asian Americans wish to affiliate with the Asian American faith community, if not their own ethnic-specific community. They are half-open by moving away from their own ethnic community, but remain half-closed by staying within the larger Asian American community.

A few Korean groups have closed their church doors for a lack of membership. Some merged with other congregations. The former usually happens in small communities while merges typically occur in large metropolitan areas.

A second-generation group with adequate support can be an authentic ethnic church that confirms both personal and religious identities. In this regard, some dynamic African American or Hispanic churches may serve as models. Sources of support include pastoral leadership, program development, physical space, and finances. The real challenge, however, lies in the desire and dedication of involved members to make this happen.

Of the four types of churches described, the most desirable one for the twenty-first-century Korean Americans is the authentic ethnic church. It is not an ethnocentric church but an ethnic-relevant church. Recent research findings support this direction for the reasons already discussed in this book.

It is time for the Korean church to rearticulate its reasons for continuous existence as a distinct ethnic church in North America. Korean Adventist members of all generations should engage in open dialogue on the future of their church. The social milieu is favorable for their continuous existence, but the Korean church members must identify their own needs and determine their future direction. Do the Korean Adventists in North America want to make the future Korean church relevant to the social needs of its members by presenting

"Christ in culture" or "Christ over culture" (Niebuhr 1951)? Do they want be an ethnically particular church or a universally open church? The choice is theirs.

IDEALS FOR THE SECOND-GENERATION KOREAN CHURCH

Like any other growing and dynamic church, the Korean Adventist church in North America should be able to respond to the desires of its members. A church that chooses to remain Korean ought to demonstrate the following qualities:

Affirming: Through church life, members affirm both their Adventist Christian faith and their Korean identity. The programs at these churches are spiritually uplifting and culturally relevant. Those who want to identify themselves and their children as Korean Americans should benefit from such cultural relevance in church life.

Growing: The church helps its members grow personally, socially, and spiritually by providing a stimulating environment. The church keeps reviewing what it has been doing and envisioning what it has to anticipate in order to remain alert and not stagnate. In response to the changing needs of its members, the church is open to new ideas and approaches. The members discover new aspects of their faith and cultural experiences. It is important, therefore, not to be trapped in traditions that have become irrelevant to the needs of the growing congregation.

Exciting: The church is supposed to be an exciting place where its members experience the joy and happiness of Christian faith. The messages they receive, the interactions they engage in, and the services they participate in generate authentic Christian excitement. Thus, attending the Korean church is one's own choice, not a decision forced by family ties or social pressures. It is one's willful affiliation, as opposed to filiation along one's ancestry line. Indeed, people enjoy the community of their faith and are proud of being members of that particular ethnic community.

Challenging: At the same time, the church helps its members become actively engaged with a new vision, mission, and action. The members clearly understand the primary and secondary concerns of their churches in their vision and mission. The ethnic church avoids being a cocoon where the members feel cozy and are insulated from the challenges of the larger society. The members engage in outreach programs to their neighbors and Korean communities in North America and elsewhere.

The Korean Adventist church in North America ought to be conscious about its image to the members of future generations. Instead of protecting a tradition-bound and exclusive small stagnant community of graying members, the church could project the image of a dynamic transforming community for all age groups. This applies to all communities of faith, but it is far more crucial to an immigrant ethnic community when it comes to attracting members of younger generations.

REORIENTATION OF THE KOREAN CHURCH FOR SECOND-GENERATION MEMBERS

The Korean Adventist church in North America is at the crossroads of a generational shift. This forces members to reexamine their orientation and priorities, which is necessary to make the church more relevant to the concerns of the upcoming generations. They may need a new church structure with different perspectives and programs. When a second- or third-generation Korean wants to join a Korean church over many other choices, that decision should be understood as an expressed desire to establish one's identity and community. This should not be overlooked.

Root-nurturing

Although it is not the primary function of the church to nurture ethnicity, the cultural needs of its members are to be reflected in church life. It is desirable for a church to provide a healthy sense of one's roots. The first-generation members take their culture for granted, but the members of the second and later generations need to learn about their heritage. One's cultural learning may come from many sources, including church life. But not many sources are as regular and dependable as ethnic churches.

The history of Christianity and Adventism in Korea, for example, should be reviewed from time to time. The story of struggling

Korean Christians during times of tribulation can be the source of inspiration. Special Korean holidays, such as the autumn moon festival and the lunar new year, can be celebrated in the Christian context. Major Korean historical events like the liberation of Korea from the Japanese colonial occupation in 1945 can be remembered and used to draw valuable spiritual lessons. The life stories of first-generation immigrants are interesting sources. The key to success with this approach is a systematic, intentional plan and preparation.

Response to Dual Identity

A majority of those who attend Korean churches in North America may desire to have an integrated (or hyphenated) identity: Korean-American or Korean-Canadian. Wherever possible, the church helps its members reduce identity uneasiness caused by duality. Help can be given by improving the church programs that focus on satisfying the spiritual longing of the members to harmoniously blend the two cultures and life experiences. Balanced exposure to and participation in the two communities will assist the integration. The leaders may develop special educational and training programs for value integrations. The biblical figures of Joseph and Daniel are good examples of dual identity: Hebrew-Egyptian and Hebrew-Babylonian.

Restructuring

As the Korean church is in transition, it needs to look at its existing organizational structures and programs. Also, the organizational goals and priorities need to be re-examined. The church must then carefully evaluate the effectiveness of the structure in responding to the needs of the members, particularly the second-generation members and their children. If necessary, bold organizational rearrangements should be attempted to maximize the church's ability to serve its members of the next generation. This is a major organizational challenge that requires strong leadership and even sacrifices on the part of the immigrant generation. The church council should coordinate the efforts to restructure the organizational arrangement at local, regional, and division levels. The key concern should be making the church more relevant to the members of upcoming generations.

Interaction

The Korean church should avoid being a closed ethnic ghetto. Overcoming this tendency, it actively engages in interaction and exchanges with other churches beyond its own national and cultural boundaries. Moreover, it is involved with the larger communities— Korean and non-Korean, Adventist and non-Adventist—for worthy causes. This way the church might be refreshed and reinvigorated by its openness to new ideas and experiences.

If the Korean Adventist churches in North America want to remain authentic ethnic churches as described previously, they need to contextualize their Christianity and make it relevant to the cultural needs of their members. The ethnic dimension of these churches is not a mere accident of the immigrant members and their family ties, but a meaningful part of their faith.

SPECIFIC RECOMMENDATIONS FOR ACTION

Below are some specific recommendations for action. They are intended to pave the way for second-generation members and their children to remain committed to their Korean churches.

Mission Statement

The Korean church as a whole needs a clear mission statement that articulates the reasons for its continuous existence as a distinct ethnic church in North America. The mission statement should take into account the concerns of the second-generation members and their children. In addition, each local church should produce its own mission statement that is relevant to its unique local conditions within the framework of the overall mission statement.

Creating an overall mission statement requires a joint effort among members of different generations. The Korean Church Council of North America should lead in establishing an overall mission statement. Such a mission statement will provide a sense of direction among the church members who choose to join or remain with their Korean churches.

Goal Setting

Once an overall mission statement is adopted, the Korean church should establish specific goals for a period of time (e.g., five, ten, or twenty years). The goals should be realistic enough to be achievable and specific enough to be measurable. Instead of leaving the church at the mercy of trends and individual wishes, the church should be intentional in directing its energy and resources to achieve clearly defined goals. In this regard, more goals should be related to future generations.

Strategic Plan

The church needs medium- and long-term strategic plans. A strategic plan lays out the methods and means for achieving collective goals. Once the plans are adopted, they have to be clearly understood by the members. Priorities should be established and limited resources should be allocated according to those priorities. Needless to say, the concerns of the future generations ought to be given high priority.

FORMATION OF A LARGER CONGREGATION

Wherever possible, small churches in the same vicinity should study the possibility of merging. The main objective is to form a larger congregation so that a sizable English-speaking group might be established. Although such a move should be beneficial to both groups, the main focus should be on the English-speaking members. A few Korean churches have already made such a move. Parents should be willing to sacrifice their priorities and convenience for the long-term benefits of their children.

Establishment of Funds for English Ministry

The greatest need of the Korean Adventist churches in North America is trained Korean American pastors who can identify with and understand the congregations they minister to. This is possible only through one's socialization in North America. As there are not enough trained ministers for English-speaking congregations, some Korean churches hire non-theology majors or non-Korean pastors for their English-speaking congregations. Also, pastors from Korea are called to English ministry after only a few years of exposure in North America. Such practices are inevitable in providing a short-term solution, but they are not ideal for the long-term development of Korean American churches.

The Korean Church Council should lead a fund-raising drive for this purpose so that anyone who is qualified for youth ministry can be supported in the form of scholarships and other incentives. No other area seems to be more urgent than this.

Reasonable Remuneration for Youth Pastors

The church council should set a minimum standard in the hiring and remuneration of youth pastors according to their training and experiences. As reported elsewhere, only a few Korean youth pastors receive a full salary and benefits from their local conferences. Clearly defined mutual expectations are healthy in a long-term relationship between a local church and its youth pastor. The youth ministry funds proposed above could be used to supplement local church support. To encourage the youth pastors to continue their ministry, a reasonable salary and benefits are a minimum requirement.

Development of Lay Youth Leaders

As most Korean Adventist youth want to pursue health-related professions, mainly medicine and dentistry, the shortage of qualified youth pastors is becoming a serious problem. To mitigate the situation, the church may consider legitimizing the use of selective lay leaders through systematic short-term educational opportunities and training. A certificate program based on established criteria would maintain a standard. In the absence of a regular youth pastor, some professionals have helped churches on weekends, and others want to get involved in youth ministry if their voluntary service is legitimized and supported. Empower Ministry, for example, is an attempt to train future lay youth leaders. Other means, such as a distance program conducted via the Internet, should be viable options for such a purpose.

Education Committee

The church council should form a centralized education committee to plan and conduct a variety of educational and training programs for second-generation members. Such programs would include not only coordinated seminars, workshops, internships, and resource information, but also scholarly research and publications.

Training Church

Using the teaching hospital model, a number of churches may be designated for a specific type of training, such as providing an internship for youth ministry and lay pastors. At least one church in a metropolitan area could serve as a training church. The designated churches would offer training programs and materials while other churches may develop specialized programs according to their location and available talents. Campus ministry, small group training, inner-city ministry, music ministry, drama presentations, and use of computer technology are some examples of specialized programs. Thus, a full-time youth pastor or a lay volunteer can learn a variety of ministry skills at different locations on a rotating basis.

English Ministry Advisory Board

Realizing the increasing importance of English ministry, an English ministry advisory board should be formed. Composed of first- and second-generation members, including both clergy and lay members, the advisory board would assist the English ministry leadership in the areas of organization, program development, finances, education, and training. The major function of such a board at the division level is to provide consistent direction and review. At the same time, integrating the diverse segments of the church may generate synergy.

Interaction with Other Ethnic Churches

Formal and informal channels need to be established for the purpose of exchanging ideas with other ethnic churches in North America, especially with other Asian-American churches. This can be done at both regional and national levels. The Korean Adventist churches may learn a lot from the experiences of African-American, Hispanic, and other established minority churches. Both Adventist and non-Adventist churches are included for such interactions. Some types of short-term exchange programs of leaders, both ministerial or laity, among different ethnic churches may promote interactions.

Implementing the recommendations in this chapter could be a huge task. It may require tremendous commitments on the part of many in the church. Intellectual input, feedback from different groups, setting priorities for the limited resources of the church, establishing study committees, logistics, and performance evaluation call for the attention of the entire church. More than any other group, the leadership of the Korean Church Council and their determination are the key to success.

NOTES

1. Han River flows through the middle of the Korean capital city, Seoul. Koreans borrowed the expression from the Germans who used to refer to their impressive post-war economic growth as the miracle of Rhine River.

2. The IMF crisis was a national, financial turmoil caused by the lack of foreign reserves in 1997. The Korean government accepted the intervention of the International Monetary Fund (IMF) to resolve the economic crisis.

3. The other sponsor was Japan. The world soccer games were played both in Japan and Korea.

Appendix A: The Vision 2020 Survey Questionnaire

> In most questions, you simply mark a check (✓) before the item fitting to your situation. Please answer each question only after reading all the possible response categories listed.

1. Where were you born? 1____ America; 2____Canada; 3____Korea; 4____Other Country.

2. If you were born in elsewhere other than America or Canada, how old were you when you or your family moved to North America? (If you were born in North America, skip to Question 3.)

   I was _____ years old, and it was in the year of 19_____.

3. How old are you now? _____ years old

4. Sex: 1____Male; 2____Female

5. Your ethnicity: 1____Korean; 2____Half Korean; 3____Other: Specify_____

6. Your legal citizenship (the nationality indicated on your passport) is:
   1____American; 2____Canadian; 3____Korean; 4____Other

7. Regardless of your legal (or citizenship) status, you identify (or consider) yourself primarily as:
   1____American; 2____Canadian;
   3____Korean; 4____Korean-American or Korean-Canadian.

8. Your parents live in:
   1____America; 2____Canada; 3____Korea; 4____Other country

9. How many times have you visited Korea? _____times.

10. Have you ever served in Korea as a student missionary or for any other task? 1____yes; 2____no

11. At present, you attend:
    1____an Adventist school; 2____other private school: 3____a public school;
    4____Other; 5____not applicable, because I finished formal education.

12. You are fluent in:
    1____English; 2____Korean; 3____both English and Korean

13. The language you speak at home is:
    1____mainly English; 2____mainly Korean; 3____both English and Korean; 4____other.

14. Overall, your Korean is:
    1____fluent; 2____fairly good; 3____limited; 4____very limited

15. Have you ever studied Korean from other(s) than your own family members? 1____yes; 2____no.

    If yes, how many years have you studied Korean from other(s)? _____years.

16. Do you wish that your parents insisted that you speak and learn Korean?
     1___definitely yes;   2___probably yes   3___not sure;
     4___probably no;   5___definitely no;   6___I'm fluent in Korean.

17. Do you regret that you did not learn to speak Korean as fluent as you wish?
     1___definitely yes;   2___probably yes;   3___not sure;
     4___probably no;   5___definitely no;   6___I'm fluent in Korean.

18. Are you proud of being Korean?
     1___definitely yes;   2___probably yes;   3___not sure;
     4___probably no;   5___definitely no;   6___not applicable

19. Would you have your children learn to speak Korean as much as they can?
     1___definitely yes;   2___probably yes;   3___not sure;
     4___probably no;   5___definitely no

20. The approximate membership size of your entire church (both adults and youth) is:
     1___less than 50   2___51-100   2___101-150   4___151-200
     5___201-250   6___251-300   7___more than 300

21. The approximate membership size of your youth church or group is:
     1___less than 30   2___31-70   2___71-100   4___101-130
     4___131-170   5___171-200   6___more than 200

22. The name of the church you are presently attending:_____

23. The name of the city where your church is located in or near (within 100 miles).
     Example: Atlanta, Chicago, and Denver.

     _____

24. What is the ethnicity of your five closest friends?
     1___mostly Korean friends   2___mostly non-Korean friends
     3___about half and half   4___different mixture

25. What do you think is an ideal worship format for English-speaking Koreans?
     1___complete joint bilingual service (translation) with the adults every Sabbath
     2___complete separate service between Korean-speaking adults and youths every Sabbath
     3___mixture of the above two worship formats (joint and separate)

26. How long have you attended the present Korean church? _____ years.
     (Enter 0 if you have attended a non-Korean church.)

27. How regularly have you attended the Korean church within the last 6 months?
     1___almost every week   2___once or twice a month
     3___once in a while   4___none at all

28. Your youth leader is;   1___male;   2___female.

29. Is your youth leader married? 1___yes;   2___no.

30. What is the ethnic background of your present youth leader? (Leader means either a youth pastor or a lay person, depending on local church situation.)
    1___Korean-born Korean   2___North American-born Korean
    3___Non-Korean   4___no regular youth leader at my church

31. Your youth leader's approximate age category is:
    1___20 or younger;   2___21-25;   3___26-30;   4___31-35;   5___36 or older.

32. Did your youth leader study religion or ministry at the college level? 1___yes;   2___no.

33. Your youth leader is fluent in:
    1___English only;   2___English with limited Korean;
    3___Korean with limited English;   4___English and Korean.

34. Who decides where you go to church?
    1___mainly my parents' choice   2___mainly my sibling's choice
    3___mainly my own choice   4___mainly my friend's choice
    5___mainly my spouse's choice   6___mainly my church leaders' choice

35. If you were free to choose a church to attend on a regular basis, which one would you choose now?
    1___my present Korean church   2___another Korean church
    3___a white church   4___other ethnic minority church

36. How often do you attend a non-Korean church?
    1___almost every Sabbath   2___once or twice a month
    3___very once in a while   4___never

37. Which church offers a better program/activity in the areas listed below? Check either Korean or non-Korean church. If you have never attended a non-Korean Church, please check here _____ then skip to Question 38.

	Korean Church 1	non-Korean Church 2
a. Better Sabbath School program is offered by:	_____	_____
b. Better Sabbath worship program is offerd by:	_____	_____
c. Better music program is offered by:	_____	_____
d. Better mission outreach program is offerd by:	_____	_____
e. Better social activities are available at:	_____	_____
f. More friends are at:	_____	_____
g. Better youth pastor is at:	_____	_____
h. More friendly atmosphere is at:	_____	_____
i. Better spiritual atmosphere is at:	_____	_____

38. Do you see yourself still attending a Korean church 20 years from now?
    1___definitely yes   2___probably yes   3___not sure
    4___probably no   5___definitely no

39. In what capacity, would you like to serve Korean church in the future?
    1___as a full-time pastor   2___as a part-time pastor with my own job
    3___as a lay leader (elder, AY leader, etc)   4___not interested in serving

40.   In 20 years, suppose you reside in a city where a Korean SDA church is established. What would be the major determining factors in your decision to attend the Korean church over other churches in the same city? Please answer all, 1 through 5. Each column represents a different degree of agreement with the statements below.

<u>5</u>=strongly agree;   <u>4</u>=agree;   <u>3</u>=not sure   <u>2</u>=disagree;   <u>1</u>=strongly disagree

	<u>5</u>	<u>4</u>	<u>3</u>	<u>2</u>	<u>1</u>
1. To continue my Korean identity or heritage	___	___	___	___	___
2. To strengthen my children's Korean identity	___	___	___	___	___
3. To maintain my tie with the Korean community	___	___	___	___	___
4. To benefit from quality spiritual programs	___	___	___	___	___
5. To merely continue my childhood habit	___	___	___	___	___

41.   How do you see the future of Korean SDA Churches in North America after the first immigrant-generation is gone? Please check only one.

1____The Korean SDA churches as I know them will continue to exist without much change.

2____The Korean SDA churches as I know them will become very different through many changes.

3____The separate Korean ethnic churches mainly for Koreans, including English-speaking Koreans, will be out of existence during my life time.

4____I have no idea as to what might happen to the Korean SDA churches in North America.

42.   How active (or involved) are you at your church?

1____very active   2____somewhat active

3____somewhat indifferent   4____very indifferent

43.   Please indicate the image of the Korean SDA churches you have developed over the years. Please check only one in each row (or pair). For instance, the first row has the 'Dull---Exciting' pair and the last row has the 'Authoritarian---Democratic' pair.

My overall impression about the Korean church (es) is:

		<------- more		neutral		more ------->		
1.	Dull	___	___	___	___	___	___	Exciting
2.	Cold	___	___	___	___	___	___	Warm
3.	Disorganized	___	___	___	___	___	___	Organized
4.	Rigid/Stiff	___	___	___	___	___	___	Flexible
5.	Unstable	___	___	___	___	___	___	Stable
6.	Isolated	___	___	___	___	___	___	Integrated
7.	Stagnating	___	___	___	___	___	___	Growing
8.	Disharmonious	___	___	___	___	___	___	Harmonious
9.	Rude	___	___	___	___	___	___	Kind
10.	Dark	___	___	___	___	___	___	Bright
11.	Exclusive	___	___	___	___	___	___	Inclusive
12.	Authoritarian	___	___	___	___	___	___	Democratic
		1	2	3	4	5	6	7

44.   Are you baptized? 1____Yes; 2____No

45.   If yes, how old were you when you were baptized? _____ years old.

46. What is your primary reason to attend the Korean church? Please check only one.
    1____not applicable, because I attend a non-Korean church.
    2____My family expects me to attend, although it is not my choice.
    3____It's my family church, and I want to continue to support it.
    4____I want to worship with my Korean friends.
    5____I feel at home at a Korean church.
    6____I appreciate the quality of church programs at the Korean church.

47. Are you married?   1___yes   2___no

48. If yes, is your spouse Korean? (If no, skip to 51.) 1___yes   2___no

49. Do you have children?   1___yes   2___no

50. Is your spouse a Seventh-day Adventist Christian?   1___yes   2___no

51. If you are not married, how important is your future spouse being a Korean descendant? (If you are married, skip to 53.)
    1___definitely important   2___probably important   3___doesn't matter
    4___probably not important   5___defnitely not important

52. How important is your future spouse being a Seventh-day Adventist Christian?
    1___definitely important   2___probably important   3___doesn't matter
    4___probably not important   5___defnitely not important

53. How satisfied are you with your overall life situations?

	Very Satisfied 5	Satisfied 4	Don't Know 3	Unsatisfied 2	Very Unsatisf. 1
My family life	___	___	___	___	___
My church life	___	___	___	___	___
My school life (only students)	___	___	___	___	___
My occupational life (only job holders)	___	___	___	___	___
My spiritual life	___	___	___	___	___
My social life	___	___	___	___	___

54. How satisfied are you with the joint bilingual service (both in Korean and English)?
    1___very satisfied   2___satisfied   3___don't know
    4___unsatisfied   5___very unsatisfied   6___not applicable

55. What is your preference on the frequency of joint bilingual services?
    1___once a month   2___twice a month   3___three times a month
    4___every sabbath   5___once every 2 or 3 months   6___none at all
    6___not applicable

56. What do you think about the separate service between the Korean-speaking adults and the English-speaking youth?
    1___very desirable   2___desirable   3___don't know
    4___undesirable   5___very undesirable   6___not applicable

57. Check if the following family members are (or were) Seventh-day Adventists.
    1____ my great-grandparents (father side)   2____ my great-grandparetns (mother side)
    3____ my paternal grandparents   4____ my maternal grandparents
    5____ my father   6____ my mother
    7____ my siblings   8____ I am the only Adventist in my family.

58. What is your impression about the adult members of your church toward your youth group?
    1____ They have done their best to work with us under the circumstances.
    2____ They could have done more for us under the circumstances.
    3____ They seem to be indifferent about the concerns of our youths.
    4____ Both groups do not get along well with each other.

59. What has been the overall relationship between the adults and youth at your church?
    1____ very satisfactory   2____ satisfactory   3____ don't know
    4____ unsatisfactory   5____ very unsatisfactory

60. What are the most pressing needs for the youth group at your church? Please select only three areas
    from the list below then rank them according to the importance of each selected item.
           1=most important need;   2=second most important;   3=third most important.

    ____ i.   Church building and other physical facilities for youth
    ____ ii.   Counseling program
    ____ iii. Qualified youth pastor
    ____ iv.   Quality worship programs
    ____ v.   Mission or community outreach
    ____ vi.   Spiritual revival
    ____ vii. Dedicated lay youth leaders
    ____ viii. Social activities
    ____ ix.   Other : specify_____

61. Please indicate the state or province (in Canada) of your residence. If you are an unmarried student
    (or dependent), write the state or the province of your parents' residence.
    Example: Florida (in America) or Ontario (in Canada)

    _____

62. What is your highest level of educational attainment as of now?
    1___ Junior High School   2___ Academy/High School
    3___ Attending College   4___ Attending Graduate/Professional School
    5___ My last degree is a BA or BS   6___ My last degree is an MA or MS.
    7___ My last degree is a doctoral degree (DDS, Ed.D, JD, MD, Ph.D, Th.D, etc.)

63. Please check if you attended (or attending) the SDA educational system at each level.
    1___ Elementary Sch.   2___ Junior High   3___ Academy/High School
    4___ Vocational Sch.   5___ College   6___ Graduate/Professional School

64. What is the highest educational achievement of your father?
    1___ less than high school diploma   2___ high school diploma
    3___ college attendance   4___ college degree
    5___ master degree (MA, MS)   6___ doctoral degree (Ed.D; MD, Ph.D, etc)
    7___ other

65. What is the highest educational achievement of your mother?
    1___less than high school diploma   2___high school diploma
    3___vocational school   4___college attendance
    5___college degree   6___master degree (MA, MS)
    7___doctoral degree (Ed.D, MD, PhD, etc)

66. What line of a future career are you pursuing or already practicing at present?
    01___Art Performance (Music, Painting, etc.)   02___Business/Finance/Sales
    03___Engineering and technical   04___Health Care (med./denstistry, other)
    05___Home-making   06___Information (computer, journalism)
    07___Law and para-legal   08___Ministry
    09___Public Service (Govt./non-profit)   10___Teaching
    11___Other: specify _____

67. How good is your father's English?
    1___fluent   2___fairly good   3___limited   4___very limited

68. How good is your mother's English?
    1___fluent   2___fairly good   3___limited   4___very limited

69. Did your father attend (or attending now) school in North America?   1___yes   2___no

70. Did your mother attend (or attending now) school in North America?   1___yes   2___no

71. What is your opinion about starting a separate youth church, mainly for English-speaking second-generation Koreans, indpependent of the existing Korean churches?
    1___strongly support; 2___support; 3___not sure; 4___oppose; 5___strongly oppose

72. What do you like and dislike about your Korean church?

    Like
    1. _____
    2. _____
    3. _____

    Dislike
    1. _____
    2. _____
    3. _____

Thank you very much for your patience. If you want to add personal comments on any of the topics mentioned in the survey, use the back of this page. Before you return this questionnaire to your designated leader, pleases go over the questionnaire once more lest any part is left out unanswered. Thank you again for your participation and prompt return.

Won K. Yoon, Survey Director

Appendix B: The Early Development of the Korean Adventist Church in the History of the Korean Protestant Church

1626   Three Dutch sailors—Jan J. Weltevree, Direk Geijsbertz, and Jean Pieterz—were caught when their ship drifted to the east coast of Korea. They were the first Protestant Christians to step onto Korean soil.

1653   Thirty-three Dutch sailors were rescued near Jeju Island when their ship was wrecked. One of the escapees, Hendrick Hamel, introduced Korea to Europe through a book on the fourteen years he lived in Korea.

1832   Dutch missionary Karl F. A. Guzlaff landed in Korea on July 17. With the help of Koreans, he translated the Lord's prayer into Korean.

1866   A British missionary, Robert Jermain Thomas, was martyred when the American merchant ship, General Sherman, was burned on the Daedong River near Pyungyang.

1879   In China, John McIntyre and John Ross translated the Gospels of Luke and John into Korean.

1884   In September, Dr. Horace N. Allen arrived from the United States.

1885   The first Korean Protestant church was established in the Whanghe province.

The Royal Medical Clinic was established by Dr. Allen in February.

Drs. H. G. Underwood, W. B. Scranton, J. W. Herton, and Rev. Henry G. Appenzeller arrived from the United States.

Rev. Appenzeller established the first school, Baejae Hakdang, for boys.

Dr. Underwood opened another school, Kyongshin Hakdang, for boys.

1886   The first school for girls was opened by Mrs. Mary Scranton and later became Ewha Women's University.

1887   The New Testament was published in Korean.

Rev. John Ross visited from Southern Manchuria.

The second school for girls, Chongshin Girls School, was established by Annie Ellers from the United States.

1888   In May, Abram La Rue arrived in Hong Kong to introduce the Adventist message to East Asia.

1903   On January 12, the first group of 102 Korean immigrants aboard the Gaelic arrived in Honolulu. Korean-speaking churches were established in Hawaii.

1904   The second Adventist church in Japan was organized in Kobe under the leadership of Pastor Kunia.

Two Koreans, Hung Yul Lee and Hung Cho Sohn, were baptized as Adventists in Kobe.

Mr. Hung Cho Sohn returned to Korea and spread the Adventist message with Mr. Key Ban Yim.

The first Adventist evangelistic meeting was held near Pyungyang and seventy-one people were baptized by F. W. Field and Pastor Kunia from Japan.

1905   W. R. Smith arrived as the first Adventist missionary from the United States.

The first training school for ministers was established by the Presbyterian church in Pyungyang.

1907   Adventist missionaries started a workers' training school near Pyungyang.

1908   The Korean Mission (Adventist) was established separately from the Japan Mission.

1909   The headquarters of the Korean Mission was moved to Seoul.

1910   Mr. Sun Il Park was baptized by American missionary George W. Caviness in Yucatan, Mexico. Park became the first Korean Adventist in North America.

The entire Bible was translated and published in Korean.

1915   Two gospel workers were ordained, thus becoming the first ordained Korean Adventist ministers.

1919   Korean Union Mission (Adventist) was organized with three regional conferences.

The first union general session (Adventist) was held repre-

senting twenty-four churches with 1,021 members.
The union (Adventist) had 131 workers.

1924   The first Korean Adventist church in North America was established in Merida, a city on the Yucatan Peninsula, Mexico. The members were Korean immigrants who came to Mexico in 1905.

1935   The Japanese government began to pressure Korean church leaders to worship their emperor. Most leaders refused to comply.

1936   Seoul Sanitarium Hospital (Adventist) was opened in the capital city.

1941   American Adventist missionaries left Korea during the outbreak of the Pacific War.

1943   The Japanese government closed the operation of the Adventist church and a number of church leaders were imprisoned.
During the war, 200 Christian churches were forced to close and about 2,000 Protestant ministers were imprisoned for their refusal to cooperate with the Japanese government. Around fifty were martyred.

1945   Japan was defeated and the Adventist church was reestablished. American missionaries returned.

Appendix C: A Brief History of the Korean American Community in the Context of Asian American History

1600	There were reports that Chinese, Japanese, and Filipinos visited Mexico.
1610	Japanese sailed to the New World.
1763	Filipino crews jumped off a ship in New Orleans and settled in the bayous of Louisiana, thus becoming the first Asian American residents.
1790	The Naturalization Act restricted citizenship only to free white immigrants.
1820	The first Chinese workers immigrated to the United States.
1840	The first Japanese resident settled in Massachusetts.
1847	Three Chinese students came to study in Massachusetts.
1848	Gold was discovered in California, and the Chinese began to arrive in large numbers.
1850	There were 4,000 Chinese workers in the United States.
1858	The California legislature banned Chinese immigration.
1860	California excluded the Chinese from its public school system.
1860s	Japanese immigrants began to arrive.
1869	The transcontinental railroad was completed.
1882	The Chinese Exclusion Act was passed by the U.S. Congress.
1900	Hawaii became a U.S. territory. There were 89,863 Chinese and 24,326 Japanese, respectively.
1903	The first wave of Korean immigrants (103) arrived in Hawaii.
1905	The Korean government ended immigration to Hawaii. About 8,000 immigrants had come to the islands over the three-year (1903–1905) period.
1907	The Gentlemen's Agreement between the U.S. and Japanese governments was made to prohibit new Japanese immigration to the United States.
1910	Korean picture brides began to arrive to marry Korean men in North America. Nearly 1,000 Korean women came until 1924.
1913	The Alien Land Act was passed in California to bar Asian immigrants from land ownership.

1921   The National Origin Act was passed to curve immigrants from southern and eastern European countries.

1924   The U.S. Congress passed the Oriental Exclusion Act, thus ending Asian immigration to the United States.

1941   Pearl Harbor was attacked on December 7.

1942   President Roosevelt signed Executive Order 9066 to evacuate people of Japanese ancestry, and more than 126,000 were forced to relocate.

1943   The Chinese Exclusion Act was repealed by the U.S. Supreme Court, and the annual immigration quota of 105 was granted to China.

1945   Upon ending the Second World War, most Japanese internees left the relocation camps mainly in the West.

1950   There were 117,629 Chinese and 141,768 Japanese in the United States.

1951   Korean orphans and war brides (GI spouses) began to arrive in America (second wave).

1952   The McCanan-Walter Act made Asian immigrants eligible for U.S. citizenship.

1954   The first wave of Southeast Asians came mainly from Vietnam.

1965   The Immigration Amendment Act reversed previous discrimination against the eastern-hemisphere (Asian) nations.

1975   The second wave of Southeast Asians (refugees/boat people) arrived following the U.S. withdrawal from Vietnam, Cambodia, and Laos.

1990   The U.S. government (President Reagan) offered an apology to the Japanese Americans and paid $20,000 to each surviving member of the relocation camps.

2000   10.2 million Asians were counted in the last census, and they comprised 3.6 percent of the U.S. population.

Appendix D: Biblical Significance of the Ethnic Minority

In a sense, the Bible is the history of a wandering minority people, the Israelites. The ethnic minority churches in North America may draw inspiration and strength from the stories of the Israelites and find their own significance in the Bible.

Throughout its history the African American church has drawn inspiration and strength from the stories of Jews. Black Christians defined their historical situations in biblical terms. During the slavery and civil rights struggles, for instance, the leaders of black churches led their followers with biblical parallels. Black sermons and speeches are replete with references to the experiences of the Jews.

The following biblical themes hold great significance for ethnic minority churches:

1. Much of the history of ancient Israel is that of wandering (migration).

2. The status of Jews both in Old Testament and New Testament times was often that of a minority in Egypt, Babylon, Persia, and Rome.

3. The biblical heroes and heroines—like Joseph, Moses, Daniel, Esther, and Paul—were shining in foreign lands where they were regarded as strangers and minority members.

4. In the Bible, God's people are viewed as "strangers," "foreigners," or "pilgrims" on earth.

5. The chosen ones are always a minority.

6. The spread of the gospel message to the ends of the earth presupposes the role of sojourners and wanderers throughout the world.

7. One is primarily responsible to his or her people in carrying out the commission of the gospel work.

8. The world is often changed by the chosen few (creative minority): salt and yeast.

9. Even a chosen few were promised to grow and prosper like the stars in the sky and the sand on the seashore.

10. The Bible promises to raise and uplift the humble and marginal people.

11. God promises that Israel will be the head of the world, not the tail of it. Smallness is not necessarily a disadvantage.

12. An ethnic minority church may serve as a refuge for sojourners.

Appendix E: Reasons for Pursuing a Multiethnic and Multicultural Korean Church in North America

Some second-generation members regard the multiethnic and multicultural church as a viable model for their future in North America. The reasons are derived from the Bible and reality as well.

1. One God and one human family: Division or separation by race or culture is contrary to the biblical concept of oneness.

2. The great commission of the gospel work depends on all people transcending cultural and language differences. The first Pentecostal gathering in Jerusalem demonstrated the oneness of all people.

3. The church should reflect and represent the multiethnic and multicultural reality of North American societies. Integration, not segregation, is to be pursued.

4. The overall Korean-speaking population may shrink as Korean immigration to North America has declined.

5. The Korean American community becomes more diverse as more people marry those outside their own ethnic group.

6. When a Korean community becomes smaller in a given area, transition into a multiethnic church is the only way to survive.

Appendix F: Reasons for Maintaining the Korean Church in North America

The continued distinctiveness of Korean Adventist churches in North America will depend upon a number of factors, but a steady commitment and support by the members of future generations is a key to its continuous existence. The reasons for commitment and support might be personal as well as social. Below are some of the justifications for maintaining Korean churches in the future:

1. To help the spiritual growth of Korean and non-Korean members who choose to join the Korean church over other churches.

2. To reach out to the Korean communities in North America and elsewhere. No other group can be more effective in reaching out to Korean people than Korean Christians.

3. To preserve and transmit the unique values of Korean culture, including values of family, education, and hard work.

4. To preserve and continue the unique spiritual heritages of Korean Christians in the areas of personal devotion, enthusiasm, sacrifice, and outreach efforts.

5. To meet the personal and social needs of Korean church members, such as identity formation, friendship, social networks, marriage, and cultural heritage.

6. To contribute to the larger Christian community by adding the Korean dimension.

7. To maintain solidarity and networks among Korean Christian communities around the world.

Appendix G: Avoiding Ethnic Traps in Minority Churches

Any ethnic minority community faces the danger of being trapped as it tends to exist in isolation and even insulation. In order to keep growing as a viable and authentic community of faith, its members need to be aware of the potential traps of their ethnic church.

1. The primary concern of an ethnic church should be the spiritual growth and development of its members. Any cultural promotion or concern should be secondary to the primary one. A church should not sacrifice spiritual well-being in the name of cultural preservation or promotion under any circumstances. The choice should be clear.

2. In any Christian community, the Christian faith is the core of its identity. It takes precedence over any cultural components.

3. Any effort to promote or preserve a cultural component may be made as long as it is in harmony with spiritual growth and development. On the other hand, any cultural trait that is detrimental to the healthy growth of a Christian community is to be disregarded.

4. An ethnic church should resist the tendency to be isolated. It should engage in dialogue and interaction with other communities. A variety of exchanges and joint programs should be attempted with other communities on a regular basis.

5. An ethnic church should avoid division among its members because of language and generational differences. It should try to maintain an integrated whole whenever possible.

6. As an organization, the church is expected to adapt to changing external conditions.

7. Most ethnic minority churches tend to be dominated by members in authority based on age, gender, and social status. Efforts should be made to give equal opportunities to every segment of the community.

Bibliography

Ablemann, Nancy and John Lie. 1995. *Blue Dreams: Korean Americans and Los Angeles Riots.* Cambridge, MA: Harvard University Press.

Alba, Richard D. and Victor Nee. 1997. "Rethinking Assimilation Theory for a New Era of Immigration." *International Migration Review* 31:826–874.

Alumkal, Anthony W. 2001. "Being Korean, Being Christian: Particularism and Universalism in a Second-Generation Congregation." Pp. 181–191 in *Korean Americans and Their Religions: Pilgrims and Missionaries from a Different Shore,* edited by Ho-Youn Kwon, Kwang Chung Kim, and R. Stephen Warner. University Park, PA: Pennsylvania State University Press.

Aronowitz, Michael. 1992. "Adjustment of Immigrant Children as a Function of Parental Attitudes to Change." *International Migration Review* 26:89–110.

Asian Greenhouse. 2007. "Nearly 100,000 Korean Students Studying in the US." Retrieved September 11, 2007 (http://wolk.multiply.com/reviews/item/69).

Asian-Nation. 2005. "Interracial Dating and Marriage." Retrieved July 7, 2005 (http://www.asian-nation.org).

Barber, Benjamin R. 1996. *Jihad vs. McWorld: How Globalism and Tribalism Are Reshaping the World.* New York: Ballantine Books.

Barret, David B., George T. Kuriar, and Todd M. Johnson. 2001. *World Christian Encyclopedia,* vols. 1–2. New York: Oxford University Press.

Berry, Brewton and Henry Tischer. 1978. *Race and Ethnic Relations.* 4th ed. Boston: Houghton Mifflin Co.

Beyer, Peter. 1994. *Religion and Globalization.* London: Sage.

Borthwick, Mark. 1998. *Pacific Century: The Emergence of Modern Pacific Asia.* Boulder: Westview Press.

Carnes, Tony and Fenggang Yang, eds. 2004. *Asian American Religions: The Making and Remaking of Borders and Boundaries.* New York: New York University Press.

Cha, Peter T. 2001. "Ethnic Identity Formation and Participation in Immigrant Churches." Pp. 141–156 in *Korean Americans and Their Religions: Pilgrims and Missionaries from a Different Shore*, edited by Ho-Youn Kwon, Kwang Chung Kim, and R. Stephen Warner. University Park, PA: Pennsylvania State University Press.

Chai, Karen J. 2001. "Beyond Strictness to Distinctiveness: Generational Transition in Korean Protestant Churches." Pp. 157–180 in *Korean Americans and Their Religions: Pilgrims and Missionaries from a Different Shore*, edited by Ho-Youn Kwon, Kwang Chung Kim, and R. Stephen Warner. University Park, PA: Pennsylvania State University Press.

Chong, Kelly. 1998. "What It Means to Be Christian: The Role of Religion in Construction of Ethnic Identity and Boundary among Second-Generation Korean Americans." *Sociology of Religion* 59(3):259–286.

Chu, Jeff, Nadia Mustafa, Kristin Kloberdanz, and Amanda Bower. 2006. "Between Two Worlds." *Time*, January 16, 167(3):64–68.

Chua, Amy. 2004. *World on Fire: How Exporting Free Market Democracy Breeds Ethnic Hatred and Global Instability*. New York: Random House.

Clyde, Paul H. and Burton F. Beers. 1975. *The Far East: A History of Western Impacts and Eastern Responses, 1830–1975*. Englewood Cliffs, NJ: Prentice-Hall.

Congressional Desk. 2005. "Moran Bill Grants South Korea Admission to Visa Waiver Program." Retrieved July 9, 2007 (http://www.americanchronicle.com/articles/viewArticle.asp?articleID=3621).

Dhingra, Pawan. 2004. "'We Are Not a Korean American Church Anymore': Dilemmas Constructing a Multi-Racial Church Identity." *Social Compass* 51:367–379.

Ebaugh, Helen Rose and Janet Saltzman Chafetz. 2000. *Religion and the New Immigrants: Continuities and Adaptations in Immigrant Congregations*. Walnut Creek, CA: AltaMira Press.

Elegant, Robert. 1990. *Pacific Destiny: Inside Asia Today*. New York: Crown Publishers.

Empower Ministry Group. 2002. Retrieved November 15, 2002 (http://www.empowerministry.com).

The Encyclopedic Dictionary of Sociology. 1991. 4th ed. Guilford, CT: The Dushkin Publishing Group.

Espiritu, Yen Le. 2002. "The Intersection of Race, Ethnicity, and Class: The Multiple Identities of Second-Generation Filipinos." Pp. 19–52 in *Second Generation: Ethnic Identity and Asian Americans*, edited by Pyong Gap Min. Walnut Creek, CA: AltaMira Press.

Gans, Herbert J. 1979. "Symbolic Ethnicity: The Future of Ethnic Groups and Cultures in America." *Ethnic and Racial Studies* 2:1–20.

Gans, Herbert J. 1992. "Second-Generation Decline: Scenarios for the Economic and Ethnic Futures of the Post–1965 American Immigrants." *Ethnic and Racial Studies* 15:173–192.

General Conference of Seventh-day Adventists. 2002. *SDA Yearbook*. Hagerstown, MD: Review and Herald Publishing Association.

General Conference of Seventh-day Adventists. 2005. "Annual Statistical Report" for 2005. Retrieved January 8, 2007 (http://www.adventistarchives.org/documents.asp?catid).

Gibney, Frank. 1992. *The Pacific Century: America and Asia in a Changing World*. New York: Maxwell McMillan.

Glazer, Nathan. 1993. "Is Assimilation Dead?" *Annals of the American Academy of Political and Social Science* 530:122–136.

Goette, Robert D. 1998. "The Urgency of Contextualized English Ministry among Korean Americans." Research paper, Southwestern Baptist Theological Seminary, Fort Worth, TX.

Goette, Robert. 2001. "The Transformation of a First-Generation Church into a Bilingual Second-Generation Church." Pp. 125–140 in *Korean Americans and Their Religions: Pilgrims and Missionaries from a Different Shore*, edited by Ho-Youn Kwon, Kwang Chung Kim, and R. Stephen Warner. University Park, PA: Pennsylvania State University Press.

Guillen, Mauro F. 2001. "Is Globalization Civilizing, Destructive or Feeble? A Critique of Five Key Debates in the Social Science Literature." *Annual Review of Sociology* 27:235–260.

Hong, Joan and Pyong Gap Min. 1999. "Ethnic Attachment among Second Generation Korean Adolescents." *Amerasia Journal* 25:165–178.

Hurh, Won Moo. 1998. *The Korean Americans*. Westport, CT: Greenwood Press.

Hyun, Kyoo Whan. 1976. *A History of Korean Wanderers and Immigrants*, vols. 1–2 (in Korean). Seoul: Sam Wha Publishing Co.

Jensen, Leif and Yoshimi Chitose. 1994. "Today's Second Generation: Evidence from the 1990 U.S. Census." *International Migration Review* 28:714–735.

Jeung, Russel. 2002. "Asia American Pan-Ethnic Formation and Congregational Culture." Pp. 215–243 in *Religions in Asian America: Building Faith Communities*, edited by Pyong Gap Min and Jung Ha Kim. Walnut Creek, CA: AltaMira Press.

Jeung, Russel. 2004. "Creating an Asian American Christian Subculture: Grace Community Covenant Church." Pp. 287–312 in *Asian American Religions: The Making and Remaking of Borders and Boundaries*, edited by Tony Carnes and Fenggang Yang. New York: New York University Press.

Kang, Bong Ho. 1987. "My Autobiography." Pp. 436–442 in *The Pioneers and Martyrs of the Seventh-day Adventists in Korea*, edited by Ryu Sik Lee. Seoul: Korean Publishing House.

Kibria, Nazli. 1999. "College and Notions of Asian America." *Amerasia Journal* 25:29–51.

Kim, Jae Shin. 1993. *A History of the Seventh-day Adventist Church in North Korea* (in Korean). Seoul: Korean Publishing House.

Kim, Jung Ha. 2002. "Cartography of Korean American Protestant Faith Communities in the United States." Pp. 185–213 in *Religions in Asian America: Building Faith Communities*, edited by Pyong Gap Min and Jung Ha Kim. Walnut Creek, CA: AltaMira Press.

Kim, Kwang Chung, R. Stephen Warner, and Ho-Youn Kwon. 2001. "Korean American Religion in International Perspective." Pp. 3–24 in *Korean Americans and Their Religions: Pilgrims and Missionaries from a Different Shore*, edited by Ho-Youn Kwon, Kwang Chung

Kim, and R. Stephen Warner. University Park, PA: Pennsylvania State University Press.

Kim, Kwang Chung and Shin Kim. 2001. "Ethnic Roles of Korean Immigrant Churches in the United States." Pp. 71–94 in *Korean Americans and Their Religions: Pilgrims and Missionaries from a Different Shore*, edited by Ho-Youn Kwon, Chung Kim, and R. Stephen Warner. University Park, PA: Pennsylvania State University Press.

Kitano, Kerrily J. and Harry H. L. Kitano. 1998. "The Japanese-American Family." Pp. 311–330 in *Ethnic Families in America: Patterns and Variations*, 4th ed., edited by Charles H. Mindel, R. W. Habenstein, and R. Wright, Jr. Upper Saddle River, NJ: Prentice Hall.

Korean Church Council of North America. 1993. *Brief History of Local Korean Adventist Churches in North America* (in Korean). Los Angeles: Korean Adventist Press.

Korean Church Council of North America. 2000. *The 7th General Session Report of the Korean Church Council*. Los Angeles: Korean Church Council.

Korean Church Council of North America. 2003. *The 8th General Session Report of the Korean Church Council*. Los Angeles: Korean Church Council.

Korean Church Council of North America. 2006. *The 9th General Session Report of the Korean Church Council*. Los Angeles: Korean Church Council.

Kwon, Ho-Youn, Kwang Chung Kim, and R. Stephen Warner, eds. 2001. *Korean Americans and Their Religions: Pilgrims and Missionaries from a Different Shore*. University Park, PA: Pennsylvania State University Press.

Lee, Helen. 1996. "Silent Exodus: Can the East Asian Church in America Reverse the Flight of Its Next Generation?" *Christianity Today*, August 12, 40:50–53.

Lee, Jae Myung. 2000. "A Study of the Growth of the Korean Adventist Church in America." MA thesis in Korean, Sahmyook University, Seoul.

Lee, Ryu Sik, ed. 1987. *The Pioneers and Martyrs of the Seventh-day Adventists in Korea* (in Korean). Seoul: Korean Publishing House.

Levitt, Peggy. 2001. *The Transnational Villagers*. Berkeley: University of California Press.

Levitt, Peggy and Mary C. Walters, eds. 2002. *The Changing Face of Home: The Transnational Lives of the Second Generation*. New York: Russell Sage Foundation.

Lien, Pei-te and Tony Carnes. 2004. "The Religious Demography of Asian American Boundary Crossing." Pp. 38–51 in *Asian American Religions: The Making and Remaking of Borders and Boundaries*, edited by Tony Carnes and Fenggang Yang. New York: New York University Press.

Membership Directory of Korean Adventist Churches in the Americas. 2001, 2003, 2005. Los Angeles: Korean Adventist Press.

Min, Pyong Gap. 1998. "Korean American Family." Pp. 223–253 in *Ethnic Families in America: Patterns and Variations*. 4th ed., edited by Charles H. Mindel, Robert W. Habenstein, and Roosevelt Wright, Jr. Upper Saddle River, NJ: Prentice Hall.

Min, Pyong Gap. 2002. "Introduction," Pp. 1–14 in *Religions in Asian America: Building Faith Communities*, edited by Pyong Gap Min and Jung Ha Kim. Walnut Creek, CA: AltaMira Press.

Min, Pyong Gap, ed. 2002. *Second Generation: Ethnic Identity among Asian Americans*. Walnut Creek, CA: AltaMira Press.

Min, Pyong Gap and Jung Ha Kim, eds. 2002. *Religions in Asian America: Building Faith Communities*. Walnut Creek, CA: AltaMira Press.

Min, Pyong Gap and Rose Kim. 2002. "Formation of Ethnic and Racial Identities: Narratives by Asian American Professionals." Pp. 153–181 in *Second Generation: Ethnic Identity and Asian Americans*, edited by Pyong Gap Min. Walnut Creek, CA: AltaMira Press.

Mindel, Charles H., R. W. Habenstein, and R. Wright, Jr. 1998. *Ethnic Families in America: Patterns and Variations*. 4th ed. Upper Saddle River, NJ: Prentice Hall.

Moll, Rob. 2006. "Missions Incredible." *Christianity Today*, March 3, 50:28–34.

Nahm, Andrew C. 1988. *Korea: Tradition and Transformation*. Seoul: Hollym Corporation.

Ng, Franklin, ed. 1998. *Adaptation, Acculturation, and Transnational Ties among Asian Americans*. New York: Garland Publishing.

Niebuhr, H. Richard. 1951. *Christ and Culture*. New York: Harper.

North American Division Multi-lingual Department. 2001. Figures on Multilingual Groups Provided at Won Yoon's Request. Silver Spring, MD: North American Division Multi-lingual Department.

Overseas Koreans Foundation. 2004. "Report on Overseas Koreans." Retrieved June 8, 2007 (http://www.korean.net/morgue/status_1.jsp?tCode=status&dCode=0101).

Pai, Young, Deloras Pemberton, and John Worley. 1987. *Findings on Korean-American Early Adolescents and Adolescents*. Kansas City: University of Missouri School of Education.

Park, Nancy Josephine. 2005. "Building Bridges, Creating Communities: Korean American Identities and Intergenerational Relationships." MA thesis, Claremont Graduate University, Claremont, CA.

Patterson, Wayne and Hyung-Chan Kim. 1977. *The Koreans in America*. Minneapolis: Lerner Publications Co.

Portes, Alejandro and Min Zhou. 1993. "The New Second Generation: Segmented Assimilation and Its Variants." *The Annals of the American Academy of Political and Social Science* 530(1):74–96.

Portes, Alejandro and Richard Schuffler. 1994. "Language and the Second Generation: Bilingualism Yesterday and Today." *International Migration Review* 21:640–661.

Portes, Alejandro and Rubén G. Rumbaut. 2001. *Legacies: The Story of the Immigrant Second Generation*. Berkeley: University of California Press.

Rumbaut, Rubén G. 1994. "The Crucible Within: Ethnic Identity, Self-Esteem, and Segmented Assimilation among Children of Immigrants." *International Migration Review* 28:748–794.

Rumbaut, Rubén G. and Alejandro Portes. 2001. *Ethnicities: Children of Immigrants in America*. Berkeley: University of California Press.

Schaefer, Richard T. 2004. *Racial and Ethnic Groups*. 9th ed. Upper Saddle River, NJ: Prentice Hall.

Thai, Hung C. 1999. "'Splitting Things in Half Is So White!' Conceptions of Family Life and Friendship and the Formation of Ethnic Identity among Second Generation Vietnamese Americans." *Amerasia Journal* 25:53–88.

Tuan, Mia. 1998. *Forever Foreigners or Honorary Whites? The Asian Experience Today*. New Brunswick: Rutgers University Press.

Um, Sang-Hyun. 2003. *The Present State of Education for Overseas Koreans and the Future Tasks*. Seoul: Republic of Korea Ministry of Education and Human Resources.

U.S. Department of State. 2006. "South Korea: ROK Visa Waiver Program." Retrieved July 9, 2007 (http://www.state.gov/r/pa/prs/ps/2006/71974.htm).

Yang, Fenggang. 1999. "ABC and XYZ." *Amerasia Journal* 25:89–114.

Yang, Fenggang and Helen R. Ebaugh. 2001. "Transformation in New Immigrant Religions and Their Global Implications." *American Sociological Review* 66:269–288.

Yoo, David K., ed. 1999. *New Spiritual Homes: Religion and Asian Americans*. Honolulu: University of Hawaii Press.

Yoon, Won K. 1989. *The Passage of a Picture Bride*. Loma Linda, CA: Loma Linda University Press.

Yu, Eui-Young. 2001. "Korean Population in the United States as Reflected in the Year 2000 U.S. Census." Unpublished manuscript, California State University, Los Angeles, CA.

Index

231